Why Winners Win!

WHY
WINNERS
WIN!

Techniques of Advocate Selling

JOHN TORQUATO

amacom
American Management Associations

HF
5438.25
.T66
1983

Library of Congress Cataloging in Publication Data

Torquato, John.
    Why winners win!

    Includes index.
    1. Selling.   2. Success.   I. Title.
HF5438.25.T66   1983   658.8'5   82-73831
ISBN 0-8144-5770-3

First Printing

Acknowledgments

Acknowledgments are far too personal and maudlin to be of any interest to the reader, but for the author they are the only way to publicly express the thanks and appreciation that are truly due others. No man is an island.

To my father, who cares and to Hiram G. Andrews, who didn't have to.

To Judy, whose patience and encouragement made it happen.

To Rosemary Carroll and Ross Olney, whose technical word skills helped me make concepts reality.

To Dennis Lahey for his cases and Alan Weiss for his contribution to Chapter 12—my professional as well as personal thanks.

To Ben Tregoe, who graciously allowed me to learn from him while I was being paid to teach what I knew to others.

To Dick Pershing and Charlie Calderaro, whose astute business judgment made this project a financial piece of cake.

To Bob Arnold, who gave me refuge, help, and advice when it was needed.

To Jack for being Jack and to Max and Bo and Sadie.

Most of all, my thanks and appreciation to Robert J. Johnston of Philadelphia. What I didn't already know about selling, Bob taught me.

My last and final acknowledgment is to whoever or whatever controls human destiny. I hope the job I did is worthy of the help I received.

God bless.

Foreword

"As in war, how well you played the game doesn't count, only whether you won or lost. Winning means making the sale." Simple and straightforward, this quote summarizes what *Why Winners Win!* is all about and why it will benefit not only the professional salesperson who wants to learn new skills and sharpen old ones, but anyone interested in improving his batting average in dealing with others and in improving his own self-understanding.

I wish I had had this book when I was with the U.S. Public Health Service. I wish I'd had it when I was working with sales and marketing people at General Motors Corporation some fifteen years ago and later at Pan American World Airways. If it was needed then, it's needed much more now. Resources are limited, competitive pressures are increasing, and the consumer wants to be sold—wants to be convinced that your product or service meets a real need and achieves quality results. This book will help you to better use your time, money, and energy; it will increase your effectiveness in meeting competition and in selling the prospective customer. In short, this book will help you win!

It will help because it's practical. It's full of very real case histories and vignettes about people selling and not selling, winning and losing. And, more important, it contains the whys that separate the two. There are ideas to be mulled over for months, and techniques to be applied immediately—tested, tailored, and refined to suit individual situations. There are the basic people types: Doers, Waiters, and Watchers. There are Need Salesmen, Relationship Salesmen, and Order Takers. There are Economic, Feasibility, and Implementive Buyers. There is the "chain of beneficiaries" concept which, when linked with the concepts of the minisale and close, provides a powerful tool for selling today and simultaneously building for future sales. There are sixteen detailed closing techniques used by advocate salespeople, so it's perfect for the new salesperson. It also offers a refreshing view of strategy and tactics for the experienced salesperson and sales manager. The "advocate process" is a tool managers can use to more effectively manage their salespeople, a tool that can be adapted to any company's present selling system.

Further, it will help because it is insightful. It links an understanding of people and their needs and motivations with knowledge that comes from the author's successful battles in the world of selling. He understands that selling is an adversary process in which each person advocates a position. He knows that every such confrontation is a win/lose situation for the salesperson. A sale is made or it is not!

So, welcome to Advocate Selling. *Why Winners Win!* isn't just a book. It's a reference library, a training course, a guidebook, and a conceptual adversary that will continually test the way you think and act. It's war—but this kind of war isn't hell, it's fun.

As you move through the pages that follow, you'll be made aware over and over again of both the simplicity and the complexity of selling. You will appreciate the fact that although the concepts presented are many and varied, John Torquato never loses sight of his central purpose: to help readers increase their effectiveness in closing the sale . . . and winning.

> Donald L. Parker
> Senior Vice President
> N.W. Gibson International

Contents

Prologue

Why Winners Win! is not about selling. It is about the dynamics of personal relationships. "Selling" has a product orientation, and only a relatively small group of our population considers itself to be salesmen. But no man is an island. Others must be convinced before anything can happen. *Why Winners Win!* is a practical guide to the psychology of selling yourself and your alternatives to other people, be they your boss, peers, associates, or spouse.

In the book I call a great deal of attention to people who are Doers. Doers make things happen. They are the shakers and movers of the world. My message is that everybody could be a Doer except for a suffocating fear of risk. Doers want to win. People who are Waiters and Watchers need to beat. If they aren't sure of their ability to beat, they won't play the game. Waiters and Watchers take losses personally and home to bed at night. Doers accept loss as an inevitable part of risk and do not consider it to be a reflection of their own self-worth. They play the game as hard as they can—but win, lose, or draw, they have the ability to step off the gameboard and be people again instead of players.

If only a handful of people overcome their fear of risk and rejection from reading this book, my labors will be justified tenfold. Fear and rejection will be converted to challenge and play.

Everyone talks about skills. Skills are necessary to achieve things. The absence of skills seems to condemn us to underachievement. Yet that condemnation is surely self-imposed. Skills are based upon knowledge. Whether or not we gather the knowledge necessary to build skills is purely dependent upon our attitude. Our attitude toward ourselves dictates what we will be. It has been my experience that most people are self-fulfilling prophecies who lament their lot in life. Fate didn't make them what they are, their attitude did, and fear of change solidified the mold.

Why Winners Win! will help anyone from any walk of life sell himself to himself and then sell that to others. The book introduces readers to the strangely denied fact that selling is an adversary process. Anyone who has been forced to sell himself a bitter truth knows the mental conflicts this generates. If you compound the contest by adding another player, the adversarial elements multiply logarithmically. Each person is an advocate of his own position. One or the other will dominate. Over the past 18 years, I have developed the dominant advocate selling process in the arena as a method to ensure winning my share of the contests. At an early age I became aware that no one could win them for me. Just like no one can do it for you.

Why Winners Win! is divided into 14 key selling concepts. Concepts 1–5 are designed to help the reader know himself— who he is and what his current strengths and limitations are. Concepts 6–8 are designed to help the reader know his buyers, for in today's complex world nothing much happens without the cooperation of others. Concepts 9–14 provide the reader with the skills necessary to ensure the position he advocates is the one that dominates.

The vignettes in the book are based on fact. All events really happened. Names and circumstances have been changed in order to avoid spending the rest of my life in court. Permission has been obtained when actual names and circumstances are quoted.

John Torquato

CONCEPT 1

Salesmen Like People
. . . and Other Myths

Salesmen today work under unbelievably adverse circumstances and pressures. This makes them love everybody, of
course.

The precepts of consular selling dictate that a salesman
must find a *win* for the customer to earn a *win* for himself, but
the salesman's boss and the corporation issuing his paycheck
have no concept of this trade-off at all. To them it's either meet
your forecast or lose.

Meet your budget or lose.

Salesmen have all the flexibility in the world to meet the
customer's needs but no authority to commit resources or initiate the policy changes necessary to do so. Naturally this
makes them love the people they deal with!

Salesmen are told they have an ethical responsibility. Unlike accountants, they aren't told what that ethical responsibility is. While trying to figure it out by himself, the salesman
finds that he's being treated as a third-class citizen by the masters who pay him and as a servant by the customers who purchase his products. Go out and sell something, his masters say,
and we'll measure how well you did after you have done it.

Bring us a product we like, his buyers say, and after we see
it we'll tell you whether you have wasted your time.

A balance must be maintained between being pushy and
being accommodating, his masters say. We tolerate no high
pressure here.

If you don't like the terms and conditions associated with

our business, his buyers say, why don't you sell your products someplace else?

Certainly salesmen like people—why shouldn't they?

Professional salesmen sell by choice, but it's a hard fact that all people sell whether they like it or not. They sell themselves into a job; they sell a product; they sell an alternative, an idea, a change. And selling is an adversary situation! Remember how tense you were in your last job interview? Salesmen go through that every day of the week! Of course they like people!

By definition, an adversary situation is one in which people have something to lose—and nobody likes to lose! If the real truth were known, you would probably find that many salesmen, those who love their work if not the people around them, consciously place themselves in adversary situations in order to experience the thrill of dominating the person who buys their alternative, the self-approval that comes of that domination, and the approval of others that is inherent in their acquiescence.

Bill Merriweather built and managed a professional sales force of over 2,000 Thermacon-Frigacon salespeople for over 25 successful years. A clutch of corporate recruiters charged with staffing Bill's sales force trooped into his office one day scratching their collective heads.

"Bill," they asked, "do salesmen really like people?"

"I wonder if it isn't a love/hate relationship," Bill replied. "Good salesmen are not altruistic. They have a product and that product is all they have to sell. If they don't sell it, how are they going to make a living? If they don't make a living, how can they have self-approval? If they don't have self-approval, how can they have self-confidence? If they don't have self-confidence, how can they sell our product effectively?

"A customer may really have a different priority for his money than the product offered by our salesman," Bill went on. "Nevertheless, if the salesman doesn't make a sale he doesn't eat. Should he walk out of the customer's office with his tail between his legs, saying 'The customer knows best'? Or does he try to find something that appeals to the buyer's natural need, greed, or fear in order to change his buyer's priority? After all, a salesman really needs to sell the product he represents rather than one the customer truly needs at the moment!"

As an example, Bill told the story of a young salesman who had been floundering on the job for six months. No amount of sales management help and advice seemed to do any good.

Then, when he was on the verge of being fired, the man's sales record took a dramatic positive turn. His sales increased sharply and his close-to-call ratio became a model for the other salesmen in the division. Management was flabbergasted. "What had gone right?" they asked themselves, obviously pleased at not having to ask "What had gone wrong?" for a change.

The new salesman simply replied, "I finally realized that in every presentation a sale is made. Either I sell the customer or he sells me. And damn it, I got tired buying all the time."

"Hey!" the recruiters countered. "Selling is supposed to be people-oriented. It's supposed to match products with needs. It's supposed to be fun—lots of travel and all that! If what you say is true, how did everything get so crazy?" They didn't believe him!

Bill explained that the adversarial nature of the sales relationship today was created in large measure by the buyers, not the salesmen. To support this, Bill quoted a recent article headlined "Act Japanese, American Car Makers Tell Their Suppliers," by Donald Wontat.*

" 'General Motors,' " Bill continued, " 'intends to slash its supplier network by half. Ford is moving in the same direction. But to implement Japanese-style relationships with scores of companies, the critics say Detroit and its support firms will have to smooth over the adversarial relationship that, at times, has matched—in depth of feeling at least—the pitched battles with the United Auto Workers Union.

" 'The Big Three have routinely pitted suppliers against each other in bidding wars for contracts on identical parts. Suppliers complained of late-hour engineering changes ordered by Detroit that compromise the quality of components—and create chaos in their plants.

" 'James McLean, President of Budd Company of Troy, Michigan, and a major supplier of stamping and other parts,' " Bill read on, " 'says there has long been a certain insensitivity among the Big Three to the special problems of suppliers.' "

Bill paused for effect. " 'A protest from a parts maker,' " he quoted with emphasis, " 'often brings the response: You want our business or don't you?' A classic application of the Golden Rule, don't you think?" Bill observed, smiling. *"He who has the gold makes the rules."*

---

* Copyright 1982, *Los Angeles Times*. Reprinted by permission.

The recruiters left, shaking their collective heads. "You might not like the way the world is today," mumbled one, "but you certainly have to accept it." If buyers treat their vendors without ethics or consideration, what can buyers expect in return? This could get out of hand.

But Bill Merriweather had bigger concerns. Several of the corporation's new products had incurred substantial R&D costs and were two years behind schedule. Corporate attention was not focused on introducing these products, and the pressure on the sales force was mounting.

In order to relieve Bill's regional and district managers from the time and responsibility of recruiting—not to mention the accompanying placement fees from search firms—corporate personnel had volunteered to create a department from its own budget whose sole function was to recruit skilled personnel for the corporation. There was a running dispute between line sales management and the personnel professors as to who could best recruit top salesmen. That disagreement was Bill's primary reason for meeting with the recruiters. Bill was of the opinion that only a line sales manager has sensitive enough antennae to recognize the true killer instinct of another top producer. But he had been unable to convince management that selling is still an art, not a science, and that salesmen couldn't be hired according to a formula. So personnel had gotten the job of recruiting Bill's sales force.

Meanwhile, one of the recruiters returned to Bill's office. The conversation that followed had the potential to be a solid aid to salesmen.

"I'm Boyd Mueller," he said formally. "I have just taken over as director of sales recruiting and this is the first time I've had a chance to sit down and talk with the great Bill Merriweather face to face. I have to admit, your observation that good salesmen don't like people shocked most of my associates. My background is in education. I spent five years as a public school administrator and ten years with a management development firm. Five years ago I founded my own firm specializing in sales training. After several years of eking out a living doing that, I realized that my next original creative thought would be my first. What I had really been doing for five years was cobbling and plagiarizing the creative things that had been done before by others.

"After much soul searching," Boyd went on, "I rationalized

that cobbling and plagiarizing is a talent in itself. I needed to find a place where my ability to assimilate the creative successes achieved by others would be productive and appreciated. So I closed the doors of my little practice, turned in my air travel card, paid off American Express in installments, and applied for the job of director of sales recruiting for Thermacon-Frigacon Inc.

"What you said, Bill, has been a revelation to my people. To help us service your division properly, could you expand a bit on some of the reasons you think selling is an adversary process and why you think salesmen don't like people?"

Bill nodded and motioned his visitor to a chair. "I appreciate your interest. It would have been a lot easier for you to walk out of here shaking your head like the rest of them. So I'll be glad to take as much time as you need to fully explain my position. Let me start with an example. Six years ago our R&D Department got fat, happy, and lazy. As a result, a new company came up with a product that competed with our mainstay, Thermacon-A. Up until then, Thermacon-A had been a cash cow. It sold itself. For years several of our R&D engineers had been advocating design changes, but our policy people wouldn't listen. They couldn't see any reason for changing a good thing.

"Those engineers left Thermacon, acquired some financial backing, and two years later formed a new company that produced the product that beat the technical pants off Thermacon-A. It was a smaller unit, a more efficient unit, and a more cost-effective unit. In addition, our competition's advertising made both the customers and us acutely aware of the deficiencies of Thermacon-A units and the benefits of theirs.

"At the time, we had 250 Thermacon-A units on inventory at a total factory cost of $25 million. Retail on those units was double that figure. We had to unload them. Pete Abbott was our top national accounts salesman. I called him into my office one day and gave him the task.

"Pete knew the drill. He had plenty to lose and not much to gain. Oh, Pete's job wasn't at stake but his reputation certainly was. We didn't have a commission plan at the time so the most that he could expect for success was a pat on the back and possibly a letter from the chairman telling him what a valuable team player he was. Conversely, had he not been able to sell the old Thermacon-A inventory, every finger pointer on the fourteenth floor who helped decide not to upgrade the engineering

in Thermacon-A units would have blamed the sales organization for its failure to unload the inventory. Pete would have
taken most of the heat.

"Pete and I are still here. He successfully dumped the inventory. In fact, he was able to achieve this objective within 90
days. I might add that he did not take my quiet recommendation to discount the units and sell price.

"After Pete placed the final order and saved the third-
quarter dividend, we all asked him how in the hell he did it. He
replied that every product has three elements to it: hardware,
software, and service. 'I knew,' Pete went on, 'that the competition had us beat solidly on hardware design. I suspected—although it was arguable—that it also had us beat on software. So
I abandoned hardware and software pitches and simply sold
service. I called on every major account I knew and was quite
up front about our competitor's new product. I indicated that
we had considered incorporating some of its ideas into Thermacon-A units for several years but felt them to be risky from the
standpoint of service. I reiterated that Thermacon-Frigacon
Inc. had grown to over a billion-dollar company solely on the
basis of its engineering integrity. We're a conservative company
because we don't take high risks and pass those risks along to
our customers. Every engineering breakthrough must be tested
for adverse consequences, just like new drugs before the Food
and Drug Administration. Remember the Thalidomide disaster,' he pointed out. 'Had that drug been allowed on the American market as soon or as easily as it had been in England, there
would have been thousands and thousands more babies born
with flippers instead of hands. Thalidomide made my point,'
Pete went on. 'Even with careful scrutiny, new changes—be
they engineering or chemical—can have unforeseen consequences. I sold Thermacon's reputation for service and integrity and I got full price for the units.'

"At the end of the applause the chairman of the board took
the unusual step of thanking Pete Abbott personally for his accomplishment," Bill Merriweather continued. "When asked
how he felt about making a presentation to customers who were
quite aware of the engineering credibility gap between
Thermacon-A and its new competitor, Pete replied, 'I felt like
the bald-headed barber trying to sell one of his customers a
bottle of hair tonic.' This broke everybody up and the chairman

asked Pete how the barber managed to do it. 'Well,' Pete went on, 'the barber's customer had asked him how he dared to sell hair tonic when he himself was bald. Nothing wrong with that, said the barber. Whether you know it or not, there are 10,000 guys out there trying to sell brassieres. We have been friends for ten years, the barber went on. I should have used this hair tonic when my hair was just thinning like yours. The barber said this as he wrapped up the package. But I wasn't as smart as you. So now, do as I say, not as I do. The deal was closed.'

"Needless to say," Bill Merriweather concluded, "after that speech, the director of research and development got his group cracking on what is now the Thermacon 1000."

"That's a good story," Boyd said, "but I don't really understand how it is germane. I can understand that you put Pete Abbott into an artificial pressure cooker. He had everything to lose and nothing to gain by accepting responsibility for unloading $25 million in outdated inventory. I can understand that he sold service and integrity when he knew he couldn't compete on product and software. What kind of person does that make him? Pete Abbott might really like people, but he was forced to choose between two very lousy alternatives from his point of view. His only choices were to refuse to do the job that you asked him to do, Bill, or get out and try to do the job in spite of a high possibility of failure. That's not a good enough criterion to judge anyone's feelings toward people in general."

"That's true," Bill went on, "but you forget, Boyd, that I specifically asked Pete to perform this task for Thermacon-Frigacon products. I could have assigned a lot of people the job, but I suspect they merely would have reported back to me what we already knew—that Thermacon-A units could not compete with our competition's new product. Only Pete Abbott had the killer instinct that I could count on to get the job done."

"Okay," Boyd said, "I guess you better define a killer instinct for me."

"Fine," Bill replied. "Let's take something simple. Let's take Pete's little anecdote about the barber to see exactly what a killer instinct is. Not everybody has it.

"The barber, like Pete, had overhead. He had a wife and a family, and if he didn't sell haircuts and hair products his business would fail and his family wouldn't eat. The fact that he was bald was a handicap. But what should he do now that his hair had fallen out—find another career? What should Pete have done when Thermacon's R&D department let him down? Flush his retirement and find a new job?

"On the other hand, the barber's customer had a real problem too. In a few short years he knew he was probably going to be as bald as a cue ball. Being a vain animal like the rest of us, the customer wanted to prevent that from happening. So now you have a classic situation of two people with totally different sets of personal objectives attempting to see if there is a ground for agreement. In spite of their ten-year relationship, each is not genuinely concerned about the other's objectives. Although he might deny it, the customer couldn't care less if the barber's business failed. Let's face it. When someone dies the first thing we think is, 'Thank God it wasn't me,' before saying, 'I'm really sorry to hear about that.' The barber, on the other hand, figured that the customer's hair was going to fall out anyway and that any kind of legitimate treatment would delay this unfortunate event. As long as the customer had any hair left he would still be a customer. Bald men don't need many haircuts. So the barber was able to rationalize selling a long-time customer and friend a bottle of hair tonic whose ability to produce results was somewhat questionable, to say the least."

"I'm beginning to see your point," Boyd said. "In other words, although they were friends and associates of ten years' standing, when it got down to serious business, both buyer and seller took a self-serving position and neither really gave a hoot about the other's personal problems or objectives."

"That's right," Bill replied. "In Pete's case, Thermacon's customers had a long-time trust relationship with him. Nevertheless, the buying motivator of safety now jeopardized that relationship. If Thermacon-A units proved inferior to our new competitor's products, our buyers' credibility would diminish in the eyes of their superiors. They did not value their relationship with Pete to the extent of their own detriment. Cold-blooded decisions like that are made every day. Pete found himself in a classic conflict of objectives with his buyers. They needed a product like Thermacon-A and, like Pete, they needed to keep their job, pay the rent, and feed their family. Pete's previous 'friends' were now his adversaries. Pete's killer instinct made itself visible when he found a way to turn their personal concerns into an advantage. Pete's buyers were not end users of Thermacon-A units. They were purchasing agents, or what's called Feasibility Buyers in the trade—buyers of a technical orientation who evaluate the benefits and features of competing products for end users and for the people paying the bills. Buyers like this need to be right all the time. But Pete knew that the definition of right is always relative to a particular point of view. He realized that even though end users of a Thermacon-A unit might be more than willing to risk changing to a competing product for the benefits promised by a new design, the end users did not answer directly to top management. Pete's buyers did. By raising concerns about possible problems with his competitor's new design, Pete was able to make the specter of potential disaster loom so large that it was safe for his buyers to recommend the purchase of Thermacon-A units until the competing new design was tried and proven. 'Let your competitors test the new unit,' was Pete Abbott's battle cry. 'The extra benefits aren't worth the risk.'

"Even though he was dealing from a position of weakness, Pete was able to find a benefit to the customer that he could rationally advocate—safety! The customer was advocating cost-effectiveness of the competitive unit and one of them would dominate. In this case it would be Pete. A question could be raised about the ethics Pete used in selling his customers what he knew to be a technically inferior product. But that question is far too simplistic. You've got to understand what Pete's customers were really buying. As I said before, an end user of the Thermacon-A unit may have been willing to take the risks inherent in an unproven product as an offset to the potential benefits. But Pete knew that an end user could not unilaterally dictate something called 'bet the company.' Only top management could take that risk, and it was very reluctant to do so. Therefore, an excellent case can be made that Pete was more ethical than his competitors. He was selling the safety of the proven Thermacon-A units compared with the risky benefits of the unproven units. From that point of view," Bill said, "if Pete was a killer, he was the most benevolent and empathetic killer on record. You could truthfully say he only had the best interests of his victims at heart."

"I think I'm getting a migraine," Boyd said.

"Let's go back to basics," Bill said. "Like the barber, our salesmen are basically nice people who have to feed their families, so they have to sell a product to earn money for food. But on top of that responsibility, look what else we make them deal

with. Every six months we have them work up a budget. Every
year we have them work up a forecast. Every month the forecast is reviewed against their performance. Every quarter the
budgets are adjusted. If a man doesn't make his forecast, he's
penalized. Sometimes he loses his job. If a man doesn't make
his budget, he's penalized. Sometimes he loses his job. And let's
face it, it's not just the salesmen who are in jeopardy. Your budget and my budget are predicated upon sales forecasts being accurate. This corporation is like the federal government. The
government hands out money to the states and municipalities—but where does the money come from in the first place?
That's right, from the states and municipalities. If the states
and municipalities failed to produce revenue, the federal government would starve to death. So would this corporation if our
salesmen failed to produce sales. But our salesmen never receive any real corporate support. At the corporate level the subject of selling to make money is treated the same as the subject
of sex. Everybody knows you do it but nobody is willing to talk
about it.

"Our top management people like to feel they are above the
selling arena and prefer to talk platitudes about job enrichment
for the worker rather than trying to help the guy who supports
them make a buck. The salesman is caught between people like
us demanding that he produce revenue, people like his buyers
trying to save revenue, and people called competitors trying to
beat him out of whatever orders and money there is out there
for anyone. Now tell me, how can a guy who really likes people
maintain his sanity, let alone operate successfully, in that kind
of environment? Everybody he meets wants a piece of his
hide."

"Okay," Boyd said, "in that context, what you say makes
sense. When I had my own sales training firm I used to teach
sales planning and strategy and a variation on the consular selling method. As you know, consular selling teaches that a win
must be found for the customer or a sale can never be made. In
finding a win for the customer the salesman also wins. The big
pizzazz of consular sales training is Win/Win stickers plastered
all over the walls and on buttons in every salesman's lapel. It is
a good program, but it obviously has its drawbacks.

"Two years ago a major company whose primary product
was the processing and sale of chemicals called me up with an

emergency. The new vice president of sales was almost beside himself. He had just put 700 of his men through consular selling. Sales soared—I mean they literally went off the forecast charts. Unfortunately, profits crashed."

Bill interrupted. "I heard about that. That was the case where the only win for the customer the salesman could find was a reduction in price and/or delivery time, wasn't it?"

"You got it," Boyd said. "Chemicals must meet an established quality standard. After that, price, terms, and delivery are the only games left to play, and the salesmen had no authority or latitude for change. They were responsible only for quotas and goals. All of a sudden, the salesmen were shortening their delivery dates, causing production costs to go off the wall. The extra-generous payment terms they gave customers cut deeply into a cash flow that was already hard hit by increased production costs. In addition, the salesmen were twisting and turning to find a way to give the customer a better price break under any guise they could think of.

"The vice president of sales had been appalled by what he considered to be a Theory X approach to sales management on the part of his predecessor," Boyd continued. "He felt that the company was losing potential sales because the salesmen were advocating the company's position to the point of ignoring the customer's objectives. The VP felt that the situation was the mirror image of the one described in the article you quoted—where General Motors in effect said to its vendors, 'If you don't want our business, go elsewhere.' He felt his salesmen were saying to customers, 'If you don't like our deal, go find a better one.' He had a point. To some extent, that really was the salesmen's position, because that was his predecessor's policy. What the new VP didn't know was the reason behind his predecessor's policies and strict autocratic control of the sales force. He simply condemned his predecessor and his policies on the basis of management theory. By definition, the 700 men in his sales force were made up mostly of Order Takers and Relationship Salesmen. Relationship Salesmen, for the most part, sell their relationship with the customer rather than their product. They sell themselves first, the company second, and the product third. Usually, Relationship Salesmen simply sell integrity. But integrity will never sell need.

"Order Takers usually don't *sell* anything, but they will provide you with what you want if they have it. An Order Taker's idea of a hard selling day is talking to ten extra customers. A Relationship Salesman's idea of a good selling day is to invite his customer out to lunch and talk about the ballgame.

"Both Order Takers and Relationship Salesmen need approval but have conditioned themselves to expect rejection. That's why the Order Taker won't try to sell and the Relationship Salesman will talk about ball scores rather than product. Fewer risks are involved for everyone.

"But don't jump to the conclusion the Order Takers and Relationship Salesmen *like* people," said Boyd. "In point of fact, these types sometime suffer more real abuse from people than the more aggressive types who are capable of standing up and confronting a customer and successfully negotiating a sale on the merits of the product alone. It is the Order Taker's and Relationship Salesman's nature to take the path of least resistance. The new VP's consular selling philosophy gave them all an excuse to go out and make sweetheart deals they knew the customer would take. Under the guise of finding a win for the customer, they gleefully beat the hell out of their competitors and quietly ignored the impact their actions were having on corporate costs and profits.

"Some of them probably even laughed. Most of the men were old-timers. They knew the score and could predict the outcome. But who cares, they said. Let's go bite the hand that feeds us for a while and make some money doing it. Through consular selling they had found a way to ignore prudent company policy and still avoid the ultimate rejection of being fired.

"By the way," Boyd added, "until then, I had always been enamored of the theory of consular selling. That job convinced me to get out of the sales training business and go back to work with professional salespeople. It was the first time I had a glimmer of your premise that most salesmen only go through the motions of liking people. I was dumbfounded. I thought that all salesmen, despite their aggression, really liked people, just the way actors do. How wrong I was. This particular bunch needed approval and sought to avoid rejection. They turned their aggression on their master when the leash was removed. What would you have done to prevent this if you had been in the VP's shoes?" Boyd asked.

"What could have been done?" countered Bill Merriweather. "From what you have told me, the VP should have known that his sales force was made up mostly of Relationship Salesmen and Order Takers. His concern about the drawbacks of aggressive, entrepreneurial salesmen—guys who sell *need*— was most probably an echo of a previous experience. If he had recognized that his present sales force consisted of Order Takers and Relationship Salesmen, he probably would have managed them differently.

"Salesmen who sell need are more secure and self-contained. They have a higher tolerance for rejection and have less need for approval of others. Their motivation comes from self-approval. Relationship Salesmen and Order Takers have the same amount of aggression as Need Salesmen. But their need for approval of others is the weak spot. By forcing Relationship Salesmen and Order Takers to perform advocate selling, the vice president's predecessor had in fact instilled an artificial backbone in a rather weak sales force. I am sure that this did not ingratiate the old VP with the sales force, which was probably why he was replaced. Management freed the slaves and the slaves gave away the plantation," Bill added with a grin. Then he became serious again.

"What should have been done is obvious. Chemicals are a mundane product. Boring to sell. An effort should have been made to find new applications, new benefits, and new features for the salesmen to talk about. The salesmen's natural need to please would have been turned outward in a profitable way. No excuses would have been accepted had they tried to turn it inward, as they did by negotiating price, delivery date, and terms that were not beneficial to their employer. In other words, give them something to advocate and make sure that they advocate it to the customer and not their employer. Whatever you think of salesmen, they are advocates. Just like lawyers. There are lawyers who win cases and there are lawyers who lose cases. I prefer the ones who win—particularly if they're working for me," Bill said. "But most important, I want one who is going to direct his efforts to selling the jury on my innocence rather than one who is going to sell me on the idea that a two-year sentence is light.

"As I understand advocate selling," Bill continued, "it is the antithesis of consular selling. Advocate selling dictates that there is some primary motivation to buy which can be utilized in every sales situation. It was safety in Pete Abbott's case. Finding this motivator is what puts the salesman in a dominant position. Consular selling, on the other hand, dictates that the salesman should use his 'judgment' as to whether the buyer's objectives are truly being met rather than use his 'skill' as a salesman to advocate the benefits and features of his own product over his competitors'. My problem with consular selling," Bill said, "has always been that its basic premise of a win for the customer gives weak salesmen an easy and acceptable excuse for the customer's failure to buy. In my opinion, psychiatrists should be skilled in counseling, judges skilled in making judgments, and salesmen skilled in closing sales."

"I'd like to agree with you," Boyd said, "but I am truly ambivalent on this point. In my opinion, consular selling was developed by the best behavioralists and psychologists this country currently has to offer. What you're saying is that a weak salesman would use 'ethics' as a reason for accepting a no from the buyer. He couldn't find a win for the customer. Whereas a strong Advocate Salesman would search beneath simple benefits and features into the buyer's fear-of-failure insecurities to sell him a product that was tried and proven but not on the leading edge of technology."

"But," Bill asked, "where is the line between incompetence and ethics? Does an incompetent who sells his employer an excuse for his failure like people any better than a killer like Abbott who sells his customer on buying what he probably truly thinks is an outdated product? Where does true loyalty lie? These are very fundamental questions everyone must answer, not just professional salesmen.

"The dominant advocate selling method is not perfect either. You and I are engaged in an exchange right now that is an example of advocate selling," Bill went on. "Even though we have common objectives to hire the most effective salespeople available, you and I are spending time testing our philosophical mettle regarding what kind of salesmen are best. I sink or swim on the results my salespeople produce. You sink or swim on your ability to recruit top people, a good number of whom are going to do the selling for this division. Yet you do not really subscribe to the advocate method of selling. As I've stated before, my concern is that the behavioralists and psychology types you find in corporate personnel departments or their entrepreneurial counterparts—search firms—are not qualified to truly evaluate and ascertain the qualities that make up a successful outside salesman. Line operating managers call those types 'goofies,' with good reason.

"Selling is still an art. It is not a science. It's always been my position," Bill said, "that it takes a good salesman to know a good salesman. Only another killer can sniff out a true killer instinct. But I am more than willing to let you and your group prove your worth, Boyd. I agree that you cannot turn a bunch of aggressive salesmen loose on customers like a pack of war dogs. If you could, the best closing technique in the world would be a .45-caliber automatic pointed at the head of the buyer. There are limits to advocate selling.

"The critical element in advocate selling is knowing when *not* to use it. The most fondly remembered warriors of history are those who tempered their conquests with mercy and a high sense of justice. Let's face it, old Abe Lincoln and his Civil War killed more Americans than Hitler, the British, or the Spanish combined, yet he is fondly remembered as a compassionate man. There is always a balance that must be achieved between aggression, justice, and compassion. No salesman should ever oversell a customer simply because he has the negotiating skills to do so. In fact it's against his best interests to do so. He'll blow all his follow-on sales.

"But how can you tell who will cross that line and who won't during a hiring interview? That is the litmus test of a good recruiter. His job is to find the people whose superb selling skills and aggressive need to achieve are balanced by a sense of fair play. That's a very big order. Some people out there are not only incompetent but basically dishonest. Unlike the Order Takers and Relationship Salesmen who take advantage of a corporate change of philosophy toward selling to bend the rules on price, terms, and delivery," Bill said, "some salesmen deliberately set out to rip off their employer. They sell themselves into a job that is above their ability. But instead of trying to grow and master the required skills of the job, they turn all their attention and energy toward hiding their incompetence. They twist and turn, lie and blame until they are caught and fired—or promoted into a different job. I had a man like that working for me once," Bill added. "Matt Gallagher needed a job badly. He had seven kids to support, and his last employer had let him go because he refused to take a foreign assignment. He had more experience in management than in sales, but he made all the right noises so I agreed to put him in the field. In four months it should have been all over, because Matt didn't really know how to sell. But it didn't happen that way.

"Like a business professor I once had at City University, Matt could talk about the principles of marketing and sales impressively and at great length. But there was no way he could practice what he preached. Unfortunately for me, a critical regional manager position opened up one month after Matt was hired. Because of Matt's previous background in sales management, personnel recommended I give him the job. However, Matt had little direct experience with sales, and Thermacon's regional managers are still required to sell. A major part of a regional manager's responsibility is to personally manage all the major accounts in his region with whom the company has maintained a successful and profitable relationship.

"Instead of managing the accounts properly, Matt decided to try to make himself look good enough quick enough to get promoted again. After all, he had gotten lucky once. For six months all Matt Gallagher did was run around taking old customers to lunch. Every time they said, 'Maybe,' Matt wrote it down as a firm order with an extended date of delivery. His forecast looked great, his backlog looked super, and for several months he was the star of the show. Then, of course, the whole thing exploded. I fired him immediately, almost lost my own job, and spent the next 12 months smoothing the feathers of our biggest customers. Would you believe," Bill said with a grimace, "that turkey had the gall to sue us for commissions and bonuses?

"The major point," Bill said, "is that salesmen are *supposed* to be aggressive. They don't have to like people. But, as the case of Matt Gallagher painfully demonstrates, that aggression must be curbed and channeled. I failed to do that. Matt, because of his own devious nature, was unable to satisfy his aggressive instincts at the customer level. He couldn't push for the order because it conflicted with his intolerance of rejection. So he took the path of least resistance and turned his aggression inward on the company. He lied to us. It was easier for him to lie to us than to sell the customer, and for a while we actually applauded him for doing it."

"That would make an interesting case study," Boyd said. "Gallagher evidently was a man who needed approval so badly that he couldn't handle the rejection of the customer saying no when he asked for the order. Conversely, he was willing to tolerate his ultimate rejection by the company and you—even his disgrace—in return for the short-term recognition and the approval of others and self-approval that came with that recognition. You are saying again that there is a love/hate relationship between salesmen and the people they are selling—be it their customer, their company, or the boss."

"That's right," Bill said. "Matt really didn't like people but he needed them for his own definition. For all practical purposes, Matt was half a person. There was something missing. Matt should have been aggressive enough to get beneath the surface with his buyers and ascertain what kind of buyers they were. Were they purchasing agents? Were they end users of the product? Were they general managers interested in profit? Were they technicians interested in performance?

"He should have done this analysis with the same exuberance and skill that he used analyzing the objectives and political climate of the company employing him. Like Pete Abbott, Matt Gallagher should have found a way to make the product he was selling meet the customer's objectives.

"If the customer were a purchasing agent, Matt could have sold integrity and safety, as Pete Abbott did. If the customer were an end user, Matt could have sold benefits and features, or 'bells and whistles' as they're called in the trade. If the customer were a technician buying a product for somebody else to use, Matt could have sold a combination of bells and whistles and integrity and safety.

"But instead of selling the customer, Matt decided to sell us. He knew us more intimately than the buyer. Therein lies the fault. Matt should have known his customers more intimately than he knew us. But he made no effort to do so. Matt was aggressive but he had no ethics," Bill went on. "He was no better than a thief. I failed to recognize this, so the company lost heavily, I lost heavily, and Matt lost heavily. It was a lose/lose/lose situation for everyone.

"On the other hand, there's the case of John Davidson," Bill continued. "John had all of Matt's aggressiveness, but he channeled it properly. He grew up in the hard-coal regions of West Virginia—a skinny kid with glasses in a family of football players. John didn't have a way to prove himself so he took to fast cars. Somewhere along the line his father recognized what was going on—at least John gives him that credit—and got the kid into stock car racing. All of a sudden John had an identity. He no longer cut school, his grades came up, and he became one of the hottest stock car drivers in an area that is as famous for its daredevil drivers as it is for its football players. John found that achieving success gave him a sort of power. He was recognized. Having received approval from others, he was able to approve of himself.

"He was about twenty-eight when I met him," Bill recalled, "and he had an absolute dynamite sales record behind him. But he was a bit rough around the edges. After six months I eased him into three-piece suits with button-down shirts and out of that tomato-red Cadillac convertible he loved to drive at 80 miles an hour. John was good but he needed sophistication. Unlike Matt, who basically had no loyalty to anyone, John could appreciate that not everybody was his adversary but understood that not everyone was his friend.

"At a sales meeting two years later I asked John to discuss with the troops the balance a salesman needs to develop between aggressively pursuing new customer relationships and maintaining the good will and repeat business of current customers. John was an expert at achieving this balance. However, some of the newer men had been attempting to squeeze increased business out of old customers so cold-bloodedly that I personally had to field the complaints. My objective was not to dampen their enthusiasm. I simply wanted to channel it toward building new customer relationships rather than squeezing the last drop of blood from the old ones.

"John was superb. He got the point across quickly and well. He explained that once a prospect becomes a customer, the salesman must react to that change, just as bears must hibernate and birds must fly south when fall finally changes to winter. The aggressive tactics used to acquire the new customer's business must be replaced by sensible management of the customer relationship. To ignore that need for a change can be fatal.

"If the customer's real needs do not fit the revenue needs of the salesman's quota, that doesn't mean the customer is now an enemy. And if the salesman tries to jawbone his buyer for additional orders, neglects him to seek more lucrative accounts, or exerts undue pressure to win points for the sales contest, he will find his reward very short-lived. His good customers will find someone new to do business with, and his new prospects may prove to be something quite different from what he expected—if they materialize as customers at all.

"Don't pressure a good customer just because you want to be a superstar—that was John's message. Salesmen who do are actually asking their customers to solve their problems. It should be the other way around. Manage your customers fairly and properly. Stifle your impulse to drop your problems in a good customer's lap or to view customers as a means of achieving your short-term personal ambitions. They have their own problems and ambitions to worry about. Treat them well and get out there on the street and generate new revenue from prospects without jeopardizing the steady flow of old customer revenue. In case you are ever tempted to question the wisdom of this adivce, John said to his audience, let me tell you the story of the stubborn little sparrow who wouldn't listen." Bill grinned as he continued with John Davidson's story.

"Once upon a time, there was a nonconforming sparrow who decided not to fly south for the winter. However, soon the weather turned so cold that the bird reluctantly started to fly south. In a short time ice began to form on his wings and he fell to earth in a barnyard, almost frozen. A cow passed by and dumped a pile of manure on the little sparrow. The sparrow thought it was the end. But the manure warmed him and defrosted his wings. Warm, able to breathe, but unhappy, he started to chirp his annoyance. Just then a large cat came by and, hearing the chirping, investigated the sounds. The cat cleared away the manure, found the chirping bird, and promptly ate him.

"The moral of John's story is (1) everyone who piles manure on you is not necessarily your enemy, (2) everyone who gets you out of the manure is not necessarily your friend, and (3) if you're warm and safe in a pile of manure, keep your mouth shut!

"The sparrow was stubborn and didn't want to conform. Like a salesman who finds his projections off by a considerable degree, the sparrow thought it was the end when he found himself covered with manure. And, like the salesman who blamed his good customers for his dilemma, the sparrow blamed the cow. Instead of adjusting to the new reality and the benefits it offered, both the sparrow and the salesman decided to make noise. The result was a disaster for both.

"John's philosophy took hold and worked perfectly. Whenever I'd notice people falling back on pressuring old customers, I'd call a meeting and have John give his little speech. What I want in a sales force, Boyd," Bill concluded, "is men with a sense of competition, strong and aggressive but not lethal. I want men who go into the arena with a mailed fist, but I want that fist concealed by a velvet glove."

CONCEPT 2

Rejection! The Part It Plays in Selling

Everybody *hates* rejection! Rejection threatens our already fragile feelings of self-worth and makes us introspective. It's a shame that we need to seek the opinion of others in order to form an opinion of ourselves, but it's true!

Franklin Roosevelt once said that the only thing we have to fear is fear itself. How true it is. Psychologists say that life is a series of rejections that begin with the frustrations of an infant whose hands are too small and muscle coordination too feeble to grasp the bright object he sees. Achievers push on and try again. Nonachievers choose a different bright object.

There are various ways to handle rejection. Some people run at it head on to find the cause and eliminate it. Others have to learn first that their own behavior is the cause of rejection by others. Still others simply take rejection for granted and develop a way of living with it.

Fear of rejection is the basic reason most people do not become salesmen. In sales the measurement of results is clear: Either the customer buys or he doesn't. Fear of rejection is also what makes some salesmen bad closers. They'd rather take a maybe than a definite no. They are hoping that the customer will say yes on his own accord. But if he doesn't, there is always the opportunity to come back and waste more time.

People who have a very low tolerance for rejection go through life either waiting for someone else to take the risks before they act or just standing back and watching the world go by.

Strangely enough, some professional salesmen seem to have retained a low tolerance for rejection. They sell themselves rather than the product, and take pride in establishing a *relationship* with a customer. This creates a desire to align themselves with a product that has an already established need—one that usually is associated with a high degree of quality and integrity.

Put a salesman who sells need through an ordeal by fire, and he'll try to prove that he can sell refrigerators to Eskimos. And he would find a conceptual way to do it. A salesman selling customer relationships would never risk that rejection. He would contemptuously state right off the bat that an Eskimo has no need for a refrigerator without ever thinking that possibly Eskimos, like the rest of us, need to keep things cool instead of just frozen. Let's face it, you can't regulate the Arctic temperature. You can regulate a refrigerator!

People who watch the world go by and people who just stand and wait couldn't care less. They would never agree to any ordeal by fire. Instead, they would prefer to keep their own self-esteem intact rather than risk it on some venture whose outcome is highly measurable and probably ill-fated from the start.

In professional selling, it is a known fact that the harder the sale, the higher the commissions! By failing to risk rejection, a substantial segment of professional salespeople have relegated themselves to a lifestyle that is far beneath their ultimate potential. They would rather not play the game than play it and lose!

Tom DeFranco grew up in the Bronx. After he finished school and thought about the kind of life he would lead if he remained in his neighborhood, Tom decided to become a salesman. He liked people and people liked him. Tom figured those qualities were the key to making a fortune in sales. Right?

Wrong! Tom's first selling job shoved him against reality with the subtlety of a 20-megaton bomb. Tom signed up as a salesman for a publisher of the New York State Metalworking Directory. Not very glamorous, but as its title indicates, this highly indexed publication lists almost every metalworking firm in the state of New York. Most metalworking shops are specialty job shops. The businessmen who own them theoretically need to know which of their peers can produce certain components beyond their own specialty so arrangements can be made to bid jointly on complex jobs. At least that's what the directory publisher claimed.

New salesmen bought a "sample" directory from the publisher for $400 and sold it for $700, pocketing $300 in commission. "You mean all I have to do is sell this book?" Tom asked his boss incredulously, "and I make 300 bucks? That's as much as I used to make in a week. How many of these do you think I can sell in one day?"

Tom's boss laughed and told him he could sell one an hour if he could make that many calls.

Tom was ecstatic. "I couldn't wait to run out the door," he recalled. "My boss stopped me midstride and said, 'Hey, hotshot, before you go tearing up concrete let me give you some pointers.' He proceeded to lecture me on how important it was to physically put the book in the customer's hands. 'If nothing else,' he said, 'the guy will buy just to be able to put it down. That book weighs over eight pounds!'"

Tom's morning was a disaster. On his first call, the owner was on vacation. On the second, the manager wouldn't see him. On the third call, Tom was determined. He barged his way into the shop and literally demanded to see the owner.

"I was such a banty rooster and so pushy, nobody dared throw me out," he recalled. "So people just pointed to the boss, a big man operating a drill press at the far end of the shop. I marched over, handed him the book, and told him he needed it. He handed it back to me and told me he didn't need it or me. I opened the book and pointed to all the companies that were listed in the directory and shoved it back at him. He shoved it back at me and told me that he already knew about the damned book and hadn't bothered to get himself listed so why would he buy it to find the names of the jerks who did. I shoved the book back at him and said it was time he stopped running a one-man band and started doing business like the rest of the human race. At that point," Tom said, "he grabbed the book, plopped it on his drill press, and quite dispassionately drilled a three-quarter-inch hole through its 2,000 pages. Then he threw me and my deflowered directory into the street. There I was in the rain with the $400 book I had scraped and saved to buy which now sported a three-quarter-inch hole directly through its center. Talk about rejection! About then," Tom recalled, "I had this funny feeling that I had a lot to learn about selling."

Tom recovered from this initial rejection because he was determined. Being determined to build up a tolerance for rejection is by far the quickest and most efficient way to deal with the problem. "Psych yourself up before a call and shake a lot afterward" is one man's advice. "Think positive even when the customer says no" is another's. "Grit your teeth and make another call—like getting back on a horse after a fall" is probably the best advice. As Tom said, "I knew there wasn't going to be any pleasant cure for the turmoil, frustration, and insecurity I felt every time I looked at that three-quarter-inch hole drilled through the middle of my brand-new sample."

Like any new salesman, Tom had a world of problems to deal with and new skills to learn besides trying to handle rejection. But once he got over the paralyzing numbness that flat-out rejection can trigger, Tom went on to spend time with his boss to develop and polish his style. And he spent a whole lot of his own time learning to relate the benefits of his directory to the results his customers wanted to achieve. Anybody can do this if he has the will. Tom wanted to make money. He wanted to escape the Bronx neighborhood in which he was raised. Selling was a skill he felt he could learn on his own, without having to attend a university that his family couldn't afford. It didn't come easy. One of his biggest burdens was learning to live with the criticism he heaped on himself every time he blew a sale. A weaker man would have walked away and adjusted his goals and ambitions to accommodate an easier profession.

Not everyone has the determination of Tom DeFranco. Some people need to be grabbed by the back of the neck and shoved smack into the consequences of their own actions before they will change. Facing up to your own behavior is like learning about a hangover. Nobody can tell you what it's like. You have to go through it to believe it.

Jim Franklin was one of those people. There was an excellent chance that Jim would have spent his entire life protecting himself from rejection—except for the fact that his humble beginnings and ambition to be affluent exceeded his fear of the unknown. Jim decided there was money in sales. His ambition was so great that his wife once commented with a disquieting seriousness that Jim was really a reincarnated English squire who was bound and determined to regain the affluence he had enjoyed in his former life. Jim had a long way to go. He was a classic example of someone who deals with rejection by rejecting the rejector. This is a common enough reaction, but it is very uncommon for people who handle rejection in this manner to remain in sales.

Of course, Jim Franklin would have had to deal with his insecurities in any profession he entered. But by remaining in sales, where rejection is an everyday hazard of the trade, Jim was forced to come to terms with his own personality—a confrontation he might have avoided in a different occupation. As a result, he grew more as a salesman than he ever could have as an accountant, and his personal rewards—both psychic and financial—made him a happier man. But the road was not easy. The longest row Jim had to hoe was learning to be just a good Relationship Salesman. Compared with selling need, selling relationships is easy. But Jim's fear of rejection and hostile attitude toward people made this a very formidable task indeed.

Jim came as close to hating people as anybody can without forfeiting membership in the human race. He was terrified by people's potential for rejecting him. Bloody centuries of religious, racial, and tribal persecutions underlie how easily fear can be turned into hate. Jim had another problem. He was short. Ever since he stopped growing at 5 feet 6, he had made a determined effort to prove that he was mentally and morally superior to everyone—an ambitious but useless task.

Jim became frustrated. What he was doing of course was selling his superiority instead of his product. He would meet a customer impeccably dressed, offer a handshake that rivaled King Kong's, and throw words like "predilection" and "bemused" into all his conversations.

Fortunately for him, Jim's first sales position was as a representative for a business tax service, a job that required a high degree of confidence, integrity, and trust between buyer and seller. Many of Jim's customers mistook his attitude of superiority for honesty and integrity and subordinated themselves to him in conversation. As a result, Jim made a decent living selling a sort of reflected confidence in his employer's tax service after he sold himself. Naturally, his success was a checkerboard. Jim dealt with rejection by mentally rising above it. From that lofty perch he looked down on prospects who said no as idiots unworthy of his concern.

Jim's need for approval was so great and his self-esteem so fragile that he could make himself feel better only at the expense of others, thus contributing to his own rejection. People who saw through him dismissed him quickly. Jim was a paradox. His desperate need for approval and defensive anticipation of rejection created a self-fulfilling prophecy.

Frank Hanson became Jim's sales manager in 1975. Frank recalls, "When I first went on a call with Jim I mistook his acute case of megalomania for an acute case of self-righteous integrity, just as some of his customers did. This triggered a negative reaction in me, since I've always believed that people who sell integrity usually need to. Ralph Waldo Emerson once commented about a speaker, 'The more he talks about integrity the faster we count the spoons.' Later I found out that deep down inside Jim Franklin was nothing more than a quivering mass of Jell-O. He was terribly afraid of people. I realized that he needed approval of others so badly that he would risk the rejection inherent in a sales job in order to experience the highs that come from making a sale. He was a personality mess, but his basic need to achieve made him worth working with.

"Over a period of time I was able to sit Jim down and point out some important things. First of all, he was not selling the results of his product. He wasn't even selling the product. All Jim Franklin was selling was Jim Franklin. This limited his ability to make any kind of sale other than a relationship sale—a sale based upon a trust established between buyer and seller that has almost nothing to do with need for the product. It was absolutely impossible for Jim to sell need, because he could never get around to talking about the product. Three-quarters of his rejections came from customers who weren't exactly sure how the business tax service Jim was selling would be of benefit to them. Jim never understood this because he simply never analyzed it. He was too busy selling himself and insinuating to others that prospects who didn't buy were basically stupid people to begin with.

"I also pointed out to Jim that his great love for pompous words created a substantial barrier between himself and the customer. There are enough natural barriers between a buyer and seller without creating artificial ones. Most entrepreneurs never bother to learn or apply the English language with any great sophistication. Debaters they are not; businessmen they are!

"Jim's continued use of $64 words intimidated some buyers to the point of anger. Be what your buyer wants you to be, I said. Don't try to change him. If the guy says damn, say damn with him. If the buyer says darn, you say darn. But for God's sake don't make him feel uncomfortable by not saying one or the other.

"Most important, I tried to teach Jim to listen to what the customer was saying. Jim was always so busy thinking about what he was going to say next that he never really listened when the customer talked. He balked at that criticism. Jim felt that if he got into a free and open discussion with the customer, he would lose control of the sale, so he resisted my advice vigorously. Jim desperately needed to *feel* he was in control of the conversation, whether he really was or not.

"Finally," Frank went on, "out of desperation, I took Jim on a call to a client that he had been unable to sell and had been avoiding for the last six months. The man was polite and agreed to see us, but I could tell from the look on his face that this customer had correctly detected Jim's 'I'm okay—you stink' attitude in their initial conversations.

"I began the call by asking the customer a series of questions about his business. Warming to the subject of talking about himself, the customer began to explain what he and his company did. Later Jim would realize that people love to talk about themselves, and if you let them you are in fact accepting them. If you accept them, they tend to return the favor by not rejecting you. With a little encouragement from me, the customer began to tell us how he and his partner had started their business during the Vietnam War and how much it had grown over the last 15 years. Finally, realizing that he was talking quite a bit and taking up our time, the customer himself raised the 'burning question' Jim had never been able to get at before.

"He was currently having to choose between buying an in-house minicomputer and retaining the services of an outside business tax service. His accountant was ready to retire, so he knew he had to do something by the end of the year. One call later, Jim and I laid out the comparisons of all the minis available and contrasted them with the various features and benefits offered by a business tax service. I give Jim credit—he understood what needed to be done and made the presentation himself. The customer bought the business tax service, and for the first time in his life Jim Franklin sold a result instead of himself. More important, he realized that this opened a whole new set of doors to him that would enable him to experience approval of others and self-approval, and to avoid his nemesis—rejection!"

Jim Franklin didn't become a raging success overnight. But he did learn how to deal with rejection. He unloaded the psychological bag he was carrying and the telephone-pole-size chip on his shoulder. In learning to deal with rejection, Jim had to learn to deal with himself. Additional successes with formerly recalcitrant customers propped up Jim's self-esteem so that he no longer had to make himself look good at the expense of others. He no longer looked upon customers as idiots or inferior people simply because they had the power to reject him. Jim learned that he didn't have to sell integrity or superiority or even himself. Instead he learned to sell the results that his business tax service would produce. He learned to listen to the customer instead of talking. Complete control of the conversation was no longer necessary. Jim realized that if he could warm a buyer to a conversation, he would gain not only the buyer's gratitude but the buyer's friendship as well—and nobody likes to reject a friend.

Most important, Jim learned not to put artificial barriers between himself and the customer. Big words and intimidating handshakes may have their place in another profession, but advocate selling requires a velvet glove. He finally understood that the natural barriers between seller and buyer were more than enough to handle without creating artificial ones to soothe the *seller's* own fears and uncertainties. Jim learned that creating barriers to protect himself from rejection in fact usually triggered the rejection he sought to avoid, and he ceased to become a walking self-fulfilling prophecy.

Jim never did learn to sell need very well. He was a natural Relationship Salesman and he stayed with products where establishing a relationship was important. But Jim was a Doer—he always had been—that's why he remained in sales despite his handicaps. In his own way, Jim showed the same determination that Tom DeFranco showed in overcoming his problems with rejection. It just took him longer because Jim was unable to accept rejection in the first place. When Tom DeFranco experienced rejection he accepted it and tried to learn the cause so he could avoid the same mistake in the future. Jim Franklin rejected rejection, so he never analyzed for cause until Frank Hanson showed him the light.

The key element to dealing with rejection is to accept it. Then it can be dealt with. As Frank Hanson said, "If you are rejected—by a buyer or simply by someone you would like to know better—you have to accept, going in, that the person has the full power to reject you at his discretion."

Dandruff commercials thrive on the rejection of one interested party by another because of snowflakes on the collar. Mouthwash commercials sell the same theme. The message of these commercials is that if the rejected party analyzes the cause of the rejection and corrects it, there can be a happy ending. That was the case immediately with Tom DeFranco and eventually with Jim Franklin.

Rejection can play an even more complex role in selling. Believe it or not, some people have a built-in belief that they are going to be rejected, accept it, and somehow still wind up in sales. Paul Findley is a good example.

All his life Paul had been told what a turkey he was. His father used negative motivation. No matter what Paul achieved he always could have done better. His brothers and sisters resented having to care for Paul, but since he was the youngest, his mother insisted. Pygmalion-like, Paul began to believe what he had heard all his life. He considered himself a failure and a loser, but he accepted it. Unlike Jim Franklin, Paul did not lash back at the human race. In fact, he became fairly passive. In the world of Doers, Waiters, and Watchers, Paul Findley became a Watcher of the first magnitude.

Paul took no risks, so he received little rejection. When rejection became inevitable, Paul settled back and accepted it as something he probably deserved. What saved Paul from a self-condemned mundane existence was a chance job that he took as a clerk in a ladies' shoe store one Christmas. Paul's quiet ways and soft good looks appealed to his customers. They would seek him out and talk to him. His solicitous Order Taker nature pleased them, for they could spend as much time looking at shoes as they wanted without making him impatient. Paul's boss put up with his style because the customers seemed to like him and in the end almost always bought a pair of expensive shoes.

One day his boss took Paul aside, sat him down, and gave him one of the first meaningful compliments he had ever received. He explained that over 50 percent of the store's business came from customers who pointedly asked whether Paul would be available when they came in. For the first time in his life, Paul experienced the euphoria of success. He now had an identity!

As his success continued, Paul's personality changed. He became a Waiter instead of a Watcher. Unlike Doers, who can seemingly take nothing and turn it into something, Waiters wait for something to happen and then react to it. Paul waited for his customers to come in. He began to sell himself, because he had confidence that he wouldn't be rejected. Once he began to sell himself, the ladies loved him even more. Paul eventually built up a following that made him the rival of his peers. The continuous approval of others and absence of the rejection he had experienced all his life helped Paul overcome his negative self-image.

As a Watcher, Paul had allowed his customers to form a relationship with him. The shoes sold themselves, thanks to the buyer's talent for purchasing a fashionable line and accurately judging the needs of the market. As a Waiter, Paul began to solicit relationships with his customers and found he could do quite well. However, he still let the shoes sell themselves on their own merit. It was part of Paul's charm. The women trusted his judgment and knew he would never try to sell them a pair of shoes that didn't look good. In reality, at this stage Paul didn't trust himself to venture an opinion on what looked good and what didn't. So he relied on his customer's good taste and sold himself instead. Only later would he change.

Unlike the intangible single-product tax service Jim Franklin sold, retail sales offer a myriad of tangible products in all shapes, colors, or styles. What didn't work for Jim Franklin worked very well for Paul Findley. Paul could sell himself and trust that his customers would eventually find a pair of shoes that met their needs. Had Jim Franklin selected a career as a retail salesperson he probably would have done well, although his compulsion to reject people who rejected him would have still caused him problems. On the other hand, had Paul Findley tried to sell a single-product intangible business tax service, he would have been a disaster. But given Paul's passive personality, he would never have landed a job like that in the first place.

Paul Findley's continued success and the confidence it gave him changed his personality once again. After two years, Paul borrowed enough money to open his own ladies' shoe salon. To his great surprise, it was his father who willingly lent him most of the money. Paul became a Doer. His shy way with people didn't change. He retained the winning relationship with his customers that he always had, but Paul was now a quiet aggressor. He was a businessman who was selling need. That didn't mean he jawboned his customers into buying shoes they didn't want. Paul always asked them questions about fashion and design. He stayed abreast of new lines. He carefully chose his inventory to meet the needs of current customers and created a reason for potential customers to visit his shop out of curiosity.

In Paul's case, his early feelings of rejection and poor self-image were the biggest plusses he had. Anticipation of rejection created a shy young man who had such an appeal that women wanted to hug him. But Paul's ability to accept rejection allowed him to take risks later in his life when he gained the confidence to become a Doer instead of a Watcher. Paul's former boss often wondered whether Paul sold anything else besides shoes—a sour-grapes reaction to be expected from somebody whose business was rejected and abandoned by a large group of local customers the minute Paul left his employ.

Paul was one of those few people whose anticipation and acceptance of rejection was turned into an advantage. Outwardly, Paul never changed. He was still the affable, agreeable, quiet huggy-bear who made his customers love him. Inside, Paul became a shrewd businessman. He began to recognize that his customers were as afraid of rejection as his salesmen were. His clerks were so conscious that the customer has the ultimate say, and thus the upper hand, that they ignored the customer's needs for personal reassurance, acceptance, and attention. Paul thought he had found a key. All people fear rejection, whether they are buyers or sellers. That fear never goes entirely away, but it can be repressed by success and self-confidence.

"Remember," Paul later cautioned his trainees, "humility diminishes as power increases, and the fear of rejection diminishes as acceptance increases. Buyers fear rejection as much as sellers," he went on. "And if you can make the buyers feel comfortable and believe you accept them as human beings they will do their very best to return the favor." Thus a key element in selling is learning not only to deal with rejection yourself but also to anticipate your buyers' natural fear of rejection and instantly let them know that you accept them, however the sale may turn out.

Jim Franklin violated this rule repeatedly. He subconsciously set himself up as the rejector by selling his integrity. The only way the customer could count on acceptance from Jim

Franklin was to buy Jim's product—so Jim usually ended up the rejectee. Paul Findley never made that mistake because the alternative simply never occurred to him. He was naturally passive and solicitous toward people. Paul's ability to accept rejection within himself allowed him to accept people in a way that Jim Franklin could not.

Fear of rejection does not always originate with the individual. It is possible for an organization to create an environment which causes normally healthy and aggressive salesmen to experience a fear of rejection not felt since they asked a girl to dance at their first sock hop. No manager or organization creates such an environment on purpose. However, the true measure of an organization is how quickly it recognizes the situation and how effectively it deals with the cause once it is uncovered. Some organizations have as much difficulty as human beings confronting their own errors. Admitting mistakes is always traumatic, especially for organizations.

Remember Bill Merriweather and Boyd Mueller? Well, they were having their problems—and organizational climate was one of them. Bill's division was experiencing a drop-off in sales that had reached alarming proportions. Forecasts were sliding from first quarter to second, then from second quarter to third. Cash flow and profits were slipping noticeably and budgeting was almost impossible. Yet none of Bill's salesmen would agree to make any significant reduction in the forecasts.

"The business will come in," they chorused. "Just give us a little time and next quarter will be the biggest we've ever had."

At an emergency meeting, Bill and his regional managers analyzed for cause. What had previously been a normally aggressive sales force that prided itself on being able to close firm deals now appeared to be settling for a series of "maybes." The problem was pervasive within the sales force, with the exception of 28 percent whose forecasts were still within the 4 percent variation that had been the norm for the last five years. Probing, digging, and head scratching revealed that the difference between the 28 percent of the sales force that was on target and the 72 percent whose forecasts were sliding was (1) length of service, (2) type of accounts, and (3) geography. The 28 percent—the good guys, as they were now being called— had been with the company longer, had focused on establishing new customer accounts, and were geographically concentrated on the East Coast, where corporate headquarters was located.

"What I can't understand," Bill exclaimed, "is what has changed. The bad guys—that 72 percent—weren't always bad guys. That's the puzzler. This problem started a year ago, but we didn't recognize it as a trend for over six months. Now we're in deep trouble. What the hell happened a year ago?" More analysis, probing, and head scratching produced recollections of a slip in the economy that was considered minor, a corporate reorganization forming additional divisions, and the opening of a West Coast production facility to expedite product delivery. None seemed to be relevant to the problem.

"Don't forget the new incentive plan," one of Bill's managers interjected. "Wasn't that made effective a year ago?"

Everybody's head shot up. Four hours later Bill asked Boyd Mueller to join the meeting. "You and I have had our differences, Boyd," he said, "but we've always been able to find a common ground. This time I'm not sure we can. Your concern over the effect of advocate selling on established customer relationships seems to have turned our sales group into a bunch of wishy-washy hand holders."

Boyd didn't agree and the real meeting got started. Two days later, Boyd had a meeting with his own people and gave them the bad news.

"Apparently I've made an error in the entry- and middle-level sales training program. If you recall," Boyd continued, "my major concern about advocate selling was that it might appeal too much to our salesmen's natural agressiveness and cause chaos with established customer relationships. I was afraid the men would pay attention to acquiring new customer relationships at the expense of the old. I overstressed the need for 'massaging' customer accounts and I talked corporate personnel into skewing our incentive plan toward repeat business rather than new. The end result has been that most of our sales force is now frightened to death to lose an established account. Instead of selling, they are accommodating. What we have done is taken a bunch of Need Salesmen and turned them into Relationship Salesmen who now have a low tolerance for rejection. There is a balance in there somewhere, but we've missed it entirely. Our salesmen are more afraid of us than of the customer. They are afraid that if they push too hard and the customer rejects them, we will react by firing them. Our own salesmen are now working at cross-purposes with us and the corporation."

At a meeting two days later between Boyd, Bill, and his district managers, Boyd acknowledged himself as the cause of the problem. "Now let's see if we can correct it. I have a two-pronged solution," Boyd explained. "With your permission, I'd like to change the agenda of the national sales meeting to be held next month at Palm Springs. Instead of the scheduled product workshops, I'd like you, Bill, to conduct a four-day workshop on advocate selling with the help of my people. I need your personal credibility," Boyd explained. "If the division president himself leads the seminar, that has impact—and impact is what we need. Don't worry about the mechanics; my people have planned and run seminars for years. Just give us your input, and we'll put the package together into a program that will change behavior rapidly if you do the delivery."

It took five months for the new policy to take hold. But early in the third quarter, things started to happen. Orders came in that had been promised for months. Not only was third quarter's forecast met, but the deficits in the first two quarters were made up and a 10 percent total increase over the year-to-date forecast was posted. The immediate problem was resolved, but the philosophical differences between Bill and Boyd remained. Bill used the near disaster to confront Boyd on the fundamental issue: Who is best qualified to identify, hire, and train a sales force—line sales management who must live with the results or corporate staff highly trained in personnel selection? Boyd was at a disadvantage and Bill knew it.

"I told you several months ago that our solution was two-pronged," Boyd said. "I know that right now you don't have any faith in personnel's ability to correctly identify advocate-type salesmen through screening and testing, but I am confident that I can prove to you very quickly that we have a system that works.

"Since last year, our people have been scouring universities and personnel consulting firms to find a viable process for screening recruits. Our objective was to develop a vehicle that would allow us to identify the candidates most suited to sell Thermacon products through advocate selling. It hasn't been easy. Apparently most university types still think that salesmen really do, or at least should, like people. Others think salesmen are born, not made. One professor even claimed that all the money spent on sales training is useless. According to her, sales training is a waste of time, money, and effort, because no one really knows how to make a top salesman out of a mediocre one.

The best we can do is make an incompetent salesman out of an idiot.

"Believe me, Bill, these people are a real joy to talk to.

"Ultimately, the university people were of some help. Their files produced the case situations necessary for our own people to develop a Situation Adaptability Evaluation Test designed to identify sales candidates who have the balance we are looking for—a combination of aggressiveness and a moral sense of justice—and who, by the way, can handle rejection positively. I personally think it's an excellent tool. We've put a lot of time into producing this test and I think it will epitomize the quality of work that you can expect from corporate personnel.

"Why don't you be the first to take the test?" Boyd said, and handed Bill three stapled pages. "Read the directions, turn the page, and go ahead."

Bill took the test. After he finished he looked Boyd dead in the eye, picked up the phone, and told the chairman himself that he was going to resign if corporate personnel was not relieved of its responsibilities of recruiting for his division.

Boyd's test was a disaster.

"I wanted salesmen," Bill said later, "who feel they have formed a business relationship with Thermacon because it has a good product. Boyd's test eliminated independent thinkers as too hard to control. I wanted salesmen," he continued, "who could establish and hold a new customer relationship. Boyd's test eliminated them as dangerous, because they could quit and work for the competition.

"In essence, Boyd's test was designed to select men who put the company first and their own well-being second. What kind of namby-pamby sales force do you think we'd have after two years of recruiting people like that? Good salesmen have to view themselves as professionals who can and do get results. It's up to the company that hires them to make sure they stay. Sure you can get some bad apples, but it's also the company's responsibility to weed them out and weed them out fast. I'd rather have one or two bums like Matt Gallagher to deal with than a whole sales force of crybabies who look to the company and me to solve all the problems they should be solving themselves.

"Advocate Salesmen have one goal in mind—make the sale. And with a company like Thermacon, which sells a repeat product and service, the fact that another sale is going to follow the first will take the edge off any killer instinct that might damage our reputation.

"Let's face it, although it takes knowledge and skills to make a successful salesman, attitude is the most important thing to consider when recruiting. Attitude is what drives a salesman to acquire the knowledge and skills he needs to successfully compete in the marketplace. Boyd's test was designed to screen out just the type of personality we wanted. As much as I personally like the man, Boyd's philosophy toward recruiting and sales training is in direct conflict with what our marketplace requires. Boyd had to go."

Boyd Mueller left Thermacon and started a sales training consulting practice in San Francisco. His clients are paternalistic companies that are more concerned with how well their salesmen reflect the company's image than with how skillfully they sell its products.

Bill Merriweather's managers have been recruiting their own people for the past two years. Last year Bill's division had record sales, and the current year is expected to exceed it by 20 percent.

CONCEPT 3

Doers, Waiters, and Watchers

There are three types of people in this world—Doers, Waiters, and Watchers. Doers do things. They take risks; they're inventive; they're creative. They make things happen. They can handle rejection without falling apart.

Waiters are more cautious. They wait until somebody else does something and then react to it. Waiters don't like rejection. They won't risk as much as Doers will. They can handle rejection, but it certainly isn't pleasant.

Watchers don't like risk at all. They are normally not creative. Usually they are ultraconservative. Watchers are the judgmentalists of the world. They are participants who try not to take part. They rarely consider the possibility of rejection, since they never put themselves in that position by choice.

Not everybody in the world can be a shaker and a mover. And, judging from the conflicts we see today at all levels of society, there are probably too many Doers in the first place. Nevertheless, progress is in fact an adversary process. Watchers can't avoid it entirely or they will lose their place in line. Waiters can't wait forever, and Doers have to recognize that the rest of the world must catch up before they can go on.

A Doer is usually known in the trade as an entrepreneurial salesman. A Doer will take a state-of-the-art product and create need for it. In the 1950s industry was still getting along just fine without in-house computers, as it had been since the Industrial Revolution. The first data processing salesmen literally sold *need*. They were great advocate entrepreneurs.

By the 1980s data processing services within most companies had become a necessity. Since many excellent main-frame systems were available, the Waiters took over the selling process from the Doers and established a personal relationship with their customers. Once need is established, Waiters form a personal relationship with a client. They provide the client with good service, excellent response, and attentiveness to his particular need. They place heavy emphasis on safety as a buying motivator. A Waiter or Relationship Salesman will say, "Hey, if the price is equal and the quality is equal, buy from me because I'll take care of you." Let's face it, it's a good way to sell.

Watchers tend to be Order Takers. They are not selling anything. They just hope the customer will sell himself on need for the product so they can take it from there. Salesmen of this nature found a niche in the gigantic data processing industry created by the entrepreneurial Doers by offering reliable replacement service. If you need a new disc drive, call up a Watcher and he'll see if he has one in stock. If he does, he'll get it out to you right away.

Until his death in the early 1970s, Harry Grossman was a retail genius. His basic belief was that stores didn't sell things, people did. At a meeting of training and development specialists from all over the country, Harry discussed the formula he used in his organization to hire, train, and evaluate his retail sales-clerks.

"Doers are people who get things done," he said. "They are usually entrepreneurs, and they range from church and ski club members to the people who volunteer their next six week-ends to complete a critically important ad hoc project at the office.

"Doers sell ideas by selling a need for those ideas. Need for change! The benefits of change! Not all of their ideas are good, and if everybody was selling change things would always be changing. The world is catastrophic enough. But remember that progressive, constructive change is an adversary process. A lot of friction is involved, but the end result is usually good for everybody concerned.

"Doer workaholics are usually the ones who make it happen. In retail selling the Doer will ask a walk-in customer where she is going to wear the dress she is examining and what she wants to accomplish with the outfit—objective-setting, data-gathering questions.

"Conversely," Harry went on, "Waiters react to need. Only

after need is established will the Waiter begin to sell a relationship with the potential customer. In a retail selling situation, the Waiter assumes that the prospective buyer knows what she is looking for. The Waiter will then sell the safety factor of the brand names displayed, the exclusiveness of the shop, or the Waiter's own willingness to be of absolute and complete service.

"Watchers operate on the premise that all things being equal—price, quality, and service—the customer will come to them for the close. Need is assumed, and no effort is made to sell. Which," Harry said, "is why you find so many lookie-loos in retail stores."

Environment and circumstance as well as opportunity and attitude dictate whether a person assumes the role of Doer, Waiter, or Watcher. Doers can move up and down the scale with impunity. The reverse is not true. Watchers and Waiters move up a notch very cautiously and with great trepidation. They do not have the self-confidence of doers and seem to possess an innate fear of rejection and suspicion of the unknown. They have not yet learned that selling alternatives is an everyday task done by everyday people. How else would the soft-drink machine ever get moved to a more convenient location, or the church picnic successfully organized? Doers can play the game hard and then step off the field without taking loss as a personal rejection. Waiters and Watchers cannot, so they usually gravitate toward positions that carry either authority in their own right or reflected authority from a mentor or boss. Thus they cannot easily be second-guessed, and their fear of rejection is greatly reduced because of their position of power and authority.

Selling is always viewed positively, since a purchase implies a positive change. But selling can also be very destructive, as the sad story of Dan Moran illustrates. Dan Moran typifies a certain breed of buyer that Advocate Salesmen often encounter in the marketplace. We will see that Dan Moran never had his company's needs and objectives clearly in mind. He did have a clear vision of his own objectives. Also, Dan changed from a Watcher to a Waiter in response to opportunity, authority, and working environment. Note what happened to Dan when he tried to be something he couldn't.

Thomas Daniel Michael Moran didn't utter an intelligent word until the ripe old age of 18 months. This was three months after his mother really began to worry. His mother said later that Dan's silence and generally passive attitude was a result of the care showered upon him by the large, nuturant Moran family. She believed Dan never needed anything until he was 18 months old. When he finally did, he simply opened his mouth and asked for it.

The rest of the family had doubts about Mother Moran's theory. They believed Dan wouldn't talk because he wasn't sure what he was going to say, and until he was sure, Dan kept his mouth shut. Dan maintained this characteristic throughout most of his life. On a double date in high school, one girl whispered to her friend that going out with Dan was almost as much fun as being with someone. Although handsome and possessing an enviable ability to articulate when he wanted to, Dan remained cautious almost to the point of fault. He was a classic Watcher. He took no risks, made no decisions, and entered into no controversy he could avoid. Although his verbal skills qualified him for the campus debating society, Dan wouldn't consider it because debating meant he would have to take a position on an issue. Dan's intelligence earned him good grades in college. But upon graduation Dan promptly joined one of the major automotive companies and began his retirement.

After completing several management trainee assignments almost unnoticed, Dan was assigned to personnel, where his ability to articulate was useful. Dan didn't particularly like the job but he was content to watch the world go around from behind his dull green desk on the thirteenth floor of corporate headquarters overlooking the lovely River Rouge. But then something happened that was to drastically alter Dan's grand design for his life. Dan was designated to be trained as an instructor for a management development program packaged by a respected outside consultant and licensed for internal implementation by Dan's company.

Dan's ability to articulate, his charming good looks, and the tight structure of the program served him very well in his new position as instructor. Dan looked great—and he sounded great. Because he looked and sounded great, people began to think he was great. Pretty soon Dan began to think he was great too. That was Dan's first error!

Dan's abilities led to a job offer with the management development firm whose program he had been licensed to deliver internally. Dan's second error was taking the job he was offered.

Thus Dan the Watcher left the lazy, cozy womb of one of the world's largest companies for the wheeler-dealer life of selling high-ticket intangibles. Until Dan made that change, he never really gave much thought to how products were sold. He had observed automobiles being produced and had noticed that people bought them. He naturally assumed this miracle was going to be repeated in his new job. Dan looked forward to continuing his successful presentation of seminars sold by others. His first rude awakening came when his regional manager and new boss asked Dan how many calls he was going to make that day on Detroit companies not currently using their service.

From that day forward, Dan mounted a concerted effort to extricate himself from the responsibility of sales. After three months of smiling, boot licking, and fast talking, he persuaded the chairman and founder of the firm to create a position for him as director of corporate personnel for the 60-man company.

Dan was back in his element. He had a bigger office and a desk that wasn't green. He ingratiated himself with the chairman and his alter ego, the sycophantic senior vice president. Every time the chairman or his yes-man needed to stick it to somebody or formulate corporate policy that flew in everyone's face, Dan could be counted on to come up with a reason that made the action sound logical, palatable, justified—and somehow even deserving!

As a Watcher, Dan now had the job he wanted. He left the details of personnel—medical plans, dental plans, life insurance, workers' comp—in the hands of his very competent assistant, Mary. This practice became so engrained that line managers routinely invited Mary to attend corporate staff meetings whenever the agenda included questions on employee benefit plans. Mary had the answers. If Mary was not invited and such a question was asked, Dan would indicate that the problem had been delegated to his assistant. And if Mary was out of the office, the question never seemed to get answered.

As his employer's organization grew, Dan was forced to make another major change in his life. Dan discarded his primary role as a Watcher and became a Waiter. Waiters basically sell relationships, and over the years Dan had developed the skills to do so. His ability to explain nasty behavior with apparently faultless logic and to cloak his superiors' selfish motives under a cloth of pure altruism won him friends and mentors. Dan began to wait for opportunities to practice his skills.

Dan Moran selected the people he liked. He marked a big invisible X on the back of the people he didn't. Dan would then mount a superficially casual but in fact intense campaign against those with an X on their back. He relied on all the classic methods—gossip, behind-the-hand whispering, and damning by faint praise.

Even though Dan's responsibility was limited to corporate personnel, he took advantage of the small size of his organization to sell line policies that benefited him personally or undermined his enemies. Not all salesmen knock on doors and sell products. Dan was a very adept and very dangerous internal company salesman. His job security came from his ability to sell top management's policies to the rest of the corporation without causing a revolution every time the Old Man tried to make a few bucks at the employees' expense. When the chairman found himself facing over 50 employees with whom he had made different and conflicting deals in order to lure them from their previous positions, Dan sold him on the idea of bringing in an outside consulting firm specializing in wage and salary administration. The consultants did the dirty work, and the chairman was able to wring his hands over martinis with these old friends and lament, "My God, I understand—they're screwing me too." Dan received a nice bonus for that.

Of course, the chairman was basically at fault for Dan's behavior, but that's another story. That revered management scientist Peter Drucker may one day mention the chairman in an insignificant footnote comparing the styles, weaknesses, and strengths of Old Man Mitsubishi and Henry Ford I. But the "why" of Dan's behavior is not important. People don't care *why* you are what you are, they care only *what* you are. There isn't enough time in the world to change a colleague's or a buyer's personality.

Dan allied himself with another Waiter, Bob Rumford, manager of corporate accounting and treasurer of the firm. The two of them then spent the next several years waiting for opportunities to sell top management alternatives that either benefited their own little fiefdoms or were detrimental to their enemies. None of these alternatives took into account in any way, shape, or form the company's stated goals, objectives, and basic beliefs. But if you heard Dan sell an alternative in the board meeting, you'd think his every waking thought was concerned with the goals of the company. One detractor quite accurately accused Dan of attempting to create an official corporate prayer.

But, as one of Dan's previous victims pointed out, there really is justice in this world. Finally Dan lost what glitter he had for the chairman. A nice bonus and a friendly farewell, and Dan was on his own. Panicking, Dan realized for the first time that he needed a corporate structure to work in. Not only did he not have a *product* to sell, but without top management to whisper to, he didn't have customers either. Dan was going to have to become a Doer. Being reasonably resourceful, he enticed his competent assistant, Mary, to leave the company and help him create a personnel consulting firm.

Dan now had a product—Mary! To his credit, Dan really tried but he had no experience at all selling a noncaptive buyer. And he really hadn't the faintest idea of the results that Mary's skills could produce for his prospects. Dan, as a Doer, failed miserably. But Mary, coming into her own, wound up with a lucrative consulting practice serving four counties in upstate New York. Dan returned to teaching seminars for the people who had sold them, driving his six-year-old Pontiac to and from the airport once a week to catch the plane that would take him to his flip charts, multicolored pens, name tags, and hotel of the week. That's where he remains today.

Dan Moran's story clearly illustrates that the world needs Watchers as well as Waiters and Doers. Everything in the universe is balanced. Herbivores eat plants. Carnivores eat herbivores. Vultures eat the remains. Shrimp eat plankton. Salmon eat shrimp. Sharks eat salmon. It is as hard for a herbivore to eat a vulture as it is for a shrimp to eat a shark—or for Dan Moran to become a Doer in this lifetime. As a Watcher teaching seminars, Dan was positive, he was productive, and he was good. As a Waiter in a position of power, he was destructive. As a Doer he was a failure! But in the ten years Dan spent as director of personnel with the management development firm, he was also a buyer. He had authority, he had a budget, and he had a big set of personal objectives that he always covered with the mantle of company goals and beliefs. So many salesmen fail to sell a buyer like Dan because they make the assumption that their buyer is truly a good company man and fail to seek out his hidden self-serving objectives.

Dan's mentors, the chairman and his sycophant senior vice

president, were also buyers. In fact, when Dan pushed a project that exceeded his authority or budget, he ran to them for the necessary approvals. Of the three, only the chairman, as founder and a major stockholder, probably had even a semblance of interest in the company's true objectives. But unless the project being proposed threatened the lifeblood of the organization, he wasn't any more concerned about company objectives than the rest of them. Like most entrepreneurs, the chairman liked to find little ways to bleed the company to maximize his own personal net worth. Unlike Dan, the chairman was a Doer. His vice president was a Watcher and Dan was a Waiter. Each one filled different roles and each balanced the other nicely. Any salesman attempting to sell them had to be instantly aware of their real roles and interrelationships if he expected to close a sale of any magnitude.

And therein lies the heart of the matter. Complex as it sounds, every salesman is sometimes a buyer, and every buyer sometimes a salesman. Every Advocate Salesman needs to understand the type of buyer he is dealing with in order to select the necessary strategy and tactics to deal with him effectively. Fish are caught with hooks. Bears are taken with a gun. God help the nearsighted salesman who inadvertently hooks a bear.

Neil White could have been another Dan Moran. All his life Neil was a Waiter. He never made things happen; he left that up to others. When something did happen, Neil would jump in when he could and try to take charge or share in the glory. When Neil was a kid, he'd wait until somebody else swiped the beer. Then Neil would always show up at the hangout and demand his share of it. In his early professional life, Neil steadfastly avoided any task that held an element of finite measurement. He waited for opportunities to ingratiate himself with his boss and his boss's peers. He rarely performed a function that had a precise beginning and end. He was a blamer when things didn't go right, and he took credit for absolutely anything successful that he could convince people he had a part in.

Unlike Dan Moran, Neil became disgusted with himself. He had the opportunity to join a fledgling firm that specialized in selling software, and surprised himself by taking the job. Like every Waiter, Neil honed his relationship skills to develop good long-term customer relationships. The going was slow. But as the repeat orders built up, Neil's initial multicall approach to selling a customer shortened considerably and he became a Doer selling need without ever realizing it. He currently heads one of his company's largest divisions and is still a superstar salesman himself in spite of the fact that he has 50 men to do his selling for him.

Neil White's short story typifies the role of attitude in shaping behavior. Skills and knowledge are important. However, attitude is the primary agent of change. Dan Moran started off as a fairly passive individual but his attitude shift took a negative turn. Had Dan possessed the skills to become a Doer he would have been a destructive Doer. Neil White, on the other hand, started off with a negative and very selfish attitude and overcame it. His knowledge and skills left something to be desired, but a positive attitude and perseverance provided him with a path to success.

Attitude, knowledge, and skills are the keys to success. A salesman's reaction to people is dependent first on his attitude, second on his knowledge in dealing with people, and third on his skills in handling the customer relationship. Fear of rejection or fear of the unknown is almost solely an attitude problem. To be a Doer requires an excellent attitude, considerable knowledge, and a sharp set of skills. Tyrone Shapiro had all those things.

Tyrone—he insisted on being called that—was a forceful man who grew up in the wrong part of Brooklyn. "My mother," Tyrone once said, "was really secretly in love with that old movie star Tyrone Power. I think she envisioned herself meeting him at one of the premieres held at the then-fashionable theaters on 42nd Street and being whisked away to spend her life under a palm tree by a swimming pool somewhere in secluded Hollywood Hills. Like most of us, my mother had to compromise. She settled for Irving Shapiro down the street who had just earned his CPA license. Things could have been worse," Tyrone said. "What do you suppose she would have named me if Johnny Cash had sung 'A Boy Named Sue' the year I was born?"

Tyrone was a Doer. Rather than change a ridiculous name like Tyrone Shapiro to something sensible, as most people would, Tyrone turned his misfortune to advantage. He never failed to dissolve his listener in laughter when he told the story of his mother's choice of names. Tyrone Shapiro worked his way through New York University by selling to the garment district. He went on to study law but couldn't resist the knock-down, drag-out competition of the rag trade. He now heads one of the largest wholesale dress distribution firms in the world.

Tyrone recently addressed a group of business school grad-uates interested in pursuing a career in sales. His task was to brief them on what he considered some of the basics of selling. "I'm not going to talk to you," he began, "about how to sell gar-ments. I am going to talk to you about how to *sell.*

"One nice thing about being a successful salesperson is that you always make a lot of money. It's as simple as that!" Tyrone went on. "But money isn't everything, psychologists say. Most people work for identity, power, and money, in that order!

"Sales jobs abound, but you may find yourself reluctant to take them. When others turn up their noses at the suggestion of being a salesperson, they are usually faulted as reacting to the stereotyped hard-sell, sucde-shoe image projected by the door-to-door cemetery plot hustlers we were all exposed to as toddlers when our mothers sent us to answer the door. Actually, they are probably reacting to an intrinsic need for identity and power. On first analysis this appears odd, because most sales-people dress, look, and act like any other professionals. They usually wear the uniform of the clientele they serve. Stock-brokers wear three-piece suits and yacht salesmen wear expen-sive Topsiders and Gucci slacks. But as a salesperson, you must deal every day with a formidable psychological enemy not present in any other profession: You are continuously faced with flat-out rejection!

"As a salesperson," Tyrone emphasized, "every time you make a pitch you are exposing yourself to the definitive answer, 'No'! It's hard to separate professional rejection from personal rejection, isn't it?" he asked his audience. "You naturally feel that a customer who does not buy your product has personally rejected you. And, because some types of salespeople actually sell themselves rather than need for their product, these feel-ings are sometimes true!

"There are three basic ranks of salespeople," Tyrone stated. "Those who sell need, those who sell relationships, and those who take orders. And there are three types of people who fill those ranks: Doers, Waiters, Watchers.

"Any one of these types can be found in any one of the three ranks of sales jobs, but under the principle that water finds its own level, the Doer who exposes himself to the higher risk of rejection by selling need usually moves up to more responsibility or on to greater challenges—making much more money all along the way!

"Let's take an example. If you are a Watcher, and as such tend to be an Order Taker, you will usually work as a retail salesperson—traditionally the lowest-paid job in the sales profession. But this is not a hard-and-fast rule," he emphasized. "There are Waiters and Doers in the retail trade too, although the Doers usually wind up owning the store.

"Here's why," Tyrone said, and his audience grew attentive. "If Mrs. Jones walks into a chic shop looking for a fur coat, you as a Watcher will greet her, chat with her politely, and show her your merchandise. If Mrs. J. doesn't buy, you may lament the nonproductive time spent with a fickle customer, but you will not feel any sense of rejection. After all, it's not your fault that the store didn't stock the fur coat that Mrs. J. wanted, and anyway you're there only to take orders.

"As a Waiter, you would probably have already known Mrs. Jones. In fact, you would have built up a relationship with her over the years. That relationship may be the very reason Mrs. Jones came to your particular shop in the first place, so 'waiting' apparently paid off.

"Unfortunately, as a Waiter you will probably also go through the mind-numbing routine of showing Mrs. Jones every fur in the house. And if Mrs. J. again doesn't buy, you will justifiably feel some personal sense of rejection but will rationalize these feelings by placing the blame on something outside of your control—the buyer bought a lousy line, the manager always overprices big-ticket items like furs, ad nauseam! Then you'll sit back comfortably and wait for another customer to come in, preferably one with whom you have a better relationship and one who will have the intelligence to take the suggestions you offer.

"As a Doer who sells need," Tyrone went on, "you would consciously invite possible rejection at the beginning of the sale by daring to ask Mrs. J. a few questions before heading to the fur rack to begin the ritual of laying out every fur in the store. The main thing you must know as a Doer salesperson selling need is simply, 'What does she want a fur coat for in the first place?'

"There are six basic concepts that motivate a buyer,"

Tyrone continued. "Of these, three are classic—self-approval, approval of others, and safety. At least two of these criteria must be met for a potential buyer to become a real buyer. Doer sales-people know you can partially meet the safety criterion by showing Mrs. J. only brand-name furs. But how can you find out what will give Mrs. Jones a sense of self-approval or approval of others? Watchers don't care! Waiters hope Mrs. J. will give them a clue during the chatter surrounding the laying-out-of-inventory ritual! Doers simply say, 'Mrs. Jones, furs are really exciting. Tell me, where and when will you be wearing your new fur? I personally want to make sure you're wearing the most up-to-date, glamorous style we have!' In fact, you are put-ting priorities on the furs you have to show her.

"Your next question depends on the answer you get to your first question," Tyrone went on. "And keep asking questions until you have a fix on precisely why Mrs. Jones is in your store looking for a fur instead of the many thousands of other places she could and perhaps should be shopping.

"At worst you will discover that Mrs. J. really just had some time to kill. If that is the case, your question will be met with the instant rejection of stony silence or a cutting remark. So be it! Just say a few nice things to Mrs. J. so she isn't too offended for having wanted to take up your time solely for her own en-tertainment, and go back to doing something important.

"On the other hand," Tyrone said, "with the right kind of probing, you as a Doer may very well find out that Mrs. J.'s husband has just been promoted and his new duties and status require her to travel with him to New York City for large com-pany meetings and socializing several times a year.

"Now you have it," he exclaimed. "The real reason Mrs. J. could indeed become a confirmed and loyal buyer! She is seek-ing the approval of others in the person of her husband, his peers, his superiors, and their wives. Mrs. Jones is also seeking self-approval, because she would not be caught dead in New York City looking like an immigrant from the provinces. And to provide her with additional safety—that secure feeling every-one needs to walk away with after having spent a large chunk of money on a luxury product—you need to show her only the styles and types of coats that are fashionable in New York City. Be sure to reinforce the alternatives she selects by presenting her with copies of advertisements from major New York fashion magazines," Tyrone cautioned.

"What you as a Doer salesperson have done," he pointed out, "is ferreted out Mrs. J.'s specific personal objectives. You have found what Mrs. J. wanted to accomplish—and you did it before you showed her everything in the store. But you did so at the risk of rejection up front. After all, Mrs. J. came to the store to look at furs, not to answer questions from the help. And if the truth were known, Mrs. J. probably didn't have the foggiest idea of what fashions were most popular in New York, and her vanity would make her resent some upstart salesperson trying to uncover that fact by asking her what she would naturally consider to be simple-minded questions.

"But remember, a sale is a series of miniconfrontations designed to move a buyer from uncertainty to conclusive action. And *you* as a salesperson can control this process if you want to. The Watcher and the Waiter," Tyrone continued, "would have let the myriad of 'laid-out goods' do the confronting for them, each never realizing that Mrs. J.'s real need was to understand what furs were acceptable fashion in New York. Thus the laying out ritual served only to further confuse a very real potential buyer and drive her into greater uncertainty.

"At the risk of rejection, you, a Doer, confronted Mrs. J. early on and learned specifically what her real objective was. Once you knew what Mrs. J. was trying to accomplish, you led her exclusively to those furs that met her objectives. And you sold need—in this case, current New York fashion—the entire time Mrs. Jones was trying on furs.

"As a Doer," Tyrone continued, "you went on to sell Mrs. J. an entire wardrobe along with the proper fur to wear during her visits to New York City. After all, Mrs. J. really did need a brand-new wardrobe. She deserved it and no one was going to deprive her of it.

"Helping the customer to consciously think out her objectives is the only way to manage the sale. Once both you and the customer have decided what she is trying to accomplish, you will have her choosing between your alternatives. Time is saved, and the seller/buyer confidence that results reinforces the safety impulse necessary to lock down a sale forever," Tyrone concluded.

"How does one go about asking objective-setting questions?" Tyrone asked. "Well, there are charming questions and there are stupid questions. But first, to be a successful salesperson, you must overcome the fear of asking questions. The only process for formulating meaningful, objective-setting questions is to pay the price up front—risk asking a stupid question! The rejection you get in response to a stupid question will enable you to tell the difference between what works and what doesn't, but it's worth it!

"In Mrs. J.'s mind," Tyrone explained, "you, the Doer, now have an identity. You helped her painlessly and successfully work through a perplexing problem that was important to her. As a Doer, you have built a power base within your employer's organization. It doesn't take too many Mrs. Joneses to make you indispensable to management. But most important, you made a substantial amount of money by taking the risk up front to specifically define Mrs. Jones' need, and then simply *sell it back to her!*"

CONCEPT 4

What People Work For: Identity, Power, and Money

In order to understand and classify a buyer, it is important to know why he is working in the first place and not languishing on a beach under a palm tree. What does the buyer receive from doing the job? Money? Perhaps. But price alone will rarely make a sale. That being the case, there must be something else!

Martha Lewis has a doctorate in psychology. She also happens to be the hottest space advertising salesman in the Midwest. She never sells price in an industry that is extremely price-sensitive. Her philosophy is that people work for rewards other than money and therefore every sales pitch should reflect that. She is a recognized master within her industry at qualifying her buyers.

Martha recently gave a lecture on why people work to a large group of associates in New York City. "Behavioralists," she said, "have long attempted to identify why people work voluntarily. The assumption in the slave-owning societies was that people would not! This led to an indentured peasant class that worked most of their waking lives and to an aristocratic ruling class that did not work at all. Later, after these societies were abolished," she went on, "it was found that in fact people would work of their own volition. Abraham Maslow did great studies in this field and identified a hierarchy of needs that begins with people working to ensure their safety and ultimately to achieve a form of Utopia that Maslow termed self-actualization. I prefer the simplistic belief that people work for identity, power, and money," she said. "These can easily be paralleled to the traditional buying motivators of need, greed, and fear—or self-approval, approval of others, and safety."

Martha explained that people need an identity—"Who am I and what am I" was the call of the 1960s and the 1970s. Gail Sheehy's runaway best-seller, *Passages,* states that "there are two disasters that can befall people in their lifetime. The first is never achieving what they set out to achieve; the second is achieving it!" Apparently there is a side of human nature that makes us feel inherently unworthy. We need to disprove that assumption within ourselves by associating with other people and things—and especially jobs—that we consider worthy. Thus we benefit by reflection! That is why the loss of a particular job—or in the case of a housewife, a home or family that she identifies with—can be so devastating. People mold their own self-image (and make it dependent) on a job, person, or environment that is beyond their total control.

The behavioralists are not convinced that power is a goal women work for. They are unanimous in that it is a goal men work for. Some experts feel that both men and women work for power, but that they apply that power differently. Men use power to initiate change—sometimes for the sake of change alone. Women usually won't initiate change unless they are discontent or threatened with the way things are. Then watch out! In this evolutionary stage of the human animal, not too many women will willingly lead an army into battle. But if someone should attack their own environment, most women will fight with a frenzy that could leave a tigress in awe. "Thus," Martha concluded, "if your buyer is a man you can appeal to his Napoleonic side. If your buyer is a woman you can appeal to her desire to protect her environment. The Napoleons conquer new worlds and new fields. The tigress protects what she has—if she likes it!"

Martha emphasized that money is usually the least common reason people work. "Oh sure, when the rent isn't paid and there is no food for the cat, let alone yourself, money becomes a dominant motivator. However, everybody has limits in making the trade-off. Having once experienced the dizzying sensation of watching three men wash windows 36 floors above the Chicago streets," she said, "I knew that there was not enough money in the world for me personally to do that for a living.

Once the safety need for money is gone, people look for things to enhance the more intangible side of their lives.

"Men tend to use discretionary money to buy the symbols and badges that demonstrate to others that they have achieved the American dream. They have risen above their station in life! Women, on the other hand, tend to use discretionary money to buy freedom and time to do those things that they always wanted to do but were too busy to get to. I remember those rules when I am faced with a buyer who tells me the cost for the ad is too high or doesn't compare with the competition."

Martha practiced what she preached. In one instance, a recalcitrant customer was the managing partner of a very large, prestigious consulting firm. He believed that professional service firms should not advertise and had resisted every onslaught that space advertising professionals had made on him for the last five years.

He was a gracious man and allowed Martha enough time to explain to her why he was going to continue his policy of not advertising the professional services his firm offered. She politely interrupted to say that that was not the purpose of her visit. His reputation was well known and she was there to ask him to write an article on the subject of mergers and acquisitions—his area of expertise—for her publication. She was not there to sell him space!

Suspicious, he countered her offer by asking whether she expected him to advertise as a result of the national exposure a published article would give him. She replied quite simply that the one was not dependent upon the other. It was her hope that his article would demonstrate the benefits of exposure in her magazine by generating business for his firm. Hopefully, this would convince him that the customers he wanted to reach in fact read her publication. He wrote the article. Two months after appealing to his sense of identity, Martha received an order from his firm for a full-page advertisement for the next 12 issues. The readers had responded and her gamble paid off.

In another situation, Martha's buyer was the vice president of operations of a major executive search firm. The VP jealously protected the interests of her employers. She routinely placed space ads but consistently rejected any effort to upgrade, expand, or otherwise increase the amount of advertising done by her firm. The tigress protected the den.

With this buyer, Martha took a bold and different tack. She

knew her company regularly oversubscribed space. It also had an annoying habit of limiting space ads to 32 pages, so if all the subscriptions materialized, the odd-lot customers were often left hanging. Being currently oversubscribed, Martha, in good conscience, told her buyer that there was no more space available in the next publication for the type of ad the woman usually took. The space was sold out. She recommended a competitive publication, timing her statement to coincide with the look of frustration that came over her client's face after the woman recovered from her initial shock.

What was she to do? The woman's status quo was threatened.

Martha rose to the occasion. Because the firm was a good and loyal customer, Martha offered to see if she could renegotiate with some of her other customers and step them up to bigger ads, thus providing a space opening for the firm. Her buyer was very grateful and she immediately agreed to an appointment two days later to discuss the result of Martha's endeavors.

As she suspected, Martha was able to negotiate only half the space needed by her customer's firm. But out of gratitude and the desire to continue advertising with the same publication she always used, her buyer agreed to put the balance of her advertising into some larger and more creative ads. The wall had been breached and the status quo shattered. And the beauty of it was that the buyer never even knew what happened. She was too busy protecting her turf.

Martha knew her buyers. She knew their psyches better than they did. As a consequence, she was able to choose a tactic that she knew would close the sale. Mao Tse-tung, whatever his politics, can never be accused of being stupid. In one of his most celebrated treatises he states that "the only successful generals in the world are those who can accurately anticipate the strategic actions of their opponents and therefore tactically outmaneuver them."

Of course, success depends on self-knowledge. Martha knew herself. She accepted and was at peace with herself. That combination is critical, because without it she would have subconsciously imposed her values on others in the best tradition of the old saying, "When Peter talks about Paul, you learn more about Peter than you ever do about Paul." She would then be anticipating her customers' reactions by projecting what her reaction would be in the situation. Incestuous thinking produces terrible sales strategies, and Martha knew it.

When Martha psyched out her buyers she made no judgments about their values. She was there to sell them, not to judge them. "I don't care why a buyer is the way he is," she once said. "I care only what he is." With that knowledge she could choose a lure that would effectively hook him. Strategy and tactics must be carefully chosen to suit the prey. Any fool knows not to shoot a rabbit with a cannon or an elephant with a slingshot. But there are thousands of salesmen out there blindly using a canned pitch on a sophisticated buyer because someone told them it would work. Even worse, some of them try to sell price. Salesmen who sell price instead of results either are unskilled, naive, and dumb or are echoing their own attitude toward money.

Patrick Farrell thought he worked for money. Somewhat like Jim Franklin, Pat had the attitude of a rich European princeling whose karma was to be reincarnated as the son of an impoverished Irish immigrant in a working-class ghetto in Pittsburgh. It seemed that his entire life was spent clawing his way back to his previous position of eminence—an objective rarely achieved without much pain and suffering. Pat's problem was that he thought everyone else had the same ambitions as he did.

Pat became a businessman and later settled into a real estate career. He was somewhat of a financial wizard and could put terms and price together better than anyone else, but he had tremendous difficulty generating need. Pat had a lesson to learn about using price as a close, never as bait. The first thing out of Pat's mouth when talking to prospects was the super terms available on the property he was trying to sell. It took him a long time to realize that instead of motivating customers to be interested in the property he was touting, his mention of price early on simply raised a red flag and alerted their suspicions. People would wonder whether the roof leaked or an expressway was due to come through the back yard sometime in the very near future. Why else would the price be so good?

People don't buy deals, they buy things. But instead of selling people the things they wanted, Pat sold them price and terms. Moreover, people are usually very ambivalent about exactly what things they want. Only after they make that decision will they begin to consider the price they are willing to pay. Psuedo-salesmen like Pat miss that point entirely. At best, salesmen like Pat are Order Takers who run around showing products they hope people need so they can quickly discuss price after the customer finally finds need on his own.

Pat's driving ambition to acquire money caused him to misjudge not only his buyers' motivation but his own as well. In his quest for wealth, Pat would plow all his commissions except bare living expenses into single-dwelling properties. He looked for price bargains but his eye was really on the payment terms he could negotiate. In 15 of his 35 years, Pat had never seen California coastal real estate depreciate. So he invested everything he had in down payments. He structured second mortgages with big balloon payments five years into the future so he could purchase as many dwellings as possible with his available cash. Pat leveraged himself dangerously, but he felt that in a crunch he could always borrow against the increased value of his properties in order to pay off the second mortgages when they came due. Not a bad strategy for the 1970s. Pat became a paper millionaire by the time he was 36. And then came the interest crunch of the 1980s. The California real estate market collapsed and so did Pat.

It was during that devastating experience that Pat Farrell learned he really didn't work for money at all. All he really wanted was an identity and the respect of others. He wanted the power that being a real estate tycoon could bring him. He had thought of money as an end in itself, but in reality Pat simply used money as a means to an end. When his money was finally depleted, 20-20 hindsight allowed him to see what he had done to himself. Pat was one of the fortunate ones. He recovered. After the bankruptcy he was able to keep his house and his car and enough cash to live on to meet minimum expenses. Pat was humbled and humiliated but he had learned a very powerful lesson: He understood what he was really working for. He finally realized that his assumption that others were motivated entirely by money was invalid as well. For the first time he was truly able to qualify his buyers and not sell them price, no matter how important price appeared to be on the surface.

"I got to the point that I could see them coming," Pat relayed to his new manager. "This well-dressed fellow and his wife walked into my office and began discussing residences in the Hillsborough neighborhood. The first thing out of the guy's mouth was price. Obviously the man was affluent, but he complained about how all the real estate ads in the paper just boggled his mind. Being from the East Coast, he wasn't used to the extra zero that you add onto the price of the house the minute you move into the state of California.

"Two years ago I would have pulled out my calculator and started to show him the excellent terms on three or four houses out of the Multiple Listing Real Estate Guide. I would have automatically put price objectives first and what the buyer really wanted to accomplish with his purchase second. I would have showed him the numbers first, and if I found a set that interested him I would have rooted through my listings and pulled out a house that matched those numbers.

"Not this time. I hoped I had learned my lesson. As my customer continued to complain about the cost of California real estate, I politely asked him why he wanted to move out here in the first place. Well, that brought him up short. As I suspected, he was one of the nouveau riche microchip tycoons who was going to move his business next to his peers and competitors in Silicon Valley. He wanted to attract their attention. This man was an outsider who wanted an instant identity. He really didn't care about price or terms. He wanted recognition and power within that little microchip fraternity he was going to join, and he wanted it now! In the final analysis, the house he would buy was like the jewels on his wife's fingers and his limousine at the curb. They were accoutrements. They were a means to an end. They were part of his badge and uniform. They had absolutely no value to him whatsoever. He could care less whether the house I sold him appreciated or not. Naturally, he didn't want to lose money but what he really was buying was P-R-E-S-T-I-G-E! Clearly he was an identity and power buyer.

"I sold him and his wife one of the biggest estates anybody has ever moved around here in the last five years, and after all his complaints about the price of California real estate, guess who notified his bank to pay cash for the house. When I think of all the other people like him who I probably turned off with my Hewlett-Packard calculator and yellow pad I could almost cry," Pat said. "But I finally had to admit it. Money is the least effective motivator. As an end in itself, money is meaningless green paper. And its worth is subject to government whims. Subconsciously everybody knows that. So now I sell results, and use price as a close. If you can discover what somebody wants and give it to him, you can find out afterward what he's willing to pay to achieve those results. And if you have him on the fence and he becomes ambivalent, a change in price or a change in terms can always be used as a close. Believe me, after ten years of trying to sell price and terms instead of results, I know what I'm talking about."

Money rarely sells, but an appeal to power and identity almost always does.

From a salesman's standpoint, it is critical to understand the true motivation of power-driven executives. These people are the shakers and movers of the world, and as buyers they are very lucrative contacts. Power-driven buyers are Doers. If you can sell one of them you almost eliminate the need to sell anyone else in the organization, because power-driven executives never manage by consensus. They don't seek the approval of subordinates, only of their peers and superiors. However, there is a danger in dealing with them. When they are flying high things can be great. When they crash, they crash hard!

Dr. Ronald Stevens was doing research on advocate selling. His objectives were to determine (1) the best sales approaches to use on a particular type of buyer, especially one whose primary motivation is power and identity, and (2) the limits, if any, that a salesman selling that particular type of person should impose on himself. Dr. Stevens was interested in self-imposed limits versus company-imposed limits because he knew that there is a moment of truth when a salesman can cross the line between the ethical and unethical, and only the salesman can accurately judge the situation. He formed a discussion group of line salespeople to evaluate a case study that he had chosen from the newspapers. The subject was an entrepreneur whose meteoric rise brought him fame and fortune and whose subsequent crash brought him anxiety and despair.

The group's objective was to examine the basic personality of the entrepreneur as a potential buyer, decide what kinds of approaches would work with him, and consider what a salesman's moral and legal responsibilities and loyalties should be toward the company he represented, his customer, and himself in doing business with the buyer.

In order to initiate the analysis, Dr. Stevens asked each member of the group to read an article reprinted from *The Wall Street Journal* and independently break down the causes of business failure into three categories—operational causes, personality causes, and combination personality/operational causes. Dr. Stevens passed out the reprint to the group.* The article began:

BLOOMINGTON, Minn—The day is etched into Jerald H. Maxwell's memory.

His family will never forget it, either. To them, it is the day he started weeping in his room, the day his exuberant self-confidence ended and his depression began, the day his world—and theirs—came tumbling down.

It was October 23, 1979, the day Mr. Maxwell was fired in disgrace as chairman and chief executive of Med General Inc. The high-flying medical products company, its growth fueled by risky sales tactics that overextended it financially, was on its way down. It would end up in bankruptcy proceedings seven months later.

For the first time in his life, Mr. Maxwell was a failure, and it shattered him. His feeling of defeat led to an emotional breakdown, gnawed away at the bonds between Mr. Maxwell and his wife and four sons, and pushed him to the brink.

"When things fell apart, they fell apart so bad I was ashamed," Mr. Maxwell recalls. He pauses and sighs, then goes on: "It says in the Bible that all you have to do is ask and you will receive. Well, I asked for death many times."

The story of Jerry Maxwell is a story of an executive's emotional problems. It doesn't fit neatly into the image of the hard-driving corporate executive. But it is all too common, psychiatrists say.

There aren't any statistics on how many businessmen suffer breakdowns because they can't deal with failure. Some fired executives, of course, simply pick up the pieces and move on to something new. The executives who have the hardest time facing failures are those who are most attached to their careers.

For them, the fall from the top can be devastating. Many know nothing but success from the time they begin climbing the corporate ladder. They work long hours, and love every minute. They thrive on the heady excitement of making million-dollar decisions. Their jobs become their lives. Dr. Alan McLean, the staff psychiatrist for International Business Machines Corp., says:

"The biggest lesson, and a very simple one, is to avoid having all your eggs in the psychological basket of work."

How to Succeed

Mr. Maxwell, who is 48, says it is a lesson he finally has learned. "Inside I kept saying, 'It's not good enough. I've got to do more.'

That's a summary of what went wrong," he says. "There's nothing wrong with succeeding, but only if you put it in perspective."

Before his fall, Mr. Maxwell himself probably would have scoffed at such advice. The son of a construction foreman, he aspired to success even as a youth. "Horatio Alger rags to riches was built into me; it drove my whole life," says Mr. Maxwell, who breaks into a grin when talking about the good days gone by. At the University of Oregon he was the president of his fraternity house and vice chairman of the Young Republicans. After college came management jobs in the construction business, his own consulting firm and, in 1970, Med General, which he helped start.

Med General was just another obscure little company until 1974, when it introduced a device designed to control chronic pain by stimulating nerves. The company's sales spurted to $6.9 million in 1978 from just $539,445 in 1973, and it was ranked in the top 10 of *Inc.* magazine's list of fast-growing small companies.

Mr. Maxwell's ego grew with Med General. The license plates on his company Cadillac carried his nickname, "Big Max," and his business cards carried the title of "field general." He was a celebrity in Twin Cities business circles by mid-1979. When Med General stock hit a high of $16.50 a share in over-the-counter trading (up from less than $1 in the early 1970s), Mr. Maxwell's 238,635 shares were worth nearly $4 million.

"Things Got Distorted"

Then it ended. To meet Mr. Maxwell's overly optimistic sales goals, Med General extended easy credit terms to its customers. And some salesmen simply shipped out goods that hadn't been ordered. As a result, sales were overstated and Med General didn't have enough money coming in to pay its bills. Mr. Maxwell says he wasn't aware of the questionable sales practices. "I gave the marching orders, and things got distorted at the other end," he says, softly adding, "But it was still my responsibility. I was in charge."

Whether to blame or not, he began showing the emotional strain and went into a hospital suffering physical and mental exhaustion in early October 1979. "I couldn't get through a staff meeting without crying," he recalls. Mr. Maxwell came out of the hospital a week later and tried to revive Med General, but it was too late. Med General's bankers demanded that the board dismiss Mr. Maxwell and another top executive because of the precarious financial condition. The ax fell on October 23.

Like most fired executives, Mr. Maxwell first reacted with disbelief. In the past, he had derisively referred to Med General's board as the "board of directed" because it always did his bidding. "I was stunned. After all, it was 'my company,' " he says. "I just went home and collapsed. I couldn't do much but sleep and search for 'why.' "

It was all the more embarrassing because Mr. Maxwell's firing and details of the company's problems were widely publicized in local newspaper stories. "I thought, 'What will people think—brokers who supported me, stockholders who invested in me, employees who worked for me—what will they think?' " he says. "Here I had it all, and all I had to do was slow it down to a manageable pace and I could have continued it. Why couldn't I have seen this?"

Overcome by the fear of seeing people who knew him, the outgoing Mr. Maxwell secluded himself at home. "I was largely dropped by my friends. It was like no contact, no interest," he says. "In all fairness, part of it was my fault because I didn't want to be contacted." His wife, Patricia (everybody calls her Patsy), adds, "He decided his life was over and he would never be able to do anything. He never said that, but that's what I think he felt."

Even now, Mr. Maxwell has a hard time remembering what he did that first year. Some days he would do nothing but sleep and read. At times he would sit in the family room and compulsively watch videotapes of movies on television, one after the other, oblivious to the rest of the family. Occasionally, he wrote long letters to former Med General associates, apologizing for letting them down. He began visiting a psychiatrist, who prescribed antidepressant drugs to reduce his anxiety.

Mr. Maxwell even avoided talking on the telephone. "For two years, he didn't talk to his mother. When she would call, he'd say, 'Tell her I'm not here,' " recalls Curtis Maxwell, 25, the eldest son, who was recuperating at home from a serious motorcycle accident at the same time Mr. Maxwell's depression started.

Mr. Maxwell's firing also was hard on his family, although the Maxwells have managed to get by financially because Mr. Maxwell receives $3,000 a month in disability-insurance payments. The Med General stock is worthless, of course.

Mark Maxwell, then a high-school senior at an exclusive military academy in suburban St. Paul, knew he wouldn't get the Datsun 280-Z sports car his father had promised him. Other students rubbed it in. Shortly after Mr. Maxwell was fired, a classmate told Mark: "I see your old man's company is going down. Looks like you're not going to be rich. What's he doing, embezzling?" Mark, now 20, punched him.

For Kevin Maxwell, now 22, it meant an end to his fledgling career as a stockbroker at a small Minneapolis securities firm. He quit because he was too embarrassed to call customers who might have lost money on Med General stock. "I was depressed. I couldn't talk to anybody," he says. "I thought angry customers were going to come after me."

The family found it emotionally difficult to adjust to the new Jerry

Maxwell, who was downcast and nervous, compared with "Big Max," who had been bossy and boisterous. "I couldn't understand my father, a real gung-ho guy, not being that way anymore," Curtis says. Mark says: "I guess I understood it, but at the same time I couldn't. We couldn't see why he wouldn't snap back. My father was my god, I looked up to him. When he said jump, I jumped. All of a sudden there was a complete turnaround. I didn't like it. I despised him."

• • •

His emotional problems worsened the second year when he attempted a business comeback and ran into difficulties. He started a new medical-products company, Omega-Med International Inc., in an effort to duplicate the early success of Med General, and enlisted sons Kevin and Mark as salesmen.

Mr. Maxwell quickly found that he couldn't handle the day-to-day pressures of running a business. "I'd get dressed in the morning but couldn't go in, or I'd put on my robe and couldn't get dressed," says Mr. Maxwell, sitting in his cramped Omega-Med office with a crucifix hanging on the wall and a Bible on his desk. "I couldn't handle getting on the phone and talking to people. I'd look at the phone and tense up my arms, fearful that people would say something negative. I feared rejection."

He had figured that his experience and contacts in the medical-products business would help. On the contrary, many potential customers would have nothing to do with Omega-Med because of the Med General debacle. "They didn't want to touch us. It was like we had a disease," says Mark, whose telephone calls to customers often weren't returned.

• • •

Mrs. Maxwell despaired of her husband's getting better and took a part-time clerical job to get out of the house. "We all decided he could be this way the rest of his life," she says. "I didn't think I could sit there another two years or five years or the rest of my life with him in that condition."

Then, last October, two years after he fell into severe depression, it began to subside. It took that long, he says, before he finally started accepting failure as a part of life. "Being able to admit that maybe I can't do everything, that I'm not the best—surrendering that belief— all of a sudden I was able to start doing things," he says. "The fear started leaving."

But Mr. Maxwell's recovery remains slow. Omega-Med recently merged with another small, financially troubled medical-products company. Mr. Maxwell, who became the chief executive of the combined companies, says that the pressure of dealing with the business problems has been hard on him. "I'm very up and down," he says. "I don't have continuing depression like before, but I'm going through a very difficult time."

After they finished reading the article, Dr. Stevens' three salesmen conferred for 20 minutes and reached a consensus on the factors that led to the collapse of Med General. There was no need to examine the cause of its success. It was apparent to all that Med General was the creative brainstorm of a hard-driving entrepreneur whose primary motivation was identity and power. He had been successful in everything he had done in his life and could build Med General by brute force and skill, in that order. Playing the role of salesman performing a post mortem on an account they had theoretically sold to, their task was now to evaluate what had gone wrong and what the salesman's responsibility was as a vendor to Med General during its lifetime. The elements they agreed on were categorized as follows:

Personality Causes of Failure
> *Past achievements "not good enough, must do more."*
> *Ego grew with Med General.*
> *Broke, bankrupt, and without the drive or energy to do it again.*

Operational Causes of Failure
> *Risky sales tactics.*
> *Overextended financially.*
> *Overly optimistic sales goals.*
> *Easy credit to customers.*
> *Salesmen shipping goods to customers that haven't been ordered.*
> *Sales overstated.*
> *No cash flow.*

Personality/Operational Causes of Failure
> *Before fall, Maxwell would not take advice.*
> *Referred to board of directors as "board of directed."*
> *Refused to slow down to a manageable pace.*

With the tape recorder running, they began their analysis.

Salesman 1   Clearly Maxwell was a megalomaniac. A guy like that is driven by self-doubts, so nothing is ever good enough. His ego was wrapped up with Med General, and when it fell apart *he* fell apart. The

way to deal with a buyer like that is to give him
what he wants and let him go ahead and destroy
himself because he's going to anyway. Look at
the way he ran his business.

Salesman 2   I tend to agree with your conclusion that he is
going to destroy himself anyway. However, if he
had been one of my customers and I saw the
risky sales tactics that he was using—such as his
overly optimistic sales goals and relaxed credit—I
would have felt personally responsible to raise the
issue with Maxwell, at least ask him how he
could get away with managing his business that
way when other companies could not. More important, I would have been concerned about the
impact on my company of doing business with a
man operating under those policies. Let's face it:
if he doesn't get paid, we don't get paid; if we
don't get paid, I don't get paid.

Salesman 3   I agree that the only way anybody is ever going to
sell a man like Maxwell anything is to appeal to
his ego. I know some salesmen that would sell a
guy like Maxwell the Brooklyn Bridge by offering
to change its name to Big Max's New York City
Crossing. The old attitude of let the buyer beware. However, we all have to play by a set of
rules or society will collapse. I don't think any
salesman dealing with Maxwell, once he got close
enough to the business to understand what Maxwell was doing, should have done business with
him. I think the salesman should have reported
what he knew to his manager and protected himself and his company from suffering major losses
by the bankruptcy of Med General.

Salesman 1   That sounds all well and good, but how many
salesmen are really that altruistic? The only
salesmen with that kind of restrictions have had
them imposed on them by either legislation or
company policy. The brokers selling Med General
stock, for example, are bound by the legislated
conscience of the SEC rules not to tout the stock
of a company that they know is in bad shape. No

such rule exists for the salesmen selling raw materials and components to Med General. Those salesmen are judged solely by their backlog of orders.

Salesman 3   I agree with that but I still feel that there is a moral and probably a legal responsibility for a salesman to react to what he knows is an unethical and possibly illegal situation. Those Med General salesmen who shipped goods they hadn't ordered to customers ought to be taken to court.

Salesman 2   That's true, but who is responsible for the overly optimistic sales goals? By his own admission, Maxwell was a tyrant and you can imagine the pressure that he put on his salesmen to sell those goods. Out of desperation I suspect that some of them met their quota the only way they could. They booked and shipped bum orders! I am not excusing them for it; I am merely saying that the fact that Maxwell was the cause of their actions should be taken into consideration.

Salesman 3   Maxwell wouldn't take advice, and he referred to the board of directors as the board of directed. That says it all. Salesmen with an ongoing customer relationship tend to know a great deal about their customers' business. In my opinion, any salesman doing business with Maxwell had a moral responsibility and a legal responsibility—not to mention the personal responsibility he had to his company—to bring the facts he knew about Med General to somebody's attention.

Salesman 1   Yes, but it's not the salesman's responsibility to tell any buyer, let alone one with an ego like Maxwell's, that he is being a jerk. That's the responsibility of management. If I ran across a man like Maxwell, I would immediately call my regional VP and tell him the situation—then let him decide how to handle it.

Salesman 2   I agree. There is an ethical responsibility that all salesmen have when selling the customer. A man with an ego like Maxwell's is very easy to appeal to. But ethics aside, from a practical standpoint, overselling a guy like that is ultimately going to reflect back on the individual salesman when word gets around.

Salesman 3   I agree. The Med General salesmen who shipped goods to customers who hadn't ordered them are going to have a hard time finding a job elsewhere in the industry.

At the end of the session, it became quite apparent to Dr. Stevens that most good Advocate Salesmen have an inherent sense of fair play and justice. Those who don't either don't last long in the business or gravitate toward some sort of hit-and-run product line that offers no repeat business and is not dependent on word-of-mouth referral. Even so, the attitude of "let the buyer beware" should prevail, and does prevail in all normal business transactions. The degree to which a salesman oversells his customer or takes a risky order is directly related to the personal risk that he assumes in doing so. He doesn't want to lose his job and he certainly doesn't want to read about himself in the newspaper. He's also terrified of being sued. The underlying threat of these potential disasters usually serves as an excellent reminder to the conscience of even the most aggressive closer practicing his trade.

The most significant thing that came out of the analysis was that each salesman agreed that it was his personal responsibility to determine whether or not he was going to consummate a sale with a man like Maxwell or turn the information he had and the conclusions he reached over to somebody with greater responsibility. The group agreed unanimously that whatever decision the salesman made, the results of the decision were his alone. He is the only one close enough to a situation like Maxwell's to wave the red flag, and his actions should be dictated by whatever moral, ethical, or legal sense of responsibility he has the second he knows that his customer is in trouble.

But the most enlightening part of the discussion as far as Dr. Stevens was concerned was that none of his salesmen analysts ever questioned the fact that the best way to sell Med General was to make the purchase reflect well on Maxwell's personal identity and enhance his feeling of power. Dr. Stevens confronted the salesmen on this point. Their reactions ranged from amusement and curiosity to incredulousness. None of them understood how Dr. Stevens could think that there was ever any other way to sell Med General.

Med General, they told him, was a corporate extension of Jerald H. Maxwell and his personality. Entrepreneurs like Maxwell are hands-on managers with a finger in every nook and cranny of the company. "I wouldn't be surprised," said one of the salesmen, "if Maxwell involved himself in the purchase of cleaning supplies and toilet paper."

"Oh, absolutely," agreed another. "You could probably sell him four boxcars of toilet paper if you offered to print his competitor's logo on each tissue."

Dr. Stevens was astounded and asked the group to form another discussion team. Their new objectives were to discuss tactics for selling a variety of products to Med General by making the presentation, application, and purchase of the product appeal to Maxwell's personality quirks. They agreed, and the tape started to run again.

Salesman 1   My background is in the service industry. If I ever tried to sell Med General something costly and disruptive to the status quo, like an in-company food service program, I would be sure to work an elaborate executive dining room and gourmet food facility into the plans and tailor my presentation to Maxwell around that unit. Certainly I would have to meet other buyers' objectives within the chain of beneficiaries, but if I became stalled or struck resistance somewhere in middle—and real—management, I would make a point to get to Maxwell in person by telephone or by letter and pitch the executive dining room. I'd spend a little money on artist's renderings that would show a dining room with pictures of Maxwell hanging on the wall and Med General logos prominently displayed. I would feature menus of a wide range but highlight Big Max and French foods, and I would ask the artist to make the man pictured at the head of the table a little bit larger than life and certainly dominant over the others.

Salesman 2   I spent a good deal of my professional life in commercial real estate. In my opinion the way to sell

Med General a lease, an office building, or space for a regional office would be to appeal to Maxwell's ego needs. If you're trying to sell him a building with corporate offices, show him what his office is going to look like and the view his visitors will have. Notice I didn't say the view that he would have; I said the view that his visitors would have. And don't try to sell him a building that doesn't have a view. If I were an architect selling Maxwell plans, I would present him with the most ostentatious design in the world and tell him that once constructed, this building would be a monument to him for centuries to come. Without taking too much liberty in order to be humorous, gentlemen, I might very well use the Vatican in my analogies during the presentation. I agree that the way to end-run a middle-management blockade is to get your pitch directly up to Maxwell any way you can. Regardless of the objections of his subordinates, if you make the frame around Maxwell's picture attractive enough, he'll buy it at any cost.

Salesman 3   I grew up in the capital equipment business. Selling capital equipment can be dull. You're talking to engineers who like to expound all day on how great they are and give you two minutes to make your pitch. Then they put the whole project out on bid like they intended to do in the first place. Meanwhile, of course, you've bought lunch. If I were selling Med General, I wouldn't appeal to Maxwell's identity; I would appeal to his power. Maxwell is the kind of guy who would buy any new piece of equipment or gimmick if he felt it would give him an edge over his competitors. If you were selling left-handed monkey wrenches and told Maxwell that he would be the first guy in three states to have them, he'd probably buy. If you came out with something that was untried and unproven but told Maxwell that by incorporating this equipment in his manufacturing process Med General would be on the leading edge of technology, he would buy. These things

would appeal to Maxwell's sense of power and
need for control. Naturally they are all wrapped
up in his identity. But "high tech," "state of the
art," and other meaningless buzzwords are what
motivate a man like Maxwell. Could Napoleon
have had an identity without a sense of power?

Salesman 1   You're right. If I were selling Maxwell insurance,
I'd structure a benefit plan in such a way as to
make his employees dependent upon him. Men
like Maxwell always preach loyalty. In fact, they
are terrified of an internal revolution. Unions
drive them into a fetal position, and just the
thought gives them hives. Maxwell would want
to lock his people up in golden handcuffs yet be
able to be known in the community as a benevolent and paternalistic employer. He would have it
both ways.

Salesman 2   Oh yes, that's Maxwell. If I were in the car business, I'd try to sell him a fleet of company cars by
explaining how much loyalty and gratitude and
adoration he would receive from his employees'
families every time they got into the car Maxwell
provided to take a Sunday drive in the country.
And, as a hooker, I'd close the deal by throwing in
license plate frames with the Med Gen logo prominently displayed in the corner.

The discussion went on but the point was clear. The way to
sell Med General was to appeal to Maxwell's identity and power
needs. It is important to remember that not only is the world
filled with entrepreneurs like Jerald H. Maxwell, but there is a
little bit of Jerald H. Maxwell in every overachiever. Any person
who has achieved anything in his life has had to pay a price to
do so. *And he is never sure whether he made the right choice.*
Smart salesmen play on those insecurities and tilt their presentation in a way that reinforces the soundness of the choice. But
in order to do so, a good salesman must first ascertain what that
choice was and estimate the price the man paid for it. That's a
skill based on judgment, and good skills can only come from
knowledge, so make sure that you know your customer.

CONCEPT 5

Need Salesmen, Relationship Salesmen, and Order Takers

People who sell need are in the high technology of sales. They are creating something new in the mind of the customer, who has gotten along just fine without the particular product that Need Salesmen are selling. So Need Salesmen usually appeal to several of the buying motivators necessary to sell the appointment for a presentation. Most Need Salesmen are Doers and are able to handle a high degree of rejection.

People who sell relationships are excellent salesmen, but they usually don't know how, or want, to sell need. A Relationship Salesman sells his own personality and service, service, service. Relationship Salesmen have a much higher need for approval from the customer and thus much less tolerance of rejection. Some Relationship Salesmen don't consider themselves to be salesmen at all. They are "customer service representatives" who maintain account relations and sell indirectly or incidentally. But sell they do, whether they admit it or not. So do architects, builders, lawyers, dentists, doctors, and housewives.

Good Relationship Salesmen who are indeed professionals are found in situations where need has already been sold. For example, customers who buy sulfur have an already established need. (Who could ever sell a trainload of sulfur to somebody who doesn't need any?) Sulfur as a commodity is usually supplied by the big producers at the same quality and price. The Relationship Salesman who gets the order is the one the customer can count on to expedite delivery, handle personal requests, work out terms with the manufacturer, and generally act as the customer's advocate within the supplier's office. These salesmen solicit customer loyalty by offering personal loyalty in return. They tend to represent major brand-name corporations. That way the high personal integrity they like to project is enhanced by the company they represent.

Order Takers fill a very definite purpose in the scheme of day-to-day sales. They have a high intolerance of rejection that manifests itself in a disembodied arm's-length attitude toward their product and customer needs. They are the catalog salesmen. "If you don't like what we have on page 12, Mr. Buyer, let me show you page 13." They let the customer sell himself and find his own buying motivators. If the customer doesn't buy, it's not the Order Taker's fault. Obviously the company did not produce or display any product that the customer wanted. Therefore, onward to the next call, and if he's lucky, today the Order Taker will complete twenty-five. Somebody will want to buy something—he hopes!

Every salesman needs to know exactly what kind of salesman he is. Otherwise, he could accept a position with a company whose skill requirements were beyond his basic ability. In addition, each salesman needs to have flexibility to change his style if he can. Need Salesmen can easily switch to Relationship Salesmen or Order Takers. Relationship Salesmen have difficulty selling need but are quite happy taking orders. Order Takers are stuck. That's all right. The world needs them too. However, flexibility is the name of the game. Unless you can sell application you cannot sell need. By being able to sell an application for a product, you have put yourself in the mainstream of sales. Customers have problems to solve. And the smart salesman identifies what his buyers' problems are. Then he generates a solution to those problems through an application of his product.

Salesmen who sell relationships have difficulty with application. They hope if they present their product knowledgeably and thoroughly, the customer will see the application himself and buy. Order Takers assume the customer knows his problem, knows the solution to his problem, and looks to the Order Taker as a product expediter who can implement the solution quickly. That is also how Order Takers view themselves.

Bill Byrd was a very good Relationship Salesman for IBM in the 1960s. Bill knew his machines and he knew his software.

He was a diligent worker, kept his client and prospect list up to date, and worked his territory methodically. Bill had no problems contacting and dealing with upper management. And his buyers could depend on him to have the answers to their application questions within 24 hours.

Bill made a good living selling International Business Machines. However, he disliked IBM's regimentation and living in the East. As a consequence, he was lured to a West Coast company specializing in data processing training. Its product was a communications program that enabled line operating managers to converse intelligently with data processing management. The one-week training program taught line managers enough about data processing to ask intelligent questions. It taught data processing people enough about the needs and objectives of line management to suggest new methods by which reports could be simplified and generated to meet management's needs. Up until now, line management had been asking for 2-page reports, and data processing, covering all bases, would return with 50-page analyses. Because of his experience with IBM, Bill felt this training filled a real need and was enthusiastic when he joined the firm.

Unfortunately, Bill Byrd failed. No longer backed by the IBM reputation, Bill could not gain access to top management people. His calls were always sidetracked by secretaries and his "leave words" were rarely returned. Bill was desperate. He could not get in front of his buyers. As a last resort, Bill tried to sell his program at a lower-level entry point. He contacted data processing people. Because he could speak their language and because he was one of their peers, Bill could sell them an appointment. However, he found that data processing people were very threatened by the communications program he was presenting. He was astounded to realize that data processing people did not really want line management to know much about the mysteries of data processing. Their technical knowledge and buzzwords were job security as far as they were concerned.

Bill changed his tactics. He went to middle-management people who were quite receptive to the program offered by Bill's firm. After all, middle managers bore the brunt of interpreting the 50-page reports that data processing delivered to line management instead of the 2-page reports they requested.

But still Bill couldn't gain access to the people who really made the decisions.

Bill's manager recognized that he was floundering and teamed him up with the top salesperson in the region. Bill was surprised to learn that Hillary West had no problem obtaining appointments with top management. Not having a product name like IBM to get her past the secretaries, Hillary had devised a substitute approach. Like Bill, Hillary would discuss the benefits of her company's communications program with middle management. However, Hillary wasn't out to sell middle management. Her purpose was to glean enough information about the problems caused by the miscommunication to effectively make a presentation to the president or executive vice president of the company.

Hillary would summarize the problems that she had gleaned from middle management into a brief letter. At the end she would ask for an appointment with the president to discuss these very real and relevant problems. However, in order to assure that the letter found its way to the president's desk, Hillary sent it as a Mailgram, which she immediately followed up with a telephone call asking for an appointment. Her success ratio was 85 percent. When she failed it was usually because she had not properly identified the problems within the organization.

Once she secured the appointment, Hillary knew she would have only five minutes after chit-chat to catch the president's interest. So she made rush calls on her middle-management contacts to tell them of the pending meeting. The middle managers were ecstatic. They needed help. They gladly joined Hillary in a little conspiracy to sell the boss because now they had common objectives. By the time Hillary met with the president, she had more data about the company than some of the company's executives. She could not only list all the major problems that misinformation had caused, but she could assign a weighted dollar figure to the impact of those problems on the organization's profits and cash flow. Bill was apprehensive before the first meeting. He thought that the president would be offended because of the proprietary nature of the information Hillary had gleaned. He was amazed when the president complimented Hillary for having done her homework. Several meetings and discussions later, top management gave its blessing to the program. Implementation was turned over to those very middle managers who had provided Hillary with information. Everybody was happy. Everybody's objectives were met. And Bill had learned a lesson about how to sell need.

Unfortunately, when Bill tried Hillary's approach on his own, it didn't work. He could successfully contact middle-management people and glean the necessary information. But when he made the presentation to the president, he simply couldn't describe the problems in a meaningful way. Instead he reverted to his old technique of describing his product in detail and letting his buyer make it relevant to the problems of the company. He utterly failed at presenting solutions. So of course he was unable to convince the president that these problems did in fact exist. That's when Bill discovered that, at best, he had been a Relationship Salesman and, at worst, an Order Taker all his professional life. Bill Byrd couldn't sell need.

That realization was important to Bill. He stopped trying to do something he couldn't. He discussed the situation honestly with his boss and worked out an adjustment. Bill left the ranks of sales and joined the ranks of client service. He no longer had to sell need, for the relationship was already established among the clients Bill serviced. Now Bill's relationship skills could play a valuable part in implementing the program he had once tried to sell. Bill's order-taking skills were very useful when things needed to be expedited and facilitated. Bill had found his niche. He lived in California instead of New Jersey and reconciled himself to the fact that he probably would never make the money he had hoped to.

It is as important to understand the character of your buyer as it is to understand yourself. There is a correlation between Need Salesmen, Relationship Salesmen, and Order Takers on the one hand and Doers, Waiters, and Watchers on the other. But the correlation is not exact. An executive vice president of a company who is a Doer may not sell his projects internally by selling need. Such an EVP has a lot of authority and power. Therefore he may use his relationship with others to sell internally. His power leads others to want to please him, so he can gain their acquiescence simply by offering them a relationship with him. This Doer EVP is a Relationship Salesman using the reverse sell. "If you buy what I'm selling, you might be good enough to join my inner circle" is his message.

This is important to know if you are going to do business with such a man because he will judge your presentation by the way he makes presentations to others. Having identified him as a Doer, you can feel confident that if you sell him, the sale will be consummated. However, in presenting need to a buyer of this type, you must also form a relationship with him—*because he expects it.* If you disappoint that expectation, your credibility will be in jeopardy. If your credibility is in jeopardy, the need you have created in his mind will be suspect and the sale will become instantly unraveled.

Conversely, if your buyer sells internally by presenting need, that does not necessarily mean he is a Doer. Many Waiters and even Watchers sell need. Waiters are less forceful than Doers and therefore will not push their programs as hard as a Doers. Watchers will rarely take the risk of presenting anything but, if their own survival is at stake, they may feel they have no choice. And when forced to, Watchers can make a very telling argument if they sell need.

If you have correctly identified a buyer as a Waiter, and you make the assumption that therefore your best approach is to sell relationships, you might be very embarrassed and disappointed. If a Waiter sells need internally he will expect need to be sold to him. A Watcher who sells need will demand the same treatment. So it's critical that you present your data in a fashion that meets your buyer's expectations.

Clearly, then, there is no simple matrix relating Doers, Waiters, and Watchers and their internal sales methods with Need Salesmen, Relationship Salesmen, and Order Takers. But there are some rules of thumb. People who sell need are usually not Watchers. (Just be careful when they are!) People who sell need can very well be Waiters, but are usually Doers. People who sell relationships are sometimes Doers, usually Waiters, and occasionally Watchers. True Watchers tend to avoid anything other than superficial relationships. Order Takers are never Doers. Only occasionally are Waiters Order Takers; most are willing to risk some rejection and involve themselves when they want something badly enough. As an Order Taker, a Watcher is in his element. There is no risk to him, no commitment on his part to buyers. And if something goes wrong with the project, it's not his fault. He is simply an expediter and facilitator trying to do his job.

Now the burning question becomes: How do you find out what kind of salesman your buyer is? A wise pundit once said, "For every problem there is a solution that is short, simple, and wrong." This does not necessarily mean that simple solutions are always wrong. In determining whether your buyer sells need, forms relationships, or takes orders, the solution is really very simple. Listen to the types of questions your buyer asks. He is demanding information in the form that he is comfortable with and expects. If he asks for application and results-oriented information, he is an internal Need Salesman. If he asks about your company's history, other customers you have sold, or technical information about the product, he is an internal Relationship Salesman. If he doesn't ask any questions at all, but listens attentively, he's probably an Order Taker. However, any of the above types can listen stoically to your pitch without asking any questions as part of the buyer's role they are playing. Test a noncommunicative buyer by asking him a question that will force him to answer in order for you to proceed.

Whenever Hillary West was faced with a group of noncommunicative buyers, she would stop her presentation and ask her chief buyer questions. "How many people do you have in data processing?" was her usual opener. It was a simple question but everybody could see that it required an answer. Having gotten a precise number or a good estimate, Hillary would ask another buyer approximately how many middle-management people there were in the organization. This too was a fairly simple question. Hillary then went on to ask the group how many of those data processing people actually interfaced with middle management. This question was more complex and usually generated some discussion. From this discussion, Hillary could pick up who was asking what kinds of questions. Therefore she could categorize her buyers and adjust her selling pitch to meet everybody's expectations. Hillary was a master Advocate Salesman. She could handle a group situation.

Naturally, it is much easier to qualify buyers on a one-on-one basis. The individual buyer is forced to reveal himself, because he cannot defer the question to someone else. Once you have a sense of the buyer's personality, you must meet his selling expectations. He will recognize that you are giving him information in the manner he prefers. Therefore you will be reinforcing his personal approach to internal selling. If you present the information in a format that is different from what he expects, you are rejecting him, his personal approach to selling, and his expectations. Rejection always breeds rejection in return.

In summary, need is sold by finding application. The application can be made by appealing to results or to personal greed, power, self-approval, fear, approval of others, or safety. Also, need does not have to be limited to the specific results a product was designed to produce. Dan Moran sold need by appealing to personal power. Need was sold to Jerald Maxwell by appeals to personal identity. Martha Lewis appealed to her buyer's self-approval when she asked him to write an article for her publication. Tyrone Shapiro's Doer salesclerk sold need to Mrs. Jones in the form of approval of others. Mrs. Jones' need for a fur coat had little to do with keeping warm. Looking good was very much her most prominent objective. Mrs. J. could have kept warm with a plain wool coat. The trick is discerning exactly what the buyer's real need is.

Relationships are sold exactly the same way and against the same buying motivators. However, a Relationship Salesman is selling himself, not a product—that is, he is selling an application of his personal service to the buyer. Therefore a person selling relationships is faced with a *two-step* sale situation where only a one-step situation existed before. First he must find a reason for the buyer to buy a personal relationship with him. After that, he must still find a reason for the buyer to purchase his product. So, in any event, the salesman must sell need. The only reason why salesmen sell relationships in the first place is because they cannot or should not sell need straightaway. If a salesman could bypass the need to sell relationships and sell need for the product directly, he would be saving himself a considerable amount of time and qualify for the black belt of advocate selling.

The way to be a good Order Taker is quite simple. Don't sell anything. If you have the opportunity to sell something—don't! Don't take responsibility for anything. Try not to offer any opinions and certainly don't try to close a sale. Just wait until the customer sells himself and asks you to process the order. Then shift into high gear, be the master expediter, and fulfill the order immediately.

CONCEPT 6

Economic, Feasibility, and Implementive Buyers

Buyer roles change with each product and the personality of each company. This fact drives salesmen crazy. The main reason salesmen waste so much time closing a sale is because they are saying the right things to the wrong people.

So it can be said to all salesmen, "Know thine enemy!"

Assuming a proper attitude toward himself, his profession, and his company, a salesman needs to gather the knowledge that will enable him to develop the necessary skills to properly advocate his product in the marketplace. Without knowledge of the buyers—who they are, what they do, and how to motivate them—a salesman is reduced to mouthing canned pitches. No application can be presented, so need cannot be sold. A good Advocate Salesman always knows to immediately qualify and classify his buyers. Nevertheless, "Who the hell is the buyer?" remains the question most commonly asked by salesmen.

In the world of business and corporations, there is *always* more than one buyer. Any sale of any magnitude is a multi-approval sale. The guy with the money clearly has to approve; the guy who determines whether the product will work obviously has to approve; and the guy who must live with it certainly has to be happy or nobody will buy anything. These three people are known as the Economic Buyer, the Feasibility Buyer, and the Implementive Buyer.

The Economic Buyer is generally in control of all the business resources. Commonly he is the chief executive officer, but *that's not always the case.* It depends on the type of product being sold. To qualify for the definition, an Economic Buyer must have the power to shift the necessary budget resources, human resources, time resources, and results expectations within the organization to accommodate the product you are trying to sell.

Usually, the Economic Buyer has a Feasibility Buyer somewhere in the wings. This buyer has another motivation. He is the man the Economic Buyer relies on to either approve or shoot holes in the boss's "good ideas." The Feasibility Buyer is more of a technician. He is not particularly concerned with a product's benefits to the organization, because he is measured more on what the boss thinks of him than on how well the company does. Performance problems are the Economic Buyer's responsibility. But the Feasibility Buyer is critical to a sale and therefore must be identified. Your pitch must be slanted to demonstrate the appropriate benefits to him. Remember, he can't buy on his own, but he sure can kill your deal if he says no.

Once a sale is made—whether it is a new piece of capital equipment or an inventory control system—somebody's life is going to be disrupted by the change. Therefore you should analyze the impact your product will have on people and systems within the organization—the chain of beneficiaries. The *most critical person* within that chain is the Implementive Buyer. Sometimes he's an end user. Usually he's in charge of the end users. This buyer can't say yes all by himself, *but he certainly can hurt you.* The boss knows that if he forces something down the throat of his Implementive Buyer, it will usually stick somewhere and not get properly digested. Thus the need for consensus selling—selling the chain of beneficiaries and selling personal benefits to each link in the chain. But before you can sell, you must identify who to sell to, what kinds of buyers they are, and how to sell them.

Max Stubal, a five-star salesman for a line of office equipment, was discussing the need to identify buyers with a group of his newer colleagues. Max began his talk by asking, "If you have a great application of our new word processing system for a particular customer, who is the best person to talk to about it—the Director of Administrative Services? Possibly," he answered rhetorically. "The DAS has the power to approve expenditures, make adjustments to the budget, make changes in how many people work where and do what within the department, reallocate shifts, and so forth. He is a true Economic Buyer. He controls all the elements that make up the economic picture as it relates to our product. His performance measurement is tied directly to results. He needs to meet a predetermined budget.

"If your idea is going to be received positively, you will have to present the personal benefits to him. However," Max challenged, "the DAS may not be the *first* guy to see after all!

"With many Economic Buyers," Max went on, "the ground must be paved first by a Feasibility Buyer. This is the guy who plays devil's advocate for the boss, the one who says, 'Yeah, boss, it's feasible—it would work.' Remember, the Feasibility Buyer is usually a staff technician. His motivation is basically approval of others and safety. He has power only because the boss consults him. If the boss finds that the Feasibility Buyer's opinions have led him down too many dead ends he will simply stop consulting him. Therefore the Feasibility Buyer is more conservative than the Economic Buyer regarding new ideas. And, he doesn't have to live with the same set of performance measurements the boss does. The Economic Buyer may take a gamble. The Feasibility Buyer won't. He'll play it safe. Remember, too," Max cautioned, "even though the Feasibility Buyer can't purchase on his own authority, he gets lots of points for presenting good ideas for the Old Man's consideration, so he can make an excellent *sponsor.*

"No matter how good your idea is, you've got to recognize that it represents change," Max emphasized. "People resist change! Why? Because change rejects the status quo and rejection is intolerable to all of us. So before opening your mouth," Max suggested, "you might think through exactly who within the organization would be most affected by the changes your idea will bring. It's best to clearly identify the person in charge of those affected—the Implementive Buyer—before you even approach the boss, since this guy can sabotage your idea even if the boss buys it. Like the Feasibility Buyer, he is not a true buyer in his own right, but he can sure be a fiery dragon if he's not handled properly.

"Fear, approval of others, and safety are the principal motivators that move an Implementive Buyer. Nevertheless," Max went on, "remember that self-approval can also be a big motivator for this guy. He must not feel that your idea and the changes it will bring are going to threaten his self-image or his status in the mind of others. If he thinks your idea is going to do either, he will probably shoot you down in flames.''

Max went on to say that he uses several tactics to sell an account. One tactic is to sell up. Here he starts with the Implementive Buyer and end users of new equipment and discusses the benefits the new equipment would bring to their particular jobs. He then takes those data and runs them by the Feasibility Buyer in a low-pitched, conversational way—finding, of course, personal benefits of a change for the Feasibility Buyer. Having sold the troops, he then has no trouble getting an appointment with the Economic Buyer—the director of administrative services. The sale is almost a foregone conclusion.

In another situation Max approached the DAS directly because he knew the man was a Doer. He was a shaker and a mover within the organization and not afraid to take risks if benefits resulted. But, Max cautioned, if you do approach the DAS directly and gain his approval, don't leave the interview patting yourself on the back too quickly. Touch base with the Feasibility Buyer and the Implementive Buyer to smooth the way for the boss when he presents them with your idea. Otherwise, that fiery dragon—resistance to change—will raise its ugly head! This is particularly important when your Economic Buyer is a Doer. His people are probably wary of him because he is always changing something. Thus, under the guise of protecting him from himself, they take a "damage control" posture every time he presents them with a new idea.

Failure to identify the different kinds of buyers and their different motivations and objectives can have disastrous consequences. Nick Margolis built a successful national business handling union/management crises. Nick's specialty, for which his firm was well known, was representing management during a union election. Once the cards were signed by a majority of the employees, the national labor laws took over and an employer was forced to have an election. There was nothing the employer could do about it, and after an initial panic, the first person he called was his attorney. While attorneys are normally very reluctant to give away business, they know better than to risk their credibility by managing a union confrontation. Therefore they would go through their directory, locate a firm like Nick's, and promptly call. Nick or his counterparts would fly down to the besieged employer's headquarters, tell him how much the campaign was going to cost him, and walk away with a contract happily signed at any price by the panicked employer.

Nick's business grew to over $10 million a year—not a paltry sum for a service corporation. Nevertheless, he wanted to expand. He thought that a related area in which he could be successful was preventing the union/management confrontation in the first place. He wanted to develop a program that would encourage employees to reject overtures made by union organizers. The alternative his group came up with was a good one. Essentially it taught supervisors how to supervise. Built into that training were examples of the usual causes of supervisory mismanagement and how they led to the unrest on which labor organizers thrive. Nick packaged his program in the latest behavioral learning model. It stressed showing supervisors how to supervise correctly rather than just pointing out what they were doing wrong—the model on which the last generation of behavior modification products had been based.

Nick's program was expensive: $1,000 per supervisor, three days off the job, and $800 a day for one of Nick's instructors. Initial sales were decent but well below expectations. Nick wasn't worried, since his union election business was a money machine that never seemed to stop. However, when a recession hit, Nick found to his stunned surprise that unions were backing off organizing. Unlike British labor unions, which seem to become more militant as the economy worsens, American labor recognizes that without employers there would be no jobs. Without jobs, there would be no unions. Labor reduced its organizing efforts, and Nick's volume and profits plummeted. After months of waiting for the economy to change, Nick realized that he had better do something fast if he was going to stay in business at all.

His board of directors met. For the first time they focused on the supervisory training program as a primary product and gave it the attention it needed. It was agreed that a concentrated effort would be made to replace lost forecast revenue by selling the union preventive training. The die was cast. Each professional was given a list of clients to call on over the next month, and a meeting was scheduled in 30 days to review progress.

The results were a disaster. Not one sale was made. It was agreed that more time was needed, so another set of lists was drawn up, and another review meeting scheduled, this time at the end of 60 days. Meanwhile the expenses of $250,000 per month continued.

At the next review meeting, there were an awful lot of long faces around the table in Nick's boardroom. The longest face was Nick's. It was quite apparent that if the company was going to continue, for the first time in its history it would have to borrow money. Nick and his associates now faced a crisis of their own. One of the more intelligent professionals suggested that Nick call in a consultant, just as their own customers did when faced with a crisis. This was a bold step because consultants do not like to hire consultants. It is an admission that they don't know everything. The gurus who are attracted to the consulting profession don't like to admit that. Later, when Nick's associates found out that the consultant was a woman, they almost had a collective heart attack.

But Jane Bloomingdale's credentials were impeccable. She had been Vice President of North America for Damian-Schwartz of New York and had spent six years as President of the Institute for Behavior Modification in Washington, D.C., before starting her own practice. Jane spent a month analyzing the company's business, marketing approach, price/packaging structures, methods of delivery, and anticipated customer base. She assigned another list—a shorter one this time—to each professional responsible for sales. Over the next three weeks she accompanied each one of them on their calls to monitor and analyze what was happening. When she finished, she called a meeting of the board of directors and gave them the news.

"The good news," she said, "is that your product is excellent. It will do the job that it was intended to do. The bad news is that there isn't any more good news. The price is wrong, the package is wrong, your presentation is wrong—and, most important, your customer identification is wrong." That criticism raised everybody's eyebrows. The directors prided themselves on having dealt directly with top management and maintained that the CEO was the guy to see. Jane agreed but explained that they weren't reaching top management. In fact, Jane said, their collective call-to-appointment ratio was dismal. And when appointments had been made, they were with old customers only. The few solid new customer appointments had been set up by a third-party referral—usually by another old customer.

Jane made the group realize that before they honestly began to sell supervisory training, nobody in the firm had made

a real sale at all. With the crisis management program, need
was indelibly established in the mind of the buyer when the
election forms were laid on his desk, so no sale had been necessary. She pointed out that rarely did a chief executive officer call
their firm. Instead, he called his attorney, who then contacted
their firm. At that point, there was no selling to be done, merely
some negotiation on price and terms. Supervisory training was
different. Instead of selling a highly measurable "No there
won't be a union"/"Yes there will be a union" result, the firm
was now faced with selling a product designed to prevent something that, in the mind of the buyer, probably wouldn't occur in
the first place. Jane pointed out that previous buyers of their
services had had no idea that their employees might wish to organize. That's why they panicked when the confrontation
came. "With that kind of attitude," she reasoned, "what buyer
who did not presently have a union would want to take medicine to prevent it?"

"In fact," Jane went on, "in every one of the few presentations that the associates had been allowed to make, the buyer
raised the objection that supervisory training designed to prevent union organizing might just call attention to a union as an
alternative, thus causing what it was supposed to prevent. The
executive who controls all the resources of the company—
money, personnel, equipment—is clearly in a position to spend
the money, commit the human resources necessary to implement the program, and benefit from the results. He is clearly
the Economic Buyer and he is the chief executive officer. But
unfortunately no CEO your people approached could be sold on
the need, so a different approach must be tried.

"What needs to be done," she concluded, "is to find a different buyer."

Jane outlined her plan. The people to approach were the
vice presidents of manufacturing or the directors of operations.
These executives are usually directly responsible for the results
produced by the hourly workers, and hourly workers are the
major target of unions. Jane believed that these managers
would be in a better position to know whether or not there was
enough unrest to create an environment that was favorable for
an organizer. They would see it first. She added that although
these Feasibility Buyers controlled some of the human resources and some of the budgets, they needed permission for

major changes from the true Economic Buyer, the CEO and/or his executive committee.

"But," Jane went on, "this situation can work in your favor. Once you show the Feasibility Buyer that his plant environment is a walking invitation to an organizer, you can make a presentation to him for the preventive cure—the supervisory program. While he cannot buy directly, you have sold him need and he will now become an internal advocate for the program. But don't make the mistake of having him try to sell the CEO himself. Let's face it. He's too used to taking no for an answer from the CEO. Use the Feasibility Buyer to get an appointment with the CEO and then lay all the hard, cold facts of his plant environment in front of him. The VP Feasibility Buyer will reinforce your statements. Now the CEO *has* to believe that something he doesn't like is going on in his plant.

"At this point, you've almost duplicated the panic situation that arises when the union organizer presents the cards to the president. The CEO will start looking for alternatives to ward off the situation. Having made your presentation previously to the vice president of manufacturing and gotten his techinical approval on the quality of the program, you can now have him describe what he feels the program will do. This sets the stage for presenting the program to the CEO yourself. Your program is excellent and any CEO with an open mind will see the benefits of it. The hard part is to get him to open his mind. Once he sees the benefits, and your Feasibility Buyer agrees that the program will produce the results he wants, the sale becomes a dead certainty. But don't stop there. There are still people within the organization who must implement the program. If they don't agree with the objectives or technical aspects of the program, they'll sabotage you in the cafeteria and the parking lot and drag their heels on implementation.

"The way around this potential problem is to sell everybody affected by the program," she went on. "Instead of trying for the close they expect," Jane offered, "surprise your Economic and Feasibility Buyers by telling them that the next step is to arrange a meeting with the plant training directors and first-line supervisors. Ask them to make sure that both groups are present at the meeting. Once the meeting is arranged, make sure that you do not use the president or the executive vice president to sell. Nobody can sell your product better than you.

"Just have them there for the silent credibility that they lend to the situation and start with the basics of selling. Ask the first-line supervisors what they think of their plant environment. If they are reluctant to tell the truth, mention some of the inside information you learned from the vice president of manufacturing. This will let them know that they can speak freely. Their evaluation will serve two purposes. First, it will create need in the first-line supervisors' minds—a sense that some preventive action is necessary. Second, it will reinforce the need already established in the minds of the Economic Buyers and Feasibility Buyers present in the room. Then begin to discuss the supervisory training program as a way to prevent unionization. At this point, direct a lot of your presentation to the director of training, because you are in a position to make him a hero if you include him in the program, and he will want some reassurance that you intend to. He's your Implementive Buyer, and after seeing how all those line managers have reacted to your presentation, he knows he's going to have a program whether he likes it or not. So be careful. He may know of another firm like yours that does the same thing. If he feels you are going to exclude him, he will make quiet recommendations—or maybe loud ones—that some other firm be used, particularly if he's sure your competition will not cut him out of the picture.

"Having gotten the consensus agreement from your Economic Buyer, Feasibility Buyer, Implementive Buyer, and basic end users, you don't have to close the sale. The sale is already closed. It's a foregone conclusion as to whether they are going to buy. Now it is down to when. The sale is made, and the only thing left to do is pick a date to begin."

At the end of Jane's presentation the board of directors applauded, and the ones who applauded most were the ones who had complained the loudest when they heard they were going to have to take advice from a woman.

Jane's analysis and advice proved correct. With barely a nickel to spare in the company coffers, money started coming in from firms which were now convinced that they had to change their plant environment before organizing resumed in the unknown but predictably near future. Nick's people found the going a little tougher than selling crisis management. On the other hand, the risks were fewer, because there was no yes/no result at the end of the program. If in later years a client was in fact threatened by union organization, they could always point out that the CEO did not maintain the training and then charge him another $150,000 to manage the campaign.

A key element in Jane's analysis was to find a mentor or sponsor within the customer's organization. This is a necessary step whenever a multiapproval sale is involved. Without a sponsor, it is difficult to get anybody's attention. If you don't have anybody's attention, your alternative is never going to get high priority. If you don't have high priority, you can't even get an appointment. It's a vicious circle. Nick had always stayed away from offering crisis management to the Fortune 1000 companies because, he rationalized, they already had the best labor experts in the world on their payroll and couldn't justify the expense of an outside consultant. In reality, Nick had no idea whatsoever how to sell to a major corporation. With smaller companies, the outside attorney had always made the sale for him. Big corporations usually have inside attorneys who don't call outside consultants. Nick never knew where to begin.

However, now that he had learned how to sell, Nick took a second look at major corporations. Many of them had divisions located in the South and other areas where labor organizing was weak. Nick found to his delight that major corporate divisions are often structured as independent profit centers, with a lot of autonomy regarding budget and resource allocations. They are responsible only for producing a predetermined profit to the parent corporation. Therefore, he was able to break down those big, multidivision corporations into targets about the same size as the independent companies he had been serving all his life. However, in order to sell to them he first had to learn how each individual corporation was structured—and he needed to identify the people who could tell him that. Jane helped him devise a strategy to achieve his objective.

A breakdown of the Fortune 1000 corporations was available through *Standard & Poor's* and *Moody's* corporate financial reports. A market research firm was hired to identify those divisions within the corporation that were potential prospects for the services offered by Nick's group. Each professional in Nick's firm was given a targeted list of accounts. But instead of making calls to generate a sale, as they did with independent companies, the professionals were instructed to set up an appointment with as many vice presidents of manufacturing (Feasibility Buyers) as they could. Their sole purpose was to gather information about the organization. They were in fact doing a research study, and they truthfully told the prospects that that was the objective of their call.

This tactic served two purposes. First, it allowed the salesman to begin to establish a friendly relationship with a buyer without the usual underlying win/lose conflict inherent in a sales situation. The buyer's guard was down. Nick's people weren't trying to sell anything, and everybody likes to talk about himself and his work. As a consequence, Nick's professionals were able to learn the nuances of the reporting relationships in each multidivisional company. They were able to learn the limits placed on the spending authority of the division president, or Economic Buyer. They were able to gather history about the division's attitude toward training and productivity programs.

Armed with this knowledge, plus casual information gleaned from conversations about plant environment, Jane and Nick were able to target some very big corporate customer opportunities. Another call was then made to the Feasibility Buyers at the targeted locations. The purpose of the call was to discuss the labor environment at the plant. Normally a vice president of manufacturing would rebuff a call of this nature, but because the relationship had already been established, Nick and his people were able to sell the appointment in an astounding 95 percent of the cases. At this point, the strategy and tactics Jane had devised earlier were implemented. The Feasibility Buyer was sold on need and technically approved Nick's supervisory training program as the best alternative for union prevention. He became a *sponsor* for leading Nick's professionals through the rabbit warren of the corporate organization to put them in front of the necessary Economic and Implementive Buyers.

Nick once commented, "You know, I was amazed. Big corporations are just like small corporations. Jane was right, there are only three types of buyers: Economic, Feasibility, and Implementive Buyers. The only difference is that in big corporations power is shared, not concentrated as it is in small companies, so there are simply more Economic, Feasibility, and Implementive Buyers to touch base with. Without an internal sponsor I would never have been able to do it."

Nick's son, Ralph Margolis, also benefited from Jane Bloomingdale's training. When his father first began to describe the concept of Economic Buyers, Feasibility Buyers, and Implementive Buyers, Ralph said that it didn't apply at all to his line. Ralph sold a highly technical data processing service that specialized in managing IRA and Keogh retirement accounts for professionals and small businessmen. Ralph knew who his buyers were. His problem was getting them to take the time away from their business or practice to talk to him. One day a very strange thing happened. A busy surgeon whom Ralph cornered in the hospital corridor told Ralph to see his office manager, who handled all his administrative work. Normally Ralph would not have bothered to take that suggestion. It was just another dismissal by a busy doctor who did not really want to change his present method of pension management. However, Ralph began to wonder. If the doctor had in fact delegated total responsibility for his administrative services, including his pension fund management, to his office manager, the manager would then become an Economic Buyer, just like the president of a division who is delegated total authority by corporate headquarters. Ralph made the call.

To his surprise, he found a ready reception. Up until now the surgeon's office manager had literally been investing the doctor's money herself on the advice of several rather expensive and not too competent financial advisory firms. The responsibility was overwhelming, and the drain on her time was making her crazy. The 1 percent fee that Ralph usually found to be a big objection was no problem at all. She wanted the responsibility for those funds off her hands at any price. It wasn't her money anyway.

Ralph went back over his list of prospects. Fully 40 percent of them had indicated that somebody else in their office was responsible for managing their pension and retirement funds. Forty-eight phone calls later, Ralph had himself booked up for the next two weeks. At the end of the month he literally turned in enough booked business to meet his quota for the year. His startled manager quietly picked up the phone and began to verify the orders. They were real. After his astonishment passed, he took Ralph out for the most expensive dinner in town.

In Ralph's situation there was no visible Feasibility Buyer. Ralph's basic error had been in misidentifying the true Economic Buyer. Later Ralph was to find that although many doctors did monitor their Keogh investments personally, *all* of them relied on some outside service for financial advice. Ralph had found the Feasibility Buyer of his product. He now made it a point to find out who the financial adviser was. As his father had learned, if some motivation could be found for the Feasibility Buyer, it would be easier to sell the Economic Buyer.

Ralph knew that financial advisers like to keep getting their fee. But they are burdened by the administrative paperwork involved in keeping track of their clients' investments. Some had minicomputers, but most did not. So Ralph was able to offer them the ancillary recordkeeping service that his company performed. This service appealed to the financial advisers' greed—not greed for money, but greed for time. Paperwork had long ago chewed into their cocktail hour and was now threatening their dinner and family time.

Ralph found three other motivators that appealed to the financial adviser Feasibility Buyers. First, their fear of making a massive recordkeeping error was eliminated, because if an error occurred it would reflect upon Ralph's company, not them. Second, the reputation of Ralph's company and the fact that it specialized in keeping records of this type provided the buying motivator of safety. Finally, when the doctor received his new computerized report in a format that he could digest in five minutes over coffee, the adviser was complimented for having enlisted Ralph's services. The doctors were so pleased they rarely asked about the additional cost. When they did, only a few raised halfhearted objections. So Ralph found the motivators for financial advisers were eliminating *fear* of error, providing *safety* from criticism, and gaining *approval of others*. Ralph had made customers out of his competitors.

Later on, Ralph was astounded to find out that even in his little business an Implementive Buyer exists. If he was unsuccessful in selling a doctor or lawyer who did not delegate his investment decision, Ralph would pass the time in his prospect's office until he found out who was in charge of bookkeeping. Chatty conversation with this person usually gave Ralph the ammunition that he needed to go back and resell the doctor or his financial adviser. The bookkeeper had the responsibility of seeing that the financial adviser received the designated portion of the doctor's income for the pension plans. He was an implementer. He moved money from one bank account to another. As a result, he was privy to conversations between the doctor and his adviser. When something went wrong the bookkeeper usually learned about it during his periodic conversations with the financial adviser or through loud-voiced complaints by the doctor after he received his statements. This information was priceless to Ralph when he was in a competitive situation with a financial adviser who refused to give him a piece of the action. In January, Ralph was named Salesman of the Year. He sent Jane Bloomingdale a personal letter thanking her from the bottom of his heart.

In summary, every product has an Economic Buyer. And even though they are not always readily visible, a Feasibility Buyer and an Implementive Buyer exist somewhere in the wings. A husband may be the Economic Buyer for the family, but his wife is the household technician, and as Feasibility Buyer she'll tell him what kind of dishwasher works best. If their daughter does the dishes, she's the family Implementive Buyer.

The important thing to remember is that a buyer's motivation depends on his position in the hierarchy and the structure of the organizational environment. Before you can work on motivation, you've got to identify what kind of buyer you are dealing with so you don't waste your arrows shooting at the wrong animal. In the next chapter we'll discuss different kinds of motivation to use on your buyers.

CONCEPT 7

Buying Motivators

Everyone talks about motivation.

"I am demotivated by my work environment," complains one worker. "Motivate your people to do better," preach the management scientists.

"I have no motivation to go anyplace," complains one disgruntled homemaker. "How do you motivate a man to do something he doesn't want to do?" complains another about her spouse.

"Morale should be high and the troops motivated," roars the general. And on, and on, and on!

Everybody talks about motivation but nobody knows exactly what it is. In order to understand it, perhaps we must first define motivate. *Webster's* defines it like this: "to provide with a motive; to impel; incite." In order to clarify motivate it seems we need the definition for motive. Motive is defined by *Webster's* as follows: "that within the individual rather than without which incites him to action; any idea, need, motion, or organic state that prompts an action."

So much for the help we're going to get from Mr. Webster.

Most people understand the meaning of motivation intuitively, but they don't know how to implement it. How do you make people do something they hadn't planned on doing? How do you change a person's mind from negative to positive? How do you interest people in a new car, a new dress, a trip to Bermuda, when they hadn't planned on spending money on any of those things? The answer is you usually can't. Most salesmen do not provide motivation. Travel agents wait until people have already made up their mind to take a vacation and then sell them a trip to Bermuda or to whatever place yields the best commission. Car salesmen sell people the biggest and most expensive model their budget can afford after they have already decided they want a new car.

So why is it that an astute Doer salesclerk can sell a woman a new dress when she really went in the store to look at handbags? The clerk has created *desire,* that's why! Desire *can* be created, and people who can create desire in the minds of others where there was none before can rule the world. Fortunately, most people with that ability are also smart enough not to want the responsibility of being Emperor. Instead, they use their skills to enhance the quality of their own lives or the quality of the lives of others.

In former generations when our arms were a little longer and our backs a little hairier, those of us who had the gift of motivating would compete to lead the pack. Then, as now, there were only six basic motivators that worked on the masses: *need, greed, fear, self-approval, approval of others, and safety.*

Consider a tribe of monkeys. Most people believe that the "dominant male" monkey rules by fear alone. Not so. The tribe could easily gang up and overwhelm him. The leader fully understands that the basic requirements of his group are food, protection, and nurturance. So he organizes the tribe into food gatherers, defensive forces, and family units. This simple act of organization meets the primary needs of the tribe and thus reduces fear. The food gatherers lead the tribe to food. By being clever and successful in finding abundant food sources, the leader is allowed to continue his rule. His subjects' natural greed for all they can eat and the feelings of self-approval and safety that come from a full stomach are the best job insurance he has. The fighting forces and family units provide the safety and nurturance the group requires. So with one simple organization of the tribe, the leader provides a social alternative that satifies all the needs of the group.

Like monkey tribes, wolf packs also have a very rigid social structure. The Alpha wolf maintains his power by utilizing approval of others as a basic motivation. If his rules are broken, the pack will turn on the violator and destroy him. If the Alpha wolf's rules are maintained, the group will approve that behavior. Conformity is required, and that instinct is bred into each succeeding generation, for mavericks don't survive long enough to mate.

Human behavior is still rooted in these primeval instincts, whether we like to believe it or not.

Need, Greed, and Fear

Someone once said that any change in life is motivated by need, greed, or fear. These are the traditional concepts taught to entry-level salespeople everywhere. This statement is accurate but oversimplified. Buying motivators usually work in tandem. An appeal to two or more motivators is always necessary to close a sale. The concept of need usually also appeals to greed. Life insurance policies promote the dividends that the policy brings. They allow the insured to borrow against the policy at substantially reduced interest rates and also provide for his death—a classic example of greed and fear working together. People really do want to have their cake and eat it too. So two positive motivators will always galvanize them into action.

Selling need is the art of creating desire where it did not exist before. From a practical standpoint, selling need is the most difficult sale to make, even though in many ways it should be the easiest. Why? Because when a salesman sells need, he is telling his buyer that the process or system he has been using to date is not as good as it could be. This revelation is a personal affront. The threat to the buyer's self-image will lead him to challenge the premise. Selling need also means selling change. People resist change. So need by itself will rarely close a deal. Need must be coupled with another buying motivator to be truly effective. And remember, need is one of the most powerful motivators that exists.

As discussed before, selling need is selling results. Different kinds of people expect different kinds of results. If your buyer works for identity, he wants everything he does in his life to reflect favorably on that identity. If he works for power, his every action every waking hour is spent enhancing that power either consciously or subconsciously. If he really is an Ebenezer Scrooge who works only for money, you can always sell him price.

But it's critical to know what kind of person you are dealing with. If you are selling refrigerators, insurance policies, or Caterpillar tractors, it's easy to find some way to make the purchase of your product feed your buyer's psychological needs, provided you know what they are. But remember, those psychological needs may not have anything to do with the overall results or solutions your product was designed to provide. Only when you're selling a product that the buyer himself is going to use do the buyer's personal objectives and the results the product yields truly merge. For example, when a man buys clothing for himself, he will buy something that fits his self-image. But when he buys clothing for a woman, he selects something that will enhance the image he has of her. He won't give a second thought to what her own self-image is. He'll assume it's the same as his. This is true for women too—although quite a few women have learned better.

The same dynamic operates when a corporate buyer makes a purchase for his employer. The unemployment lines are full of out-of-work buyers whose image of their company was different from the company's image of itself. But even those buyers with a more accurate perception of the company's self-image cannot totally eliminate that primeval cry of "What's in it for me?" So if you're selling widgets and you know you've got the best widgets in the world, stop at some point during your presentation and ask yourself, "What is buying a widget going to do personally for the prospect I'm talking to?" Maybe the answer is absolutely nothing because he's simply a purchasing agent. So be it. Think about what motivates purchasing agents. Their job security is dependent upon (1) buying products that are unassailably "safe" and (2) making the best deal possible. So there are your motivators. By proving to your prospect that your widgets will produce the best results possible, you've eliminated the fear factor that is present in every professional purchasing agent's mind when he is buying a product beyond the scope of his own technical expertise. Need has already been established and fear has now been removed. You know that if you give him the best deal possible, he'll buy. If you don't want to sell price the risk is yours, but you have accurately discovered the way to close that sale if you want to.

When people talk about greed as a motivator they think of money, food, sex, or some other form of overindulgence that is basically fun. Not so! If you perceive your buyer to be a shy or reticent person you may have your sights on an individual who is starving for the approval of others. People who are Watchers are usually good prospects for this type of motivation. Load them up with approval. Their appetite is boundless. Share yourself with them. Get personal. Their greed for approval of others knows no limits. Buyers who are Doers can be equally greedy. Our old friend Jerry Maxwell of Med General Inc. was a Doer, but he was greedy for power and identity.

Remember, greed alone will not make the sale. There must be a second motivator. If your customer needs widgets, and your widgets are good, then the approval that you lavish on an insecure Watcher will close the sale. Conversely, if your buyer is somewhat insulted when you confront him with a product or service that makes a buggywhip of his previous system, he can usually be lulled into forgiving this indiscretion if you *quickly* demonstrate the great benefits that will accrue if the buyer changes his traditional ways. Naturally you will tell him what wisdom he possesses for perceiving these benefits. The buyer's greed will take over from there. Greed and need are excellent companions.

Fear is a major motivator. The late David Perry, a stockbroker and successful financial services salesman, said, "I can sell a man faster on the fear of loss than I can on the prospect of gain." To prove his point, he told the story of a successful executive who isolated himself from salesmen and relegated them to lesser members of his staff—to their eternal frustration! No matter what benefits were offered, this man refused to change his rule. That was the way he did business.

"Nobody could sell this guy," Dave recounted, "and everybody had given up on him. When I took a shot at him, everybody was amazed that I not only got an appointment but sold him a $150,000 package. How? I called him up and told him that I wanted to see him right away because, if I didn't, he stood to lose $35,000 on his present investments. It is a weakness in mankind to avoid loss," Dave said. "And when faced with the prospect of losing some of his hard-earned wealth, the man's defenses crumbled. He spent an additional $150,000 to protect the $35,000 he stood to lose. All I did was analyze his present investments and find one that needed to be strengthened. The *fear* of losing got me in the door and the man's natural *greed* for more money allowed me to sell the additional package."

Fear is a particularly powerful motivator among Waiters. They have a great fear that they will make a mistake. By showing a Waiter that the purchase of your product cannot in any way come back to haunt him, you are halfway home. All you need to do is to find another motivator and the sale is closed.

There is another dimension to fear—fear of the un-known—that is not so easily turned to advantage. Why some people will not fly airplanes in this day and age is unclear. But the primeval fear of the unfamiliar remains. Therefore, an Eco-nomic Buyer who is unfamiliar with the technology of a pro-posed new product or service will always have a Feasibility Buyer standing by to advise him on its technical practicality. An Implementation Buyer may very well know that he needs the *result* your product is designed to produce but he has no knowl-edge about budgets, profit, and cash flow. Therefore, he fears that his commitment may somehow undermine that mysteri-ous, amorphous process called generating profits *and* cost him his job.

Fear can also be a positive motivator, particularly among Feasibility or Implementive Buyers. If you already have the tacit approval of an Economic Buyer, the fear of disagreeing with him will calm otherwise troubled waters in all but the most un-usual cases. The only way to deal with fear of the unknown is to give your buyer enough information so that the unknown be-comes familiar. Only then will he relax and allow you to move to the next step in the sale. In other words, you must alleviate the fear before you begin working on motivation.

Never fail to keep in mind that there are three burning questions you must ask yourself when trying to make a sale. First, what will the product you are selling do for its end users? Second, what will the product do for the organization for which the end users work? Third, and most important, what will the purchase of the product do for the individual you are trying to sell? Make a match between your buyer and the motivation you are planning to use to sell him. Is he an Economic Buyer, a Fea-sibility Buyer, or an Implementive Buyer? Does he work for identity, power, or money? Is he a Doer, a Waiter, or a Watcher? Does he respond to need and results or is he seeking a relation-ship? All these clues will help you identify your buyer. And don't forget, there are many buyers you *have* to sell in the chain of beneficiaries to make the sale stick.

Self-Approval, Approval of Others, and Safety

Need, greed, and fear are only half the arrows in your motivational quiver. There are three others: self-approval, ap-proval of others, and safety. These concepts are not new. Peter

Drucker wrote about them extensively as motivators years ago. Nevertheless, they seem to have been omitted from most sales training programs, possibly because nobody knew what he was talking about.

All buyers need self-approval. This is particularly true when a buyer makes a substantial investment in the product you are selling. In a complex sale, self-approval, approval of others, and safety will vary with the different levels and types of buyer you are dealing with.

For example, a president and general manager of a profit center feels a sense of self-approval when he buys an expensive productivity system that he feels will help him meet his strategic business and return-on-investment goals. On the other hand, his executive vice president may go along with the package simply because he is seeking the approval of the general manager and because it seems safe to do so. The Old Man is hot on the idea and the EVP has more to lose by turning it down than he does by going along. Finally, the people to be involved in the actual implementation of the system have their own set of motivators. They will experience self-approval because they were singled out and chosen to participate. They will experience the approval of others who envy their opportunity to participate.

But safety is a problem! All the participants will fear that their new visibility also brings measurability! Unless the salesman deals with that fear, the entire program will fail. The trick is recognizing the anxieties of absolutely everybody involved in the sale and finding a benefit that relieves those anxieties. That is what motivation is all about!

In our example, the general manager solicited the "approval of others" when he asked the salesman to discuss his productivity system with his executive vice president. He was also subconsciously asking whether there were any risks involved—fear and safety! So a separate motivator must be chosen for each link in the chain of beneficiaries.

In his lecture to sales trainees, Tyrone Shapiro used the example of Mrs. Jones buying a fur coat, and an entire new wardrobe, in order to gain approval of her husband and his new peers in New York City. Once her safety factor was assured—the clothes were the latest style—Mrs. Jones gained self-approval for being able to find chic New York clothing on the West Coast. A very simple example of a very complex situation, one that sellers are faced with every day of the week. Mrs. Jones did not have her objectives clearly in mind when she entered the store. Only by astute questioning and evaluation was the sales-clerk able to ascertain Mrs. Jones' real motivation. Unless a salesman is able to pinpoint why a person is talking about a particular item in the first place, it will be next to impossible to *provide* a motive for buying.

When Martha Lewis was unable to sell need for advertising to the managing partner of a prestigious consulting firm, she appealed to his need for self-approval and approval of others by asking him to write an article for her publication—no strings attached. The resulting inquiries from potential clients who had read the article did what Martha had been unable to do. They clearly demonstrated to him the value of and need for advertising! Thus Martha turned what most salesmen would consider to be a dead prospect into a live one by appealing to that basic human need for self-approval and the recognition of others.

Failure to pay attention to the buyer's need for self-approval and approval of others is very dangerous. Tom DeFranco found that out. Recall that Tom's first pitch consisted in confronting his customer with the fact that, in Tom's opinion, anybody who didn't buy the New York Metalworking Directory was a dummy or worse. Tom's rather unusual presentation earned him a three-quarter-inch hole through the middle of his $400 sample directory.

Our old friend Jim Franklin turned off more prospects for his business tax service than he turned on because he was so busy seeking their approval that he never even thought about giving them his. But little Paul Findley turned the disadvantage of his utter inability to sell need into an advantage by lavishing graciousness and approval on his customers in a nonthreatening way. Like Martha Lewis, Paul Findley made his customers feel so good about themselves that they found need for Paul's product on their own. Selling self-approval and approval of others is a very powerful weapon indeed. Relationship Salesmen love it and use it well. And when the ability to sell self-approval and approval of others is coupled with the ability to sell need, watch out! People who have mastered these skills are capable of selling anything.

Safety is of course one of the most powerful motivators available to Advocate Salesmen. Safety and its flip side, fear, exist in every creature, from bugs that crawl underground to men who walk on the moon. Safety is not a thought process; it's an instinct. Often our pursuit of safety is grounded in logic. But when it is not, we will rationalize. Dropping the atomic bomb in 1945 to make the world safe for everyone perhaps says it all. So if you appeal to safety, whether real safety is involved or not, you are appealing to a very basic instinct to which even the most diehard logician will respond. But like all buying motivators, safety must be coupled with another appeal in order to galvanize the customer to action.

Pete Abbot sold Thermacon's outdated inventory by selling the safety of its proven technology over the new technology of Thermacon's competitor. However, need was already established. If the customers to whom Pete was selling did not have a built-in need for Thermacon's products, the safety motivation alone would have been meaningless. Need must always be sold first before safety can be applied as a close. What is the point of selling all the safety gadgets on an electric stove if the buyer likes to cook with gas?

Safety and fear look so much alike that they are hopelessly intertwined in people's minds. Yet they are actually on opposite ends of the motivational continuum. Safety as a motivator makes a person feel comfortable doing what you ask him to do. Fear as a motivator makes him afraid that if he does not do what you want him to, he's going to pay a horrible price. It is like a negative sell. David Perry sold his customer a $150,000 financial package by frightening him into realizing that he might lose $35,000 on his present investments if he didn't take David's advice.

Fear coupled with the motivator of self-approval or approval of others can produce some interesting results. Tyrone Shapiro and Harry Grossman both knew that the retail salesperson's greatest weapon is making customers afraid that their friends will disapprove if they aren't well dressed. Many buyers have walked out of a store with a $300 suit when they intended to spend only $150 because an Advocate Salesman skillfully convinced them that the $150 version was simply not flattering. If you detect a fear in a customer, the best thing to do is eliminate that fear by providing him with all the reasons it is safe to buy your product. Fear as a motivator is a broad sword, not a rapier like self-approval and approval of others. However, it does do the job well.

Matching motivation with a buyer is like looking at a prism. Each time you change the angle something different meets your eye. For example, Doer workaholics who seek identity and power are prime prospects for self-approval and approval of others. However, an Economic Buyer may not necessarily be a Doer. He may have risen to the top of the corporation by being a Waiter. Even though he controls all the resources of his profit center, he may respond best to approval of others and to safety rather than to pure need. Most Waiters do. After all, what Waiters usually sell internally or externally is relationships. It all depends on the political climate of the company paying their salary. Watchers and Order Takers almost always respond to safety and self-approval. They want to feel good about themselves, and the best way to achieve that goal is not to rock the boat or make any changes.

People who are truly motivated by money are in a category by themselves. They usually want money for the approval of others that money brings, or sometimes for the self-approval that comes from simply being rich. You can bet that one of the primary motivators of the money-driven person is safety. If you couple safety with greed you're almost certain to have a deal. Such people will always experience approval of others and safety on the day the check clears the bank.

CONCEPT 8

The Chain of Beneficiaries

Almost every successful sale has a ripple effect on the buyer's environment. A sale is a form of intervention. If a salesman sells a buyer a book, space must be made someplace in the buyer's home for the book to be placed on a shelf. Will that upset the decor and symmetry the buyer has striven to maintain?

The purchase of a new car affects not only the family's resource priorities but every member of the family as well. Will the new car be as comfortable to drive as the old one? Save gas? Go fast? Be sporty? Fit in the garage? Be easy to park? Who will get first choice at driving the new car?

Those examples are simplified, of course. Nothing is simple these days. Selling a new business system has an impact on an entire organization—from marketing and order processing through inventory control, distribution, and fulfillment. Replacing a competitor's data processing system with a different make and model represents a major change, with major organizational impact.

The chain of beneficiaries in a sale includes many people in addition to the Economic, Feasibility, and Implementive Buyers. It encompasses all those people who will be affected by the change resulting from the purchase of a product. Most of these people have no say in whether the product will be purchased or not and play no direct role in the implementation procedure. But if care is not taken to identify them and deal with a possible negative reaction on their part, you may never be able to make another sale to that company. Whoever sold the federal government on the idea of minting the one-dollar Susan B. Anthony coin sure learned that lesson the hard way.

Within the organization, the purchase of a new product affects different groups in different ways. Naturally, a change in the type of mainframe equipment will have a major impact on everyone in data processing. But data processing departments are cost centers, not profit centers. They simply produce information to be used by others internally. Any data processing salesman worth his salt will gain the confidence and approval of the recipients of that information before he tries to sell data processing management on the idea of ramming a new system down its end users' throats. In fact, as any good hardware salesman knows, no major change in data processing equipment can occur without the approval of end users.

In the insurance and employee benefits business, the Economic Buyers are usually a combination of line and financial managers examining price versus benefits. Personnel executives act as Feasibility Buyers judging the technical points and fine print of the contract. Lesser personnel staff usually serve as Implementive Buyers. But woe be to the agent who fails to survey the needs and wants of the employees whose personal health, safety, and security will be affected by any change the new plan brings.

The Honorable Tip O'Neill, venerable speaker of the House of Representatives, is a wise old politician from South Boston. O'Neill once said that he learned the hard way that everybody likes to be asked. An elderly woman whom he had known for years, and for whom he had raked leaves, shoveled snow, and run errands as a child, once commented to him after a successful election, "I want you to know, Tip, that I voted for you anyway." Flabbergasted, Tip mumbled that he had never doubted she would—had she considered not voting for him? "Everybody likes to be asked, Tip," she replied. She gave him a kiss and walked on.

A politician has many constituencies. He must deal with the power brokers, but if he does not solicit and gain the approval of the people who will benefit from his services in office, he simply will not get elected. The same is true for salesmen. A salesman may be able to deal with a small group of buyers appointed to evaluate his product, his company, and himself. But for satisfactory implementation and repeat sales, he had better pay a lot of attention to the ultimate end users and other people affected by his product.

Selling the chain of beneficiaries is a variation of the Japa-

nese system of vertical decision making—that is, involving all
the people who have to live with a decision in making that decision. It works very well.

Don McCormick had a powerful track record selling business systems. He called on the New Jersey headquarters of an
international firm of business consultants to try to interest
them in implementing a standardized order processing system
for their worldwide offices. Up to that time, the Princeton Institute for Research Analysis had processed all its orders by hand.
Telephone or handshake agreements were made by salespeople, and letters of confirmation outlining the arrangements
were processed 10 to 15 days after the fact. There was no standard system, only general policy and guidelines. Deviations
from the norm became visible to management only well after
the time was ripe for negotiation or change. Cost controls were
nonexistent and the only real way to measure profitability was
to count the number of checks that cleared the bank at the end
of a given month. Don thought the situation was ripe for a new
system. He was correct. Both the chairman and the president of
the company recognized that their phenomenal growth over the
last five years had made their order processing system obsolete.
But they didn't know what to do about it. Don probably could
have signed an order on his third call. His company had expertise and credibility in the marketplace to back up that expertise,
so the Economic Buyers were satisfied.

However, instead of closing the sale, Don chose to have the
president send him a simple letter of intent. Don knew such a
letter wasn't binding but it did involve a commitment on the
part of the president—the minisale technique we will examine
later. Don was putting off the big sale because he knew that
without the cooperation of many other people within the organization, his system would never stick. And Don had a lot of other
products to sell the Princeton Institute for Research Analysis
once he made people happy with the system he was selling
them now.

After receiving the letter, Don asked the president to identify key functions within the organization from which he could
form a committee to write the specifications for the new order
processing system. The president complied and Don made sure
the committee included as many good Feasibility and Implementive Buyers as he could identify by evaluating their job de-
scriptions. Headquarters people and line and staff groups from

field offices and major overseas offices were included. Don arranged several group meetings with these people and talked with them individually at geographical areas of convenience.

By involving the very people who would have to live with the new system in building its specifications, Don reinforced what he had known all along. People like to be asked their opinion of something that they will have to live with *before* they have to live with it. In addition, in some of the West Coast and Latin American offices, distinct differences in the marketplace became visible to top management for the first time. Simple adjustments in policy to accommodate these differences eliminated a subtle irritant that had been nagging the organization for years. In Europe and Asia similar differences were identified, and changes were readily made. Because most of the firm's top management people were from the United States and were located on the East Coast, they had made the classic error of any high-growth company in assuming that the culture of every marketplace is the same as it is in New York. Historic pricing, packaging, and order processing policy reflected that pompous assumption.

At the end of six months, Don arranged for the president to call a meeting of the entire committee for final approval of the new system. Last-minute changes were made and the product was given the go-ahead. Don was so unconcerned about closing the sale that he ordered the equipment from his company before he even sent the final contract up for the president's approval. The formal close was anticlimactic.

Three months later, the terminals were installed, the equipment tested, and the system implemented. Where normally there would have been major and minor complaints from end users, there were instead compliments and platitudes. In addition, whenever a problem did arise, instead of complaining about it loudly, the local people merely implemented a corrective change. If approval was necessary, they knew who to talk to to get the job done, thanks to Don's careful selling technique.

Vince Towne and Harry Lenkoff were far less successful than Don McCormick. They had no concept of the chain of beneficiaries. In fact, Vince and Harry didn't consider themselves salesmen. Vince and Harry had made a considerable amount of money as building contractors in California's booming Orange County market. But in the housing slump of the 1980s, Vince and Harry found themselves with a hammer and nail in each hand and no place to pound. So they began to hustle just like everybody else. Harry had a relationship with a large regional cable TV company that was expanding rapidly on the West Coast. They began talking to the resident manager, and after some negotiation and a few architectural drawings, they signed a preliminary contract to build 14 district offices and relay stations for the system. Their ship had come in. However, during their negotiations, the cable TV company was purchased by a major New York communications conglomerate which was expanding its network to include cable and satellite systems across North America.

Against the advice of others, Vince and Harry decided not to take their preliminary architectural plans to New York for review by their buyer's new parent. They were afraid of rocking the boat. It was a local job anyway, they told themselves. Two months later the sky fell in, and Vince and Harry resembled a pair of wild-eyed Chicken Littles as they commiserated in the bar across the street from their office. What they had failed to realize was that every parent likes to know what the children are up to. The first thing that New York did after making its purchase was to examine its new acquisition's budget and contingency expenses. Vince and Harry's contract constituted a major contingency expense. The parent corporation had no control over it, so the contract was canceled.

Vince and Harry then proceeded to compound their mistake. Instead of flying to New York, hat in hand, with their preliminary contract, drawings, plans, and the now necessary justification, they sat in their friendly bar and pounded the table, cursing the duplicity of the resident manager. He was an immoral man who didn't keep his word, they said, using his lack of morality as a sanctimonious justification for their plight rather than facing the hard-core reality of responsible line management and justifiable dollars and cents. They were small-town boys afraid to play a big-time game. The rules by which they normally played didn't work in the big city. Ten months later, a new contract for the 14 district offices was let to a firm with which the New York parent was familiar. Harry and Vince are currently learning from their lawyers the sad truth about trying to collect monies owed from a major corporation that has the time, money, and patience to tie you up in court for years.

Unlike Don McCormick, Vince and Harry needed to implement a reverse form of vertical decision making. They had started at the bottom, gotten tacit approval for their project, but failed to carry it through the chain up to the very top. In point of fact, when the regional cable TV company was sold, Vince and Harry's Economic Buyer changed. They simply failed to realize it. The California company no longer totally controlled all the resources within the organization. Major expenditures like those proposed by Vince and Harry were now beyond the authority of the West Coast executives with whom they had dealt. Had Vince and Harry been as good a team of Advocate Salesmen as they were professional builders, they would have known what to do. But like most technical people, Vince and Harry did not consider themselves salesmen. Even though someone had to say yes and give them money before they could build something, Vince and Harry simply thought of themselves as builders. Therefore the skills they developed and refined were technical skills related to stress and strain in the pouring of cement rather than skills for selling the job in the first place. As a result, these nonsalesmen lost a $13 million contract they thought they had in the bag.

Don McCormick recognized that a sale is a series of mini-confrontations; Vince Towne and Harry Lenkoff did not. Don recognized that he could have closed his sale early after his meetings with the chairman and president of the Princeton Institute for Research Analysis. Instead he chose to make each of these meetings a minisale in his overall sale of the project. Having the president sign a letter of intent was an important minisale. Having the president formulate an order processing task force of specific people Don wanted to sell was an even more important minisale. Through a series of minisales and closes, the "big one" was a foregone conclusion. Vince and Harry, on the other hand, stubbornly clung to their original contact and insisted on calling him a buyer. When he failed to deliver, they damned him instead of searching for a new buyer. Vince and Harry's most glaring error was their failure to realize that the only thing that never changes in this world is the fact that everything changes. Their buyer had no choice but to subordinate himself to his new masters in New York if he wanted to continue making his house payments.

The stories of Don McCormick and of Vince Towne and Harry Lenkoff obviously involve large companies and very high-priced products. Let's deal for a moment with the average salesman's problem, on a small scale. What do you do when the

person who uses your product isn't the person who buys it?
How do you reconcile the differences in objectives, measurement, and attitude between an end user and a purchasing
agent—not to mention all the beneficiaries in between—and
still keep everybody happy? An Advocate Salesman must not
only make the sale but make sure it sticks. That can be a hard
row to hoe.

Purchasing agents are evaluated on how well they achieve
overall cost reductions for their company. They don't have to
use the product, so what do they care about the minute differences in benefits and features between similar products that so
delight an end user?

In a highly technical business, the end users have more
clout than the purchasing agent. In a hospital, for example, the
administrator makes the purchases, but the doctors, nurses,
and patients are the ones who determine what products to buy.
In less technical fields this is not the case.

Al Thomas sold law books and business and tax services to
law firms, corporations, banks, and other institutions. He was a
recognized research expert but his products were very competitive. In addition, he knew that a law library was an enormous
expense for most firms, and that an office manager was usually
responsible for keeping these costs in line. The office manager
thus served as a purchasing agent, and the manager's frustration came from the fact that each one of the attorneys had his
own preference for indexing research material. It was a
lose/lose situation for the office manager, who usually ended
up basing purchase decisions on price. The office manager
could win on that.

Al was shrewd. He knew if he tried to sell the office manager
directly, he would have to give up price. If he tried an end run
on the senior partners, he ran the great risk of turning the office manager into a dragon who would find ways to procrastinate and sabotage the final order as punishment.

Al sat down and worked on a strategy for his sale. He talked
with the office manager at one large law firm and presented her
with a compromise. He understood her problems. Having af-
forded her that recognition, he asked her to understand his position. The result was a meeting among Al, the office manager,
and key end-user attorneys within the firm. The objective of the
meeting was to discuss the research priorities of the firm for the
next fiscal year. But by arranging the meeting in the first place,

Al controlled the sale. His credibility as a researcher was such that he was the only vendor present. As a result, he was able to make a full presentation of his entire product line, some of which wound up replacing competing products that had been on the shelf for years. Instead of selling a product, Al had sold approval among the chain of beneficiaries. He gave a little on price to make the office manager look good, but not nearly as much as he was prepared to. He structured the sale and closed it by successfully focusing everybody's attention on the *perceived value* (rather than the *actual value*) of his products vis-à-vis his competitors', and nobody even realized what he was doing!

Selling Consensus

Selling consensus is somewhat different from selling each member of the chain of beneficiaries. A consensus sale usually involves a group of *unrelated* and *independent* buyers. Each buys separately. But because of the need for approval of others and for safety, a single buyer who is inclined to purchase usually will not unless his peers agree that it is a good idea. No one wants to be the first on his block with an Edsel.

Carol Smithers was excellent at selling consensus. At one time in her career she represented Analytical Applications Inc., a firm that offered a logical problem-solving process for hands-on mechanics, troubleshooters, and machine operators whose behind-the-scenes knowledge, intelligence, dedication, and skills run the mighty American production machine. At that time, training in the logic of troubleshooting for this group of workers was unheard of. The only training materials they received were techinical manuals related to the pieces of equipment they were supposed to operate and fix. After getting used to the fact that this advocate for radical departure was a woman, the group vice president of manufacturing of a major conglomerate agreed to allow Carol to make a presentation at his next monthly meeting with his division presidents and plant managers. He carefully explained that each one was head of his own division and was responsible to the corporation only for profits. The parent corporation "offered assistance" (jammed something down their throats) only when profits were off, so each executive could say yes or no on his own. Carol could not expect any help from the EVP. She readily agreed.

Had Carol been foolish enough to expect to close even one out of ten of these executives she would have been disappointed. Instead, Carol carefully gathered her data and designed her presentation around establishing her product's credibility. She knew she would have to overcome the traditionally held beliefs that hourly workers should be given only mechanical training if she hoped to get her potential buyers to take the chance. As a result, at the end of her presentation Carol took the unexpected step of telling the group that she did not expect or even want them to say yes or no at this time. Instead, she wanted to leave the room for a few minutes and have the group choose one plant for her to visit—a plant with a major production problem. By combining her expertise in the problem-solving process that her company sold with the hands-on knowledge of the workers at the plant, she promised to find the cause of the problem within two weeks, provided management made all the data and resources associated with the problem available to her. She cautioned the executives to make sure that they chose a concrete problem. "Discoloration on the packages off line No. 4 is a clearly defined problem," she explained. "The morale problem at the Detroit plant is a problem situation, not a precise and defined problem." They agreed.

Ten minutes later they called Carol back in the room, and a division president stepped up to the easel. "Normally, Miss Smithers," he said, "I might be embarrassed presenting you with a problem like this. But the problem is a very real and very costly one which has arisen in our Canadian manufacturing operation. This particular plant," he went on, "manufactures tampons for both the Canadian and Eastern U.S. markets. Several times during the last year we have had major complaints from both consumers and physicians about strings that break on the tampons during removal. Some consumers have even had to have the tampons removed by a gynecologist. Our product is currently not part of the toxic shock concern, but this situation, coupled with the furor over toxic shock, could literally drive us out of business. I can promise that you will have the full cooperation of the entire staff and organization of our Quebec facilities. They are as desperate as we are to correct the situation. However, just to make sure, both the group vice president and I will personally contact the line and manufacturing people involved to ensure their undivided attention to your needs."

Carol was at first ecstatic but later a little uneasy. She had absolutely no manufacturing experience and she was not an engineer. But she had been with her firm for several years and was quite adept at using the logical problem-solving questions which had made her company famous as a vehicle for eliciting only the essential data surrounding a problem. This technique eliminated the confusing array of data that usually arises in brainstorming sessions geared at problem solving. Two weeks later she had the answer to the problem, and after the corporate VP verified the solution, he accompanied Carol personally in a company jet to a meeting with the division presidents, who had now begun to seriously consider her approval.

The division presidents were clearly delighted over the solution to the problem, but what they were really dying to know was how she had arrived at it. "Quite simply," she said, making a mental note to herself to write *Remember humility* on the blackboard 100 times. "The problem was clearly defined. A certain percentage of the tampons were experiencing a production failure. These were not caught by quality control. But your entire production was not affected. *Where* the problem occurred was clear. The problem was confined to the Quebec plant, as evidenced by the geographical area that the customer complaints came from. So only the Quebec plant was in trouble. It's when I got to *when* the problem occurred that I began to get some confusing feedback from your people. Therefore I began to suspect that *when* was the root of the problem. However, there didn't seem to be any particular regularity associated with when these complaints were reported. Sometimes one or two months would go by before any complaints would come in, sometimes as little as two weeks. So I merely asked 'when' questions for the next two hours and traced back as precisely as I could the exact date when each complaint occurred since the problem began 14 months ago.

"In response to one of these detailed 'when' questions, one of your very bright production engineers observed that the complaint pattern we had graphed out on the easel looked very similar to his overtime schedules for the past year and a half. The only difference was the months in which the complaints occurred. A hasty comparison between the complaint graphs and the overtime graphs was very revealing. The complaints began with unerring and eerie accuracy exactly one month after the start of overtime. And the complaints tended to last as

long as the overtime lasted. Needless to say, we now had a chorus of people asking what was done on overtime that was not
done when the plant was on its regular shifts. The plant manager volunteered that Machine 5 was brought into operation in
order to increase productivity and to limit the length of time he
would have to keep production on overtime. Overtime was
costly. He added that Machine 5, while an older piece of equipment, had recently been overhauled. Then he blinked, slapped
his forehead, and added, 'Fourteen months ago!' That triggered
a rush to Machine 5, and the rest is history. Machine 5 was in
excellent shape. It produced at a slower rate, but like its newer
sisters, it had a triangular blade that was programmed to de-
scend and cut the continuous line of string fed into the wrapper
at a very precise and prescribed length. In overhauling the
equipment, someone or something had evidently banged
against the knife and created a serrated edge. That serration
caused the blade to catch the string lightly well above the point
where it was supposed to be cut—only enough to weaken it not
break it, so nobody noticed. The bottom line was that the entire
bulk tampon production from Machine 5 was defective."

Carol walked away from that meeting with a firm order of
$275,000 in her pocket—an unheard of figure for her company.
What Carol had done was gather together a group of independent buyers and sell them all simultaneously. Carol had sold
consensus. It's hard enough to put a consensus sale together
simply for presentation, let alone be able to close it. But after
demonstrating need, Carol had no problem selling the other division vice presidents who had similar problems. The ones who
thought they were geniuses and could solve their own problems
were too afraid not to go along with the program. They knew
they would look like fools if a similar problem developed in their
operation and they had refused the benefit of Analytical Applications training. So Carol had need, fear, and approval of others
going for her—not to mention safety and greed, because all the
plant managers were on an incentive plan and corporate headquarters had agreed to pay the cost of her company's training.

How could Carole lose? It takes only one motivator to get a
sale going and two to close it. But it took real courage for her to
tackle a problem in the other guy's sandbox. In effect, Carol's
attitude made the sale. She already had the problem-solving
skills taught by her company. She knew that she could gain the
content *knowledge* about the equipment from the plant employ-

ees by utilizing her company's questioning technique. But she was the only one in her firm who had the conviction necessary to take on the risk of a consensus sale that turned out not to be any risk at all. Think about it. What did Carol have to lose? You're right—nothing!

Though there are quite a few differences between selling the chain of beneficiaries and selling consensus, the biggest difference is that the former involves a multiapproval sale. Numerous people have to say yes. Few if any can say no or the sale becomes unraveled. Carol could have walked away with only two or three of the independent buyers in her pocket, but Al Thomas could not have walked away from his meeting on law books without selling everybody involved in the use of his product. Don McCormick could have sold the president and chairman quite quickly, but he knew implementation would have been rough at best and a disaster at worst. So he sold everybody in the chain of beneficiaries whether he needed to or not. Conversely, Vince and Harry needed to sell a consensus at least between their Economic and Feasibility Buyers before they could hope to close the sale, but they failed to do even that. The concepts of selling the chain of beneficiaries and making a consensus sale are related in theory, but in application they are as different as a zebra is from a horse. The expert Advocate Salesman knows the difference and treats each one as the different animal it is.

CONCEPT 9

Selling Concepts and Priorities

Time is money, as the saying goes. It is particularly true in sales. Commission plans and quotas are geared to last year's average territorial sales. Naturally any competent organization will add 20 percent to assigned quotas in order to effectively reduce the commission plan. Thus real "big bucks" are kept out of reach of the average producer. Advocate Salesmen consistently break the commission-plan bank. And, because of their track record, they are in a strong position to negotiate their next year's quota rather than stoically accepting it in order to protect their jobs.

The key to using time effectively is not to buy a Maserati that breaks speed limits in order to make more calls. The key is to sell concepts instead of products—then sell priority! Selling concepts gives you a much wider field for presenting your products once need is established. Selling priorities simply ensures that your product is first in line to be purchased. Let's examine each of these techniques in detail, for they are critical to the success of an Advocate Salesman.

Selling Concepts Rather Than Products

A product is a product. A concept can be anything! Selling concepts rather than products gives you the flexibility to represent your product in any way you want to.

Any product can be sold as a concept. In fact, selling a concept can be easier and more rewarding than selling a product. For example, an Order Taker selling glassware will put a glass of a certain design on the table and tell the buyer they cost 10 cents apiece. A Need Salesman selling concepts will ask the same buyer how he could possibly do without a versatile utensil costing only 10 cents that will blend with any decor, be attractive in and by itself, hold liquids and solids and, with a minor adaptation, gas. He can have as many of these wonders as he wants, up to 14 dozen cases.

Any product can be turned into a concept if you focus on the results and benefits it is going to produce. After all, selling need is selling results, so putting the two together as a concept creates a powerful synergism. That synergism is beneficial to both the salesman and the buyer. Burglar alarm salesmen who sell burglar alarms don't make much money. Burglar alarm salesmen who sell *safety* and *security* do. Once the loss replacement cost from a potential burglary is made visible to the buyer, the cost of the system will pale by comparison. In fact, price is only lightly discussed because the thrust of the presentation is the safety and security of protecting valuable belongings. That old "fear of loss" motivator works effectively again.

Retail salespeople who sell television sets usually find themselves trapped into a technical comparison of one make versus another. Ultimately they face a price comparison. Instead, they should present their product in terms of the comfort, ease, and range of home entertainment the line provides. Cost comparisons should be made, not between competing models, but between competing media—the price of a movie, play, or live show from Las Vegas versus the cost of watching it in their homes. The customer will be forced to face the real reasons he is buying home entertainment in the first place and the sale will be 100 percent easier.

All the good salesmen whose stories we have examined so far have sold concepts. But they didn't start out that way. Each one had to learn how to do so.

As a novice salesman, Al Thomas was told by his manager that lawyers and accountants were the best prospects for his product. Need was already established and it was simply up to Al to point out the superiority of his product over the competition. Most important, his manager advised, provide service, service, service! Essentially Al's boss was telling him to be a good Relationship Salesman. So Al became one. After three months of mediocre earnings, Al had the good fortune to have lunch with a very successful owner of a brokerage house in the city.

He gave Al some advice. "Any tangible product can be sold as an intangible concept. Moreover," he went on, "this method of selling is not only good; it is easier and better than laboriously explaining the technicalities of your product.

"When my customers call me to talk about stocks," he explained, "and I make my best commissions on bonds, I can't switch them in midsteam or they will resent my changing the subject they called about. Instead," he went on, "I ask them what their objectives are in buying certain stocks. Inevitably, I am able to pull the conversation up one conceptual notch and talk about 'financial security.' This allows me to discuss a wide range of investment alternatives, including bonds. Products are merely alternatives to achieve a result. What conceptual result does the individual want to achieve by purchasing a particular product? That is the point to address in making a sales presentation."

Al took the advice. He went home and thought about the results that his services would produce. They provided up to-date, factual, and easy-to-find information on legal and tax changes as they occurred. Attorneys and accountants needed to have this information to field inquiries from their clients.

Al focused on the fact that those accountants and attorneys charged their customers between $50 and $100 per hour for that information. Al's most expensive service cost only $400 and the digest service was only $125. Aha! thought Al. I think I've found myself a new market. And he *had!* Armed with this information, Al went directly to the businessmen. He sold them the benefits of having a timely report in a service that was easily indexed. They could answer their own questions rather than have to pick up the phone and incur a $50 bill every time they needed to be brought up to date on legal and tax changes. In many cases Al was able to train his buyer's secretary in using the service. The secretary became the first person the businessman would consult on a particular question before he called his attorney. The added benefit to Al's new buyers was the fact that when they did call their attorney they knew enough about the subject to ask specific questions. Thus they reduced the time it took to get to the heart of the matter.

Al broke all records selling legal services his first year and was honored as Salesman of the Year at the company bash that December.

After a year of placing hundreds of these services in the hands of businessmen, Al made a remarkable discovery. Legal and accounting firms that had hitherto been wed to competing services now began to add Al's line to their libraries. So many of Al's customers were quoting the service Al represented that the professionals were having problems using his competitors' services to answer their questions. The indexing was entirely different.

Al had made an important discovery. His company viewed itself as a publisher for legal, accounting and professional service firms. Al redefined his company's objectives in his own marketplace by correctly stating that his company published timely and well-indexed information on legal and tax matters for businessmen, individuals, and the legal, accounting, and professional firms that serve them. This conceptual change in market definition was ultimately adopted by his employers. But it took two years of smashing success from Al to open their eyes. "No one likes to admit to being stupid, particularly when it comes to defining one's market." Al laughed. "But I give the top people credit. They did admit it. Then they did something about it. There are some firms that would have fired me for what I did."

When Max Stubal sold word processors, he rarely mentioned specific features of his equipment to anybody but an end user. When talking to an Economic Buyer, Max would make his presentations primarily in the conceptual context of cost reduction, increased efficiency, and elimination of manpower through automation. When talking to a Feasibility Buyer, Max would present the concept of efficiency in more technical terms to demonstrate the value of his equipment vis-à-vis present equipment. He would prove to the Feasibility Buyer that the cost reduction benefits he had presented to the Economic Buyer were indeed feasible.

However, when talking to an Implementive Buyer Max changed his tune. Implementive buyers and end users stand the risk of losing their jobs to automated equipment. Max wasn't stupid enough to think they didn't realize it. Instead, Max sold them the personal benefits of being trained to use the new state-of-the-art equipment. He told them how much their individual workload would be reduced by eliminating boring retyping. He usually had his Implementive Buyer and end users so excited that it didn't occur to them that someone might lose a job. Max counted on an odd fact of human nature. No one ever expects to die. Only the other guy does that.

After Pete Abbott unloaded the Thermacon-A inventory, he sold the massive new Thermacon 1000 conceptually. Pete never sold a Thermacon unit to an Economic Buyer on the basis of technical features. Instead, Pete sold increased productivity, because general managers are concerned about productivity. Manufacturing managers *are* concerned with technical comparisons, but they are also responsible for productivity. So with them Pete discussed the technical nature of the Thermacon units only as much as he had to in order to convince these Feasibility Buyers that his units really could increase productivity. Like Max Stubal, Pete Abbott compared the technical features of the Thermacon 1000 with those of his competitors' units only with Implementive Buyers and end users. By that time the sale was 90 percent closed.

Pete summed it up this way: "If I tried to sell the Thermacon 1000 as a product instead of a concept, I would be limited to doing exactly that—selling huge Thermacon units to each buyer. I can just see myself in some customer's office leaning over the desk with my nose in his face pointing at a feature in the brochure. What a waste of time! By selling a concept, I am able to gear my presentation to appeal to any of the motivators to which my buyers may respond. My time is not spent talking about microcircuitry and blinking red lights; my time is spent talking about problems on a level that interests my customer so I can ascertain what he needs and what motivates him. That knowledge is more effective than a double-barrelled shotgun when I go for the close."

By selling a concept rather than a product, an Advocate Salesman has a much wider arena in which to identify need. So it is much easier to find a need that appeals to the motivations of a particular buyer. "How many salesmen," Pete added, "waste their time talking about technical features—bells and whistles—to an Economic Buyer who is impatiently waiting to return to the production reports on his desk? It has never ceased to amaze me," he finished, "how some guys never learn."

It doesn't take any real skill to sell conceptually, simply the knowledge that every product is bought in order to *produce a result.* Never sell telephones, always sell communication. Never sell automobiles, always sell transportation. That is really what the customer is buying. Only a change in attitude is necessary to switch from selling a product to selling a concept. Like Al Thomas, once the seller thinks through the results that his products can achieve, he will find many additional applications for it. The application of results is the only way to sell need, and there has to be need before any product can be sold.

Selling Priorities

It's not enough to sell need conceptually. You must also establish a priority for that need. All of us have more needs than we can afford to satisfy, so we put priorities on them. Nobody has everything he wants. Nobody! That includes the late J. Paul Getty! Would Getty have put a pay telephone in his house for his guests' use if *he* really believed he had all the money he would ever need? So let's take a hard look at selling priorities.

"Nobody ever has enough life insurance!" That's the hue and cry of the multitude of insurance salesmen roaming this planet. It's a true statement. But a buyer has many more pressing needs that cost money. After all, he's not dead yet! Why, then, do people buy life insurance? Because some salesman has sold the fear of leaving loved ones destitute as a higher priority than meeting current financial obligations. That includes using discretionary cash for fun and entertainment while the insured person is living. That's a tall order, but good insurance salesman meet it all the time.

Why is it that "clearance sales" in retail stores (and all the advertising hullabaloo and promotion associated with them) do not attract hordes and hordes of buyers to take advantage of the super-low prices? Quite simply, the products on sale usually don't have a great priority for the buying public that day. Price can dictate priority only if need has already been established— and *that need must have a sense of urgency.*

Major corporations have multitudes of needs. If you are selling a supervisory training program that is geared to increasing productivity, you must focus on immediate productivity gains as the vehicle to sell priority, not the program itself. All corporations pay lip service to training, but they pay a great deal of attention to productivity increases that attract everyone's attention. Capital equipment investment is also designed to increase productivity, but if you can persuade a general manager that training will do it faster, he may well change his priorities. He can take the money out of his capital equipment budget if there is none left in the training budget. As the Economic Buyer, he controls all the company's resource allocations. In other words, he can alter budgets with impunity if he sees a bigger and quicker payoff for his bucks.

If you're selling word processors you'd better talk about the benefits, output, and clarity of communication that will occur immediately upon installation. Technical features don't interest anybody but the operators, and they regard the machines as toys. Your customer obviously has some current capability for word processing. Chances are he will decide to live with it even if he's not absolutely satisfied—unless you build need and show him how you can bring immediate benefits to him that far outweigh the other decisions on his desk that are competing for his dollar priorities.

Selling priorities is not unlike selling concepts. In fact, selling priorities is the next logical step in a conceptual sale. You have to sell priorities before you can close the sale. No priority, no close. It's as simple as that.

Closing sales is the name of the game. Maybes and thank-yous don't do anything except waste people's time. Knowledge of what you have to sell—of the benefits it will produce—is critical. If you don't know the benefits, you will never be able to ascertain why the customer needs your product. If you can't figure out why he needs it, there isn't any way in the world you can convince him that he needs it *now.* Imagine trying to convince somebody that there is a bright shiny object on inventory somewhere in the warehouse that will do great things for him. Never mind what those things are. Buy the product now, take it home, and find out for yourself!

Need Salesmen and even Relationship Salesmen recognize the importance of selling priorities in order to close a sale. Order Takers do not, and the retail business is rife with so-called salesmen who don't know their products. Remember Harry Grossman lecturing his trainers on the types of salespeople he wanted on the floor of his stores? Harry maintained that stores don't sell products, people do. Harry backed up his theory by quoting an article by Carol McGraw about Stanley

Marcus, retired chairman of that merchandising phenomenon Neiman-Marcus Inc.*

Stanley Marcus leans forward at the lectern and tells a group of retail sellers that their profession has "gone to hell."

The 77-year-old Marcus, often called the Merchant Prince, because of his half-century of leadership at Neiman-Marcus, is not one to mince words. He looks out across the sea of faces at the annual meeting of the Fashion Island Merchants Association and lets the other shoe drop.

"You are boring your customers to death."

There is a communal nodding of heads and applause as Marcus recites a litany of sins committed by the retail industry, and then offers some tips for salvation.

Salesmen Lack Information

Two years ago, he says, he decided not to buy anything unless it was "sold" to him. "I saved about $43,000."

One car salesman didn't ask him to test-drive a new model. Another merchant didn't know that his shop stocked a fancy cigar, even though a $14,000 color ad for the item had appeared in the morning paper the day Marcus spoke with him.

Marcus retired as president of Neiman-Marcus in 1977. His son, Richard, now holds the title. But the older Marcus is still very much involved as a consultant to Los Angeles-based Carter Hawley Hale Stores, Inc , the parent of Neiman-Marcus.

He is director of three corporations, and owns his own consulting firm. He also publishes high-quality miniature books through his own publishing house, Somesuch Press, Dallas.

Played with Thread

But retailing is still his first love. "Sure, I miss it; it's like divorcing a wife after 50 years. You miss her whether you liked her or not."

Marcus literally cut his teeth in the retailing business. His parents would bring him to their Dallas store, set him on the floor in the ladies' alteration department, and let him play with spools of thread while they minded the store.

Marcus in later years turned the store into a showplace for trendy specialty items and says he was the innovator of the first high-fashion catalog.

The Neiman-Marcus Christmas catalog became famous for its outlandish "his and hers" gifts for people who had everything.

"I would have never bought the stuff," he says, but adds that his favorites were his-and-her camels (for $4,125) and matching mummy cases.

Home Computers

Marcus believes that the advent of electronic retailing—the use of home computers to shop for merchandise—will be one of the industry's biggest challenges in the future.

While some industry experts don't expect computers to reduce store traffic, Marcus warns of that possibility if retailers don't give the customers what they want.

"Why wouldn't a customer prefer a computer to a store where he can't find the salesperson, or where the salesperson doesn't know anything about the merchandise? The computer catalog can tell them exactly what they want to know about the product, and it doesn't have bad breath," Marcus says.

After reading the article to his training group, Harry commented, "Did you notice that Stanley Marcus said his favorite products were his-and-her camels for $4,125 and matching mummy cases? Now, tell me," Harry admonished, "how do you sell his-and-her camels or mummy cases if you don't sell priority? I'm sure each of you, even if you wanted his-and-her camels or mummy cases, would not have such items far up on your priority list. I doubt the people who can afford his-and-her camels or matching mummy cases have those purchases very high on their priority list. But Stanley Marcus sold his-and-her camels. He sold matching mummy cases as well. And you can't convince me that he did it without selling priority. Sure, he appealed to greed and approval of others. He created need by convincing people they would benefit from being the first on their block to have his-and-her camels or matching mummy cases. That's *how* he sold priorities. Believe me," Harry emphasized, "if he hadn't been able to sell priorities and unload those camels and mummies, I wouldn't have wanted to be in the shoes of the guy who cleaned up the warehouse at night.

"More important," Harry Grossman concluded, "Stanley Marcus accurately points out that a knowledgeable computer is more useful to a buyer than a salesperson who knows nothing. A computer is the world's perfect Order Taker."

Harry Grossman's pronouncement is true in all levels of the sales profession. Order Takers will be the first salesmen automated out of a job. Computers and electronic mail are more efficient and certainly cost less than people. Not only do computers lack bad breath; they don't need vacations or get sick. The only reason a salesman has a job is to sell. That doesn't mean to *attempt* to sell. It means *sell.* As in war, how well you play the game doesn't count, only whether you win or not. Winning means making the sale. You can't make the sale without selling priority for your product over that of another competing for the same dollar.

Hillary West and Jane Bloomingdale both sold priority very well. When Jane, Nick, and their internal sponsor finally made the CEO realize that his plant environment was ripe for union organizers, he literally "found" the money to buy Nick's preventive medicine. After Hillary West forced her Economic Buyer to face the cost resulting from miscommunication between managers and data processing, he immediately adjusted time and budgets to accommodate her proposal.

In summary, the best way to sell priority is to relate it to risk and to cost. You *must show* the buyer that it is going to cost him more to delay purchasing your product than it is to buy it. Jane pointed out the risk/cost of failing to "cure" a potential union organizing situation immediately. Her buyer already knew what unionization of his employees would cost him in dollars and cents. Hillary simply took the direct cost of current problems and showed her buyer that the root cause of those problems was miscommunication between managers and data processing. He took it from there.

The Marcus example is an excellent vehicle to illustrate what is meant by selling need. Obviously, only a lonely Egyptian "needs" a camel or a mummy case. But Neiman-Marcus sold them to people who had a pronounced need for the approval of others. The people who bought Stanley Marcus's his-and-her camels or matching mummy cases knew what it would *cost them in status* if they were second on their block to buy them.

Risk/cost priority selling appeals to all motivations. In the above examples we have Jane Bloomingdale—need and fear; Hillary West—need and safety; Stanley Marcus—approval of others, greed, and self-approval.

Always match need with the motivation of a buyer. If you are able to find an application for your product *in a context that meets that motivation* ("Throw a party and surprise your friends—greet them on his-and-her camels!"), you will surely have sold need. The degree of need sells that priority.

CONCEPT 10

The Sale as a Series of Miniconfrontations

If a sale were not a series of miniconfrontations, salesmen would simply lie in wait in the parking lot beside a buyer's car, jump out, and yell, "Do you want to buy this typewriter or not?" and throw an order form and pen in the buyer's face.

The first confrontation is selling the appointment. You are negotiating for the buyer's time. A buyer is jealous of his time unless he has nothing to do and just likes attention—in which case he's probably not really a buyer. He wants to know why you need his time. Your job is to convince him that his time would be well spent. But in doing so you must only give him a *peek* at your product benefits, with a promise of more to come. You are now in a next-step situation.

Having granted you time for the presentation, the buyer now anticipates some reward. At this point he is aware of the product you are selling and expects you to begin the conversation with all the benefits you promised if he met with you. Your next confrontation is to ignore his expectations and instead start asking him self-serving questions designed to test the assumptions behind your selling strategy.

If you're selling typewriters you'll want to ask him what kind of *output* he expects to get from his word processing department. If you're selling commercial real estate you'll want to ask him what *results* he wants from space utilization. And then you'll tie all his answers to another question about the ratio of resources to results. That way you can get a handle on what objectives he wants to accomplish and what his spending limitations are.

The degree of skill that you demonstrate in getting honest answers to these questions will dictate the accuracy of your pitch to this customer's particular buying motivators and closing impulses.

Your third confrontation will involve ironing out the differences between the results the customer expects and the results that your product can produce. This confrontation should be followed by a confrontation regarding the results that the customer expects *for the amount of resources he has to spend!* You will find that this last confrontation is the major one. It is called the Elastic Confrontation. You are testing to see if the buyer has additional resources, and he is testing to see if you have additional results for him. This is the negotiating stage.

Remember, a customer who is combative and asking questions adversarily really wants to be sold. Nonadvocate salesmen have the bizarre idea that a selling environment must always be subdued. They think any adversarial discussion is to be avoided, as it represents an argument. Advocate Salesmen know that a buyer who is arguing is merely verbally expressing the conflicts going on in his mind. He's choosing between the results he expects, the resources he has, and the salesman's particular alternative. Argument is a very positive sign. If you handle the Elastic Confrontation properly, the close is a foregone conclusion. Sometimes the data involved in the buying decision will be too complex to handle at one sitting. Or you may simply bungle your presentation. Your first clue that something has gone wrong will be a confused "maybe" in response to your magnificent and brilliantly executed close!

Therefore, your next step is to go back to selling another appointment. The confrontation cycle repeats itself until you know enough about why the customer might want your product and what his resources are to make a presentation that will have a binary yes/no result. Recognize when you are in a sale and *sell only the next step.* Why try to sell a product when what you really want is an appointment?

One old and grizzly sales manager brought home that point in a sales meeting. Observing the young bucks in front of him who were complaining about the difficulty of getting appointments with a proper buyer, he asked them if they had the same problem meeting women. After the chorus of "nos" and "boos" subsided, he said that he thought not, because he had observed that when a young man wants to meet a young woman he tries to sell the first date, not the consummation of a marriage.

The problem corrected itself quickly.

Selling the Appointment

What are some of the techniques successful salespeople have used to get appointments? As we saw in the Hillary West/Bill Byrd story, Hillary's strategy was to gather vital information about company problems that her product was designed to correct. She gathered this information from middle-management contacts she had made, who were easier to see than the Economic Buyer. Utilizing the data obtained from these Feasibility Buyers, Hillary was able to devise a hard-hitting letter that was relevant to problems currently on her Economic Buyer's mind. Therefore, rather than being offended by her delving into company matters that were truthfully not Hillary's business, the CEO was in fact grateful that someone was going to take up his time dealing with *his* problems for a change. After all, most CEOs are looked to by their employees as the paternalistic geniuses responsible for solving all the problems that employees cannot solve themselves.

Hillary added impact to an already powerful letter by sending it as a Mailgram. With electronic mail now available from the United States Post Office at only 32 cents for two pages, many Advocate Salesmen are taking advantage of this service to keep in touch with prospects they don't have time to see in person or call on the telephone. Mailgrams and other electronically transmitted correspondence almost always get through the secretarial screen. In the future this may change, but the time is still ripe for the inventive Doer to capitalize on this current hole in his buyer's mail-screen mitt. The biggest waste of a professional salesman's time is being forced to make "cold calls." But many companies still feel that it is the salesman's responsibility to generate leads. The wiser companies give their men some help. One of the best methods for softening a prospect is to keep you and your company's name in front of him so he is at least familiar with both when you call. If he feels he knows you, he'll accept your call.

Another successful Advocate Salesman devised a newsletter as a vehicle to generate interest in an annuity insurance program he was selling. This salesman subscribed to the Commerce Clearing House and Prentice-Hall looseleaf tax services, which provide readers with up-to-date information on changing U.S. tax laws. Most of the information is taken from government releases and is therefore in the public domain. When the salesman used copyrighted material, he obtained permission to reprint it. His newsletter wasn't really a newsletter at all. It was a condensation—a *Reader's Digest* "highlights of tax headlines"—for people who bought annuity insurance policies. The newsletter referred the reader directly to the source publications for further details or advised the reader to call his accountant or tax lawyer for an opinion.

The salesman printed the newsletter on high-quality paper and had it set in easy-to-read, attractive type. He knew that when the product and the salesman are unknown, the buyer is forced to judge the quality of both by the quality of the correspondence he receives. Correspondence must not only *look* expensive; it must *be* expensive if you want to put people in the correct frame of mind to part with their money.

On the back of the newsletter he superimposed his company logo over a list of impressive customers who were currently buying annuity insurance. This list, like any referral list, required the customers' permission. But once acquired, the list gave this advocate genius the firepower he needed to send out as many newsletters as his budget could afford. He started out on a monthly basis; later he stepped up to semimonthly. The results were phenomenal. Not only were the customers interested, but their telephone calls to accountants and attorneys generated a whole new host of relationships for him. After a while, the accountants and attorneys, grateful for the extra billings they were getting through the newsletter, began to return the favor by tossing inquiries about annuity insurance his way—questions that he could work up in his letter. But the real benefit to this advocate entrepreneur was the response he received from the follow-up telephone calls he made to newsletter recipients. Yes, they remembered his name, and yes, they knew of his company. They weren't always interested. But over a five-year period he calculated that fully 50 percent of the people to whom he had sent a newsletter bought something from him. More important, 25 percent of those who did not referred him to someone else who did. In fact, the newsletter was so well received that he began to get calls for subscriptions. Not being greedy, he did not charge for the newsletter. Why let $10 stand in the way of a potential $10,000 commission? A good assistant can put together a "headline" newsletter easily. Most product lines have specialty publications, from *Packaging Magazine* to the *Financial Service Weekly,* that are excellent sources for headline information and for referral for in-depth reading.

But the telephone remains the best instrument for securing an appointment. There is no magic wand in telemarketing sales—it is a grind no matter how you look at it. Even so, there are some tricks that good Advocate Salesmen use to make sure they get through to the buyer.

One trick is to make sure that you know both the first and last name of the prospect you're calling and also his present position. If you don't have that information, call up the internal operator or receptionist and tell her that you are trying to reach a certain executive with a certain title but are not sure of the exact title or spelling of his name. She will empathize with you, because this situation happens to her on an hourly basis. She will look up his name and title in the directory and give you the correct spelling. Armed with that information, complete the call to his extension. When his secretary answers you can now ask, "Is Mr. Smith in?" She will naturally respond with the question, "Who is calling?" And you can take it from there. However, if you want to try to get by a secretarial screen, when the secretary answers with "Mr. Smith's office," simply state in a flat, commanding voice, "Put him on please."

One salesman used first names. In this situation he would ask, "May I speak to John, please?" Depending upon the secretary and her enthusiasm (or lack of same) for screening calls, a positive assumptive approach on the telephone can put you directly in touch with the person you're trying to see. After that, you're on your own again.

Remember to sell the *appointment,* not the *product.* One highly successful organization kept its salesmen in front of customers where they should be by developing an internal telecommunications group whose sole purpose was to generate appointments for salesmen. The Advocate Salesmen loved it. The other ones quit. Management loved it because close-to-call ratios were easily tracked. Help and support could be given the minute a weakness showed up. Instead of having to wait until the salesman turned in his report at the end of the month to evaluate productivity, the sales managers could monitor the salesman's calls on a weekly or daily basis, since the telemarketing group had control of the salesman's schedule. However, not just any secretary or clerk makes a good telemarketing specialist. Nor does just any sweet voice get an appointment with a busy buyer. Data about specific prospects must be provided to the telemarketing group by the salesman for whom they are attempting to secure the appointment. The Research Department provides the rest. The telemarketing specialists can then speak intelligently about the buyer's company and indicate that their salesmen have some alternatives to offer and would like to meet with the buyer. Like Hillary West, the telemarketers use a little bit of prior knowledge to gain credibility and convince the buyer that his time will be well spent. Most buyers consent to the appointment.

If your company does not provide a telemarketing group to keep you working at top efficiency, the advice remains the same. Research your prospect before you make the call, and then make sure that you sell the appointment with the data that you have. *Don't try to sell the product.* Every executive is jealous about his time—or at least thinks he should be. He will try to avoid carving what he knows is going to be a half-hour out of his day if he can sell you on making your pitch by telephone. Advocate Salesmen sell; they don't buy. They will refuse, even if the refusal costs them the appointment. There is always another day to call back.

Telemarketing people don't have this problem. Since the buyer thinks that the telemarketing person is a secretary for the salesman, he is forced to either make the appointment or do without the benefit of whatever that important thing was that the salesman had to tell him. Some very good salesmen have split some big commissions with wives who take a little time out of any busy homemaker's day to generate mailings and follow them up with telephone calls for appointments with her husband. Naturally, the salesman's wife would identify herself as his secretary, which in this case she certainly is.

CONCEPT 11

The Minisale and Close

Any sale involving more than two people is essentially a multi-approval sale.

To delay making a presentation until everybody is present is foolish. To attempt to close one buyer when the approval of another is obviously needed is not only foolish; it's logistic suicide. Therefore, the concept of the minisale.

Each buyer can be sold against his own set of objectives and the next step in the sale is permission from him to see the additional buyers involved. Most salesmen focus on selling their product. Advocate Salesmen focus on selling as much as they can at each presentation. In the case of two or more buyers, selling the next step becomes the minisale. The close is obtaining your buyer's approval to proceed with implementation.

As you review the closing techniques presented in this chapter, remember that there isn't a close in the world that will work if at least a tiny bit of *need* hasn't been created. A closing technique aptly applied is designed to shorten the time between the initiation and finalization of a sale—the time it takes to move a buyer from ignorance of your product to awareness, to interest, and finally to action. The beauty of a powerful close is that only a little bit of need has to be present in the buyer's mind for it to work. A good close will work on the buyer's *impulse to possess* as long as that element of need is present. Can you imagine what it would be like if no close were ever introduced into a sale? A buyer who needed something would ultimately, through laborious inspection and his own decision-making process, have to convince himself that he absolutely needed a particular product and then buy it. This happens when people purchase a product from vending machines. That's why vending machines are limited to the kinds of products they can sell. A vending machine is an Order Taker in purest form.

Remember that buying is not a logical art. The buying impulse is emotional. The desire to have something and to take it impulsively is universal. The term "impulse buying" is not limited to the casual shopper. All people have an impulse to possess. This is human nature. Advocate Salesmen appeal to that "impulse to possess." Remember, motivation equals reason. Impulse equals emotion. Motivation is designed to give the buyer a logical reason to do what his emotional impulses are telling him to do anyway. The close supplies the impulse to buy *now*.

The following closes have all been used effectively by professional Advocate Salesmen. We will examine each of them in depth later in this chapter.

1. *The Assumed Close.* "I have just called my company, Mr. Schwartz, to guarantee shipment within the time frame we discussed last week—we will bill you at the end of the month as usual."
2. *The Reverse Close.* "I don't think your order qualifies for our company to assign an on-site installation engineer. But, if we could increase the order by 20 percent. . . ."
3. *The Secondary Question Close.* "Which title company would you prefer to handle the escrow of this building?"
4. *The Confrontation Close.* "Please sign right here and I'll process the order immediately."
5. *The Cost/Price Close.* "I saw our new price list at a meeting this morning, but until it's officially announced, I'm going to write the order up at the old price."
6. *The Objection Close.* "I understand your problem, sir. Therefore my company will accept responsibility for arranging the transportation and include only the direct cost in your billing."
7. *The Action Close.* "If that design is available I will have to reserve it immediately. May I please borrow your telephone?"
8. *The Negotiated Close.* "I know you only need two cans of our developer, but I can only sell it by the case."
9. *Integrity Close Number One (Your Integrity).* "Things

aren't normally done that way within our company, Mr. El-
bert. However. . . ."

10. *Integrity Close Number Two (The Buyer's Integrity).* "Mr.
Hawkins, a customer like yourself deserves only the best of
quality and service. Therefore. . . ."

11. *The Service Close.* "I really wish I could give you the discount you want. However, I can arrange for our route man
to make an extra stop each afternoon."

12. *The Safety Close.* "I can assure you, Mr. Hamilton, my
company will guarantee it."

13. *The Substitution Close.* "Before you ask, Mr. Kramer, I
should tell you that, unfortunately, our vice president is
committed during the weeks that I would like to schedule
your seminar. However, if you can give me a firm commitment, I can arrange for the chairman to speak instead. I
happen to know that he is free on those particular dates."

14. *The Personal Greed Close.* "Each year our company spon-
sors a conference for our major customers and their families. Usually it's held in Barbados."

15. *The Hero Close.* "Naturally, sir, we will publish the results
of your new system in our bulletin to the industry."

16. *The Imminent Change Close.* "If we place the order now
before the strike vote is taken, I can assure delivery on the
date you want."

The minisale and power close are important to master if you
intend to be a successful Advocate Salesman. If you recall, Nick
Margolis had Jane Bloomingdale show him and his group how
to sell. The key to Jane's approach was never to sell people more
than they could buy. A Feasibility Buyer could not purchase
Nick's labor management service. But he could approve the
concept and help Nick sell the Economic Buyer who could purchase the actual service. So Nick called on a Feasibility Buyer
not to make a revenue-producing sale for his firm but to sell the
buyer on the need for those services. The close Nick used was
designed to enlist the Feasibility Buyer as an internal ally and
sponsor.

Remember Al Thomas? He didn't try to sell law books to the
office manager. Instead, he sold the concept of arranging a
meeting with the key end users of his services. It was at that
meeting that he made the sale. If Al hadn't closed the minisale
for the meeting, the major sale would never have been made.

If you recall, Max Stubal used the minisale technique to sell office equipment. Most salesmen feel that talking to an Implementive or Feasibility Buyer somewhere in the chain of beneficiaries is a waste of time—or, worse, a reflection of poor selling skills. Max disagreed. He was quite aware that all these people had to be sold anyway, at some point in time. So Max allowed the buyer's availability to dictate where he would begin the sale in the chain of beneficiaries. By correctly identifying an end user as an end user, Max knew the limits of what he could sell that person. Max got end users enthusiastic about his product by selling the bells and whistles of his line, but he did not embarrass them or himself by asking for an order they couldn't give. Instead, Max made a minisale that would serve him well when he made his major pitch.

He knew that when the time came the end user would enthusiastically approve of any change Max was able to prompt top management to make. More important, Max knew exactly where he was in the sale. Historically, he knew it took a fixed amount of time to sell his product properly and implement the purchase. However, unlike a baseball player, Max didn't have to get to first base before he ran to second. Max could move either way. He would focus on the Implementive Buyer or the Feasibility Buyer, whoever was more readily available. And if he failed to make his minisale, Max could always take another turn at bat. He would simply find another Implementive or Feasibility Buyer to replace the link in his chain.

Ultimately, Max knew he was going to have to convince an Economic Buyer to authorize the purchase, but Max didn't care which path he took first. They all led to the same place and took an equal amount of time. Max also knew that if he didn't cover everybody in the chain of beneficiaries, he would end up spending as much time after the sale as he had before the sale—and putting out fires is a lot more dangerous than preventing them in the first place.

Martha Lewis made a classic minisale when she convinced the managing partner of a major consulting firm to write an article for her publication. Once he was certain that she was not going to ask him to advertise in her publication, Martha's minisale became a nonsale in his mind. True, Martha was gambling on reader response to convince the general partner of the need for advertising his company's services. But there's nothing wrong with that. It's just good salesmanship.

Martha recognized that she had been singularly unsuccessful in selling buyer need. So she used the minisale to create a situation that would lead the buyer to convince himself. That's an accomplishment any Advocate Salesman would be proud of. Any sale has to be closed. Whether the sale is a minisale that requires a miniclose, or a full-blown presentation that requires a shark-biting grab, closing is still the name of the game. Doers initiate a close, Waiters wait for an opportunity to ask for the order, and Watchers hope the customer sells and closes himself.

Need Salesmen are powerful closers. Relationship Salesmen hope their personality and goodwill will encourage the customer to ask them to write up the order. Order Takers don't care. Of the hundreds of techniques that are used, the 16 closes that follow have proved to be the best. If you consistently choose one particular close over the others, you are limiting yourself. Not only does each situation and product dictate a certain kind of close; each buyer and his particular motivations will respond best to a certain type of close. That's called tactics. Closes are like arrows in a quiver. Each one has a different tip to do a different job. Make your selection wisely, or you'll wind up shooting at a bear with a practice arrow.

The Assumed Close
The Assumed Close simply takes for granted that the customer is going to buy. The salesman proceeds as though it has never crossed his mind that the customer might not buy. Therefore he moves busily from selling to implementation, and if the customer lets him do it, then in fact the sale is closed. The Assumed Close is an excellent tool for closing a minisale or a major presentation. As a telephone technique for getting appointments, it is invaluable. Instead of asking for an appointment, simply tell your buyer that you are going to be in town the next week and that you are checking his availability on a particular time and place. Never ask whether or not he wants to see you—he may tell you no!

Jane Bloomingdale used the Assumed Close extensively in teaching Nick Margolis how to sell supervisory training programs. Instead of asking an Economic Buyer for the order, Jane would thank him at the end of the meeting and tell him (not ask him) that she was going to arrange a meeting next week with his plant operations people to get the program started. If he didn't object, the meeting was on and that part of the deal was closed. If the buyer did object, Jane knew that she had more selling to do, or that an objection was still sitting somewhere in his mind that she had to surface and rebut.

The Assumed Close is the best technique for dealing with "maybes." If the customer does not have the guts to say no but gives you a qualified "yes" in the form of a noncommittal but still positive statement, move on to the next step in the sale and see if he drags you back. Maybe he really does want to be led, and as long as you're going down a path to which he does not object, you may as well continue. If you do lead him across some ground about which he has real objections, you will hear about it immediately.

The basic premise of the Assumed Close is that if the customer doesn't say no, he has really said yes. Therefore this technique must be tempered by the moral, ethical, and legal considerations in any good sale. Always confirm all the critical data—most certainly, terms and price—of an assumptive sale before the order is placed. Jane wrote a detailed set of instructions to the vice president of manufacturing on how to structure the meeting to which she had assumptively gotten the CEOs approval. She then wrote a letter to the CEO, referred to her conversation with him, and attached a copy of her instructions to the VP. Instead of saying, "Unless you provide me with information to the contrary, this is how we will proceed," Jane would offer her Economic Buyer a way out on a very positive tack. Her escape-clause paragraph read, "I believe I have covered all your objectives and ours in the attached letter to your vice president of manufacturing. However, if there are any additional objectives that you want us to consider, please let me know immediately."

Jane's deals always stay closed.

The Reverse Close
The Reverse Close requires a high degree of skill, since the salesman is, in effect, jeopardizing the sale by threatening to take the order away. Al Thomas used this close very effectively. He would write up an order for law books while mak-

ing his presentation and would lay it on the table during discussions with a buyer. He found to his delight that every time he pulled the order form away to put it back in his briefcase, his customer would reach for it. This behavior was, in Al's opinion, an oddity of humankind—something about how people refuse to relinquish anything they possess, whether they really want it or not. That order form was the customer's and, by God, he was going to sign it one way or the other.

In more complex selling, of course, the Reverse Close is not quite so simple. When selling Thermacon products, Pete Abbott always isolated the exact benefit or feature his buyer was hooked on. Then he would often withdraw that benefit unless the buyer added to the order or did something else that benefited Pete. In one instance, Pete sold a substantial order of five Thermacon 1000 units for delivery in May and three more units for delivery in October. Pete had correctly ascertained that his buyer had a desperate need for May delivery. He also knew that his buyer was a Waiter who tended to procrastinate or change his mind if circumstances varied. So the units ordered for October could easily be subject to change or cancelation unless they were packaged together and prepaid.

The buyer had repeatedly delayed his purchase decision. As a consequence, Pete truthfully explained that the May delivery date was going to be difficult for his production people to meet. In point of fact, Pete knew that the May delivery could still be met, because he had another customer scheduled for May who didn't really care if the equipment arrived in July. As the account manager, Pete could authorize such a substitution. However, he kept that card very close to his vest. As things now stood, his manufacturing people could not meet a May delivery date of five Thermacon 1000 units. Pete wasn't afraid of the competition filling the order, because his buyer was already a Thermacon user, and many of the competition's products were incompatible with Thermacon units. The customer naturally went white. Pete let him stew for a full 45 seconds and then added, "There may be a solution to your problem."

At this stage of the game, the customer was willing to do almost anything to get a firm order for five Thermacon 1000 units in May. The buyer was now selling the seller. That's why this particular close is called a Reverse Close. In the end, Pete was able to put all eight Thermacon 1000 units into one firm package with a minimum of five to be delivered in May. The buyer got what he originally ordered and Pete walked away knowing that the deal couldn't be canceled because, if it were, the man couldn't get his five units in May.

Unethical? There are always some who would say so—Boyd Mueller, for example. But those people usually belong to the generation that encouraged women to dress seductively, be charming and flattering, and exude what was then called the "come hither" look. After all this equipment had its desired effect and the male who had come hither was sweating profusely, the woman was then expected to tell him the terms of the deal. "You can look but don't touch. If you want to touch, we have to get married." The philosopher who said, "Right is relative to a particular point of view" knew what he was talking about.

Remember, the key to the Reverse Close is knowing what part of the sale has your buyer hooked and then denying it to him until he pays a higher price or concedes something more than he planned that is of benefit to your company and you.

The Secondary Question Close

The Secondary Question Close is a beauty. It resembles the Assumed Close, with several refinements. For arranging appointments, it is invaluable. Here the salesman simply asks a buyer whether Tuesday or Wednesday would best suit his schedule. Counting upon people's natural need to respond positively in relationships, and also relying upon their conditioning since childhood to do as they are told, the salesman would focus his buyer's attention on whether Tuesday's schedule was lighter or Wednesday's would be better— rather than on whether the appointment should be made in the first place. Only after making the appointment and hanging up the phone *might* the buyer wonder why he was having a meeting at all.

Good automobile salesmen use the Secondary Question Close regularly. "Would you prefer all three initials on the door of your Mercedes 450 SL, or just two, Mr. Buyer?" A commitment to a personalized nameplate on the side of a car requires the dealer to go to some expense that is not transferable if the customer reneges on the sale. The customer is subconsciously aware of this; and if he agrees to it, regardless of the number of initials, the salesman knows that he has the buyer hooked. So his next questions are related to the color of the car and delivery time, all of them secondary questions that assume the sale is a fact.

In a sale involving more complex products or multiapproval buyers, the Secondary Question Close focuses on implementation. One bulk chemicals salesman claims that price is rarely a problem for him—in spite of the fact that his product is very price-sensitive—because he focuses the buyer's attention on secondary aspects of the sale. Details like date of delivery and method of transportation are important to the buyer, but not to the salesman. As a result, the customer usually accepts the standard industry price instead of going through the ritual of trying for a discount. The Secondary Question Close works very well for this salesman.

Jane Bloomingdale and Nick Margolis refined their assumptive technique by adding major elements of the Secondary Question Close to finalize an order. Jane would always ask an Economic Buyer to choose between two small details in the training program that really should have been decided by the Feasibility or Implementive Buyers. But knowing that Economic Buyers like to mess around in everybody else's sandbox, Jane was able to focus the CEO's attention on the details of *how* the supervisory training program should be implemented rather than on *whether* it should be implemented. After all, it was assumed that he was going to implement the program, wasn't it?

The Secondary Question Close has been around a long time. It's roots can be traced back at least to prehistoric days when the first caveman said to the first cavewoman, "Your place or mine?" And remember, if your buyer won't play your secondary question game, you haven't lost the sale, you've simply lost the close. The secondary question is an excellent trial close. It doesn't anger the customer by forcing him to make up his mind before he is ready; nor does it embarrass him into having to say no before he is convinced that he really doesn't want to buy. The secondary question also allows a salesman who is afraid of rejection to test the water without risking the humiliation of having a full-blown close rejected. A negative reaction to the Secondary Question Close merely tells the salesman to move off into different areas, back up and resell, and then try another close.

The Confrontation Close

The Confrontation Close is simply asking for the order. Good Need Salesmen usually avoid the Confrontation Close. They prefer more subtle closes that keep the avenues of negotiation open. Relationship Salesmen use this close quite a bit because a positive response reaffirms their feelings of self-worth. However, Relationship Salesmen rarely ask for the order until they are absolutely sure that the client is going to buy. They prefer instead to keep talking until the customer himself makes the close. When forced to make any kind of close at all, Order Takers favor the Confrontation Close. However, an Order Taker will risk trying to close a sale only under great duress and pressure from management.

The Confrontation Close is used frequently in retail sales. However, even mediocre retail salespeople prefer the subtlety of the Secondary Question Close. To force the customer to make up his mind, they will ask, "May I wrap this up for you?" rather than, "Would you like to buy this?"

In certain industries, such as investment sales, the Confrontation Close is mandatory. For example, if a stockbroker uses any of the more subtle closes described in this chapter, his buyer can deny that he placed an order. So stockbrokers must ask for an order directly. So must commodities brokers and any other salesmen dealing in the securities market.

In any business that requires a detailed contract, the Confrontation Close should be used for safety's sake. Jim Martin's company sold specially designed and engineered equipment to contractors for nuclear power plants. Every sale Jim made involved a substantial investment on the part of his company for the preliminary work and studies alone. As a consequence, after a meeting with a buyer to discuss a transaction, Jim would end each conversation with "Do we have a deal or don't we?" This forced the man's commitment, which Jim would reinforce with a handshake. Jim would then follow up with a contract before any expenditures were made. That way, there was no subtlety or duplicity and consequent misunderstanding on the part of either party—and no surprises in the contract. The rule is: Cover all the bases and get a verbal agreement; then get a detailed contract between buyer and seller.

Certain types of salesmen prefer the Confrontation Close, or asking for the order, because it fits their particular personality and method of doing business. If you recall, Jim Franklin sold his superiority, which came across as high integrity to the customers who couldn't spot what Jim was really up to. At the end of a presentation, Jim would routinely and formally ask the customer for the order. It matched his style, and if the truth were known it never occurred to Jim Franklin to handle a close in any other way. Somewhere, sometime in Jim Franklin's life, he had learned that the way to sell something was to ask somebody if they wanted to buy it. At that point, the chapter on how to close permanently snapped shut in his mind and Jim never thought of the subject again. Closing every sale by simply asking the customer for the order suited his black-and-white mentality.

By the same token, certain types of buyers respond positively to the Confrontation Close. Advocate Salesmen use it when confronted with a buyer like Jerald Maxwell, whose driving force is identity and power. Asking a man like Maxwell for the order puts the salesman in a very vulnerable and subordinate position, because the buyer has the power to say yes or no. But buyers like Maxwell thrive on power. Any good Need Salesman knows that regardless of the positive response he had gotten from previous subtle and trial closes, in the end it is always best to ask a man like Maxwell for the order so he has an opportunity to be a benevolent monarch and say yes. But Need Salesmen don't try the Confrontation Close until they are absolutely sure their buyer is going to say yes. Then they use it as a formality or an ego sop to their buyer.

No particular skill is required to use the Confrontation Close. However, a great deal of skill is required to know *when* to use it. As the name implies, it is a confrontation: The customer will buy or not buy. If the customer says no, the salesman has lost ground that he may not be able to recover. That's why more subtle closes are more powerful and safer for most situations. A customer who remains basically undecided or ambivalent or who still has a valid objection will be forced to react negatively to the Confrontation Close. The other types of closes will uncover that hidden objection if they don't succeed in closing the sale. Then the salesman has the opportunity to deal with the customer's objection, whatever it is, and build up to a close again. The Confrontation Close doesn't let you do this, so be sure to use it with caution. It creates a win/lose situation, but it's a great close and very effective if you know *when* to use it.

The Cost/Price Close

Most novice salesmen think that the Cost/Price Close means giving the customer a break on price or selling terms and conditions, as our old friend Pat Farrell did in selling California real estate. Not so. The Cost/Price Close is a highly intricate technique that is effective only when it is introduced at a proper time. Need must be established clearly in the buyer's mind before cost or price can be used as a close. Pete Abbott used the Cost/Price Close whenever he sold Thermacon products to purchasing agents instead of end users. And he never gave away a dime of the company's profit. Pete's first step was to determine whether his buyer had instructions to issue a purchase order or whether he was just shopping. Once Pete had satisfied himself that his buyer did have the authorization to purchase equipment, his Cost/Price Close was to inform the buyer of the new prices that were scheduled to take effect shortly. This was the buyer's incentive to buy now rather than later. An old technique that still works. But Pete could back up his statement, because inflation, production costs, and unit prices were always under review. And in Pete's tenure with the company, he had never seen prices go down.

Al Thomas regularly used the Cost/Price Close to sell law books and services. His subscribers were well aware that the cost of their library had increased year after year and thus were not prone to argue when Al told them that if they ordered now he could reserve the service at the previous year's price. One of Al's competitors, a large looseleaf law and tax service, had a reputation for aggressive and somewhat unethical marketing techniques. The company actually encouraged its salesmen to offer cost/price alternatives like "Buy now to guarantee this year's price next year." The company had a built-in means of raising prices, so the system was a real stroke of genius. If last year's service cost $400 and the state had a 6 percent sales tax, the total bill to the customer was $424. The salesman's reorder printout therefore carried the price of $424. The customer could check with his bookkeeper to confirm that in fact last year he had paid $424. However, after the order was processed, a bill would come through for $424 *plus* 6 percent sales tax, for a new total of $449.44. In addition, the great bulk of Al's competitors did business by direct-mail renewal, on which they paid no sales tax even though they collected it. Naturally, no commission was paid on the tax.

In practice, the Cost/Price Close is a useful foil to a buyer who is relentlessly attempting to beat an Advocate Salesman down in price. Instead of responding to the customer's demand to reduce the price, an astute Advocate Salesman will counter by telling the customer that not only must he refuse him a discount but he must advise him that if he delays his purchase much longer he is going to be faced with an increase in price rather than a discount. The cost/price counter to a discount-determined buyer will almost always test the buyer's real commitment to buy.

Until the decline of the California real estate market, aggressive real estate salesmen would use the "Buy now because the price is going to go up tomorrow" close to stampede buyers and greedy speculators into closing a real estate deal now. Because what they said was true and because they were so effective at using the Cost/Price Close, California realtors created an inflated real estate market that was rivaled only by the super-heated stock market of 1929. Speculators and homeowners alike knew that single-dwelling properties were increasing in value at a rate of 22–25 percent per year. With interest rates at 9 percent and holding, that was too good a deal for anyone to pass up. After all, coastal property in California was rarely on the market long enough to get into the multiple listing,* so having a house was literally as good as gold until the crash of the 1980s. Then, of course, the piper was paid for a closing technique that had worked exceptionally well.

The Objection Close

"Always close on an objection" is the baffling advice new salesmen hear from their managers. How can you possibly close on an objection? If the customer is objecting, he obviously doesn't want to buy. Not true! If the customer is objecting, he is either negotiating with you or arguing with himself about the pros and cons of your product. His objection is usually nothing more than a verbal reflection of that internal argument.

Bud Wright was a master of the Objection Close. Bud sold real estate in the high-priced bedroom communities of Con-

---

* A confidential record prepared by local real estate associations for real estate agents only.

necticut, and he learned early in his career that unless people build a home from the ground up to their own specifications, any house they buy is a compromise between what they want, what's available, and how much money they have. As a consequence, Bud would listen while his prospect told him all the things that were wrong with the house. Then Bud would break off the meeting and say, "Let me do what I can about this." He would schedule a meeting for later in the day. Then Bud would pick up the telephone and discuss the buyer's objections with the owner.

"For the right price," Bud pitched the owner, "we can agree to change all the things about the house that he objects to and close the deal today." The owner usually went along with Bud because Bud used the magic words "the right price." Armed with the ability to deal with the customer's objections, Bud had a decided advantage at his next meeting with the buyer. The buyer was prepared to reinforce, discuss, and negotiate with Bud all the objections that he had originally brought up. Bud would sit back and relax as the man ticked off what was wrong with the roof, the cellar, the cracked cement in the patio, and the broken stained-glass windows. At the end of this diatribe, when he was sure that the buyer had exhausted himself, Bud simply asked him why he was interested in the house in the first place.

Inevitably the buyer's response was, "Except for all the things I've told you about, it's a good house."

"In other words, you'd buy it," Bud retorted.

"Yes," said the buyer. "I'd buy it if those things were fixed."

"Done," said Bud. "All the things that you mentioned will be corrected to your specifications and we'll write that into the contract of sale." Bud usually had to repeat this three times before the incredulous buyer realized what had happened. But in 90 percent of the cases the buyer proceeded, because Bud had done a good job of screening the serious buyers from the lookie-loos who were just trying to take up his time.

Handling customer objections is an art in itself. Customer objections are inevitable in sales. It is a rare product that is a perfect match between the buyer's need and the seller's inventory. Some compromise is inevitable between the customer's desires, the product alternatives available, the cost of the product, and the amount of money the customer can afford to spend. Handling objections is the litmus test of the professional Advocate Salesman.

One of the best ways to handle an objection is to simply ignore it. If it's a valid objection you can count on it to come roaring back at you like a line drive. If it's not, it probably will never be heard from again. An objection also provides the pro with the perfect opportunity to close. When you couple the Objection Close with another powerful technique like the Assumed Close, you have a tremendous amount of firepower going for you. Al Thomas used this approach with the lawyers to whom he sold books and services. Nit-picking objections are a lawyer's stock in trade, and Al was a master at dealing with them. First of all, if he couldn't ignore an objection, Al would pause, using the silence to unsettle his buyer and to gain time to evaluate the validity of the buyer's objection and think of a way to overcome it. If the solution was costly or if Al did not feel that the objection was valid, Al would couple the Objection Close with another close that would obviate all but the most serious objection. If the objection survived, Al then knew that he had to deal with it or spend his time somewhere else.

Here's a typical situation in which Al applied this technique:

"I agree that the weekly report features and digests your service contains are very valuable and timely material, Mr. Thomas, but as I told you before we are very busy here and I simply don't think we would have time to read it." Al noted that his buyer used the imperial "we."

"Yes," Al replied, "an awful lot of the digest services published in the past were as bulky as magazines and contained a great deal of detail. You have subscribed to digests like that in the past, haven't you?"

"Yes we have."

"Is your firm an association of lawyers or is it a professional corporation?" Al would ask.

"It's a professional corporation. Why do you ask?"

"All the lawyers here work for you. Therefore you'll want at least all the junior ones to have our service so they can keep up with changes until they are experienced and knowledgeable enough in their field not to need it like you."

Meanwhile Al would be busily writing up the order. He was proceeding on the assumption that although his buyer could speak for himself, the buyer's smug self-confidence did not extend to his staff attorneys. Al used the Objection Close along with an assumptive approach—combining the motivators of fear and safety—to wrap up the deal. When a buyer makes an objection, he's sticking his neck out 24 feet, and a good Advocate Salesman recognizes it. An objection is a two-part statement. Not only does it say "I don't like this particular feature of your product." It also implies that "if your product had a certain feature I would buy it." That's the chink in the buyer's armor and the beauty of the Objection Close.

Bud Wright used the Objection Close to wipe the table clean of all his buyer's objections. He eliminated the cause of the objections so the buyer had no choice but to buy, unless he wanted to look like a fool. Al Thomas correctly evaluated his buyer's objection as a reflection of smug security and professional self-confidence. But he knew that smug people need the rest of us bumbling fools in order to have something to measure themselves against and feel smug about. So Al used the buyer's objection to close him by accurately recognizing that the buyer thought less of his subordinates than he did of himself.

The Objection Close is a very powerful technique indeed.

The Action Close

The Action Close is very subtle. It doesn't require a high degree of skill, because nothing needs to be articulated except an action. No verbal subtleties are used here. Advocate Salesmen merely do something positive that makes the sale a fait accompli unless the customer intervenes directly.

One of the best techniques is the "call the office" action. If the salesman makes his presentation assumptively, never giving the customer time to say yes or no, he can reach a point where he finishes up his presentation by saying, "However, I am not sure I can guarantee the delivery date so let me call the office." Then he reaches for the customer's phone. If the customer doesn't stop him, the salesman knows that he's 99 percent home. He should then call his office and talk to somebody about delivery dates. The salesman should finish his call by saying, "Okay, but I want you to block out 37 cases of left-handed widgets for delivery to Celanoid in 24 days." If the customer doesn't object, the salesman is home free. If he does object, the salesman can simply look at him, smile, and truthfully say,

"That's all right, Mr. Buyer, I'm glad to have those widgets blocked off anyway because I have several other customers who are going to skin me alive when they find out that we're almost out of inventory."

The salesman has now created and demonstrated an urgency about delivery of his products in the mind of the buyer. He can now begin his recovery by saying, "Evidently I've missed some objection that you have about buying these left-handed widgets, Mr. Buyer. My apologies. Will you please tell me what your objection is?"

The buyer is now obligated to stop fencing and tell the salesman the truth, because he thinks he has caused the salesman some embarrassment. In point of fact, this type of Action Close puts the salesman in a win/win position. Either the buyer goes along with the close or the buyer feels that he somehow misled the salesman into thinking he had an order and embarrassed the man with his company. Once the objection is on the table, the salesman can deal with it straightaway.

Another successful Advocate Salesman combines the Action Close with the Secondary Question Close. Although he is the proud owner of several 18-karat-gold pens, this salesman never uses any of them to close an order. At the end of his pitch, the salesman picks up the order form that he placed on the buyer's desk when the presentation began and—with a nod for permission—reaches for a pen from the desk penholder that he spotted early in his pitch. The customer is distracted but not offended by his actions. But the significance of having a salesman put a pen to an order form is not lost on his subconscious. Therefore, if he is sold, he'll let the salesman continue to write up the order. If he's not, he'll feel called upon to blurt out his objection and the selling process can begin again.

Relationship Salesmen like the Action Close because they usually have a good enough relationship with their customer to borrow a pen or use the telephone without causing alarm. It's a very personal act. It implies a kinship. In order to be a close, however, it must initiate *implementation* of the sale. There are many actions a salesman can take to divert the customer's attention from a dangerous line of discussion, but unless the action triggers implementation of the sale, it is not an Action Close.

One highly successful salesman who made his presentations with a flip chart and multicolored felt-tipped pens used to drop a pen and ask someone else to retrieve it in order to break up a discussion with his buyers that had taken a bad turn. Another would interrupt the conversation to check some figures related to the discussion and use that time to devise a tactic to deal with the situation. Or he would change the subject completely. These are action techniques used to control the *selling process*. They are designed not to close the sale, merely to control it. Only an action that closes the sale deserves to be defined as an Action Close. Be aware of the difference!

Jane Bloomingdale's great Action Close at a precipitous moment during the meeting with her Economic Buyer was to stand up and announce that she had better get going to her meeting with the plant supervisors if the program was going to be implemented as planned. By taking an action that signaled the implementation of her program, Jane commanded the situation and forced the buyer to choose between interrupting her or allowing her to proceed as she had informed him.

"If the buyer had a real objection that he hadn't told me about," Jane said, "he would say, 'Well, wait a minute, Jane, what about . . .' and out would pop the objection. If the objection was merely a nag and not thoroughly thought through, the buyer would call my name as I was going out the door and remind me to be careful about something. If his concern was serious enough to be a problem later on, I would stop dead in my tracks," Jane went on, "and deal with the situation right away if I could. If I couldn't, I would ignore him and continue out the door to my meeting. But I was now armed with the knowledge that I was going to have problems down the road and usually all I needed was a little time to find a way to deal with the objection."

The Action Close forces the buyer to make up his mind. Being polite is probably part of his nature so if he has to physically restrain you from picking up the telephone, he isn't sold in the first place and the Action Close came too soon. Like any close, timing is all important. An Action Close is rarely a trial close. You can offend the buyer by taking an action to implement a sale if he doesn't feel that you have any good reason to believe that he is willing to buy your product at the time of your action. This can happen very easily, for example, if the Action Close is tried too early in the presentation. The buyer would know very well what you're doing and would probably invite you to leave his office. The Action Close works well on any kind of buyer with any motivation. It also works well coupled with any of the other closes, including the Confrontation Close. For example, "While you're signing this order, Mr. Buyer, I'll use your phone for just a second to call my office and reserve a firm delivery date before our Distribution Department closes." Buyers like a properly executed Action Close. It shows that the salesman is not a person to waste time or to overlook important details. He's the kind of get-up-and-go guy you can rely on to take care of you properly.

The Negotiated Close

The Negotiated Close is very basic. Negotiations can be over price, delivery dates, or benefits and features of the product. But the only way to implement the Negotiated Close is to start playing a game of give and take with your buyer early in the sale. Otherwise you are just in the normal selling process and have no real chance to close the sale through the Nego- tiated Close. For example, a discussion about benefits, payment terms, and delivery dates is the average day-to-day dialogue of the mediocre salesman. But an Advocate Salesman will say to his buyer, "If you are satisfied with the payment terms, I will see what I can do about delivery dates," thus setting the stage for a trade-off. Coupled with the Reverse Close, the Negotiated Close can be a formidable weapon. If the salesman knows that the buyer's hot button is tied to benefits and results, he can ne- gotiate a fast close by indicating that those benefits won't be available unless the buyer acts now. Or, more positively, if the buyer acts now, he will get more of the benefits he dearly loves than if he waits until later.

In order for people to negotiate in good faith, each party must need and want something from the other. If need is not sold there can be no negotiation. If there is no negotiation there can be no Negotiated Close. There isn't a close in the world that will work if a little bit of need hasn't been created. But a good close can shorten the length of time it takes to make a sale.

Retail stores offer lots of customer services that are a verita- ble gold mine for a successful Negotiated Close. The fact that a garment is going to need alterations is a beautiful trade-off point for a strong negotiated closer. So are immediate product availability and home delivery. Historically, however, only Doers and Need Salesmen use the Negotiated Close in the retail business. Waiters and Watchers are likely to give away these services without gaining a concession from the customer (such as a decision to purchase now rather than delaying a week). Order Takers have the odd habit of forgetting that everyone in the store supposedly works for the customer. If an expensive dress has to be altered and the customer needs it by Friday, an Order Taker will pick up the phone and call the overworked and underpaid tailor in the back room to verify a Friday delivery. After about ten seconds of abuse, the Order Taker shrugs his shoulders and tells his customer it's impossible to have it by Friday. Let's face it, if the dress is expensive enough, somebody in the store can change the tailor's priorities. "But that's up to someone else," thinks the Order Taker. "I don't get paid to do that." The Order Taker avoids potential rejection like the plague, and that includes rejection by an overworked and underpaid tailor. He doesn't care that he has just missed a solid opportunity to negotiate a close.

Again, it is important to remember that the art of selling is the art of negotiation, but the Negotiated Close requires using that natural process to close the sale, not just to generate interest! It's amazing how many salesmen fail to remember why they are in front of a buyer in the first place. Closing is the name of the game. One highly successful salesman says that he always offers the customer 50 percent less than what he wants when negotiations begin and asks for exactly 50 percent more than he wants in return. It takes a strong will to do this but the message is clear. In using the Negotiated Close, make sure you leave enough room in every proposal that you advance to in fact negotiate later. For once you've given away all you can give, the buyer controls the sale. He now knows what your best terms are and can always shop the deal.

Integrity Close Number One

Integrity Close Number One is known as the *Gone with the Wind* Close. Can't you just hear Scarlett O'Hara saying, "Oh my goodness gracious, Mr. Butler, I couldn't possibly do anything like that. Whatever do you take me for?" It is also known as the Sanctimonious/Self-Righteous Close. Harvard and Stanford Business School graduates use it on each other with impunity. Here are some lead-in examples:

"The quality of Apex products is unsurpassed, as you know.

You are free, of course, to investigate other alternatives, but our inventory is limited."

"I beg your pardon, sir, Rolls Royce automobiles do not experience mechanical difficulties. If I sell you one, you can count on my word for that."

"The very reason our worldwide network of offices and consultants exists is to prevent the kinds of problems you have from occurring."

In and by itself, Integrity Close Number One will wrap up many a deal that couldn't be wrapped up before. Coupled with the Negative Close, it can be a knockout.

Essentially, a salesman using Integrity Close Number One is intimidating his buyer. Companies that stress excellence and quality or have a popular proprietary product usually have a very inflexible attitude toward negotiating price, terms, and conditions. Therefore their salesmen do not have the flexibility to correctly implement a strong Negotiated Close. Faced with a buyer who is attempting to force negotiation when none is possible, a good advocate salesman will stand as tall as he can and inform his buyer, "Things just aren't done that way in our company!"

This close has the effect of belittling and shaming a buyer—and therefore has its dangers. But as we all learned as children, belittlement and shame are powerful tools to motivate people to do what you want them to do in the first place. In the hands of a real expert, Integrity Close Number One can be devastating. If from the outset the salesman knows he is going to use Integrity Close Number One and adopts the correct posture and bearing necessary to support it, that salesman is going to close many orders solely on the basis of his perceived integrity. And if he really does have room to negotiate, he is going to be a tiger in the marketplace, because in those few instances when the Integrity Close doesn't work on a customer who has been set up for it, the salesman can always switch to the Negotiated Close and use the policy flexibility that he was saving all along.

The two best situations in which to use Integrity Close Number One are when you have a whole lot going for you—in terms of your company's reputation, your product's credibility, and your position in the marketplace—and when you have *none* of these things going for you. In the first instance, you are appealing to your buyer's natural desire for brand names. Brand names carry with them the implied motivator of safety.

Why do people buy Cadillacs when a host of other smaller and cheaper cars are more efficient and just as comfortable? Because the excellence of Cadillac automobiles has been instilled in the customer's mind along with the built-in approval (or envy) of Cadillac owners. General Motors has made most of its profits from selling these gas-guzzling "street cruisers," as they are called in Europe. Naturally, the buyer who seeks the approval of others always gains self-approval when he is successful. So integrity, and the excellence that it implies, is a powerful close to use.

Conversely, if your product is unknown, your company is new, and you don't yet have a position in the marketplace, Integrity Close Number One is ideal, because, like the new kid on the block, nobody knows anything bad about you. Just make sure you are impeccably dressed, look successful, articulate well, and make the buyer feel that he is talking to someone special. If you use any printed material about your company or product, make sure it reflects the highest-quality artwork and paper. It is human nature to make judgments, and everybody knows that first impressions, accurate or not, carry the most weight.

If you are able to interest a buyer in your product, you can expect him to start negotiating with you. At this point, the Integrity Close is the right arrow to grab from your quiver. If you eliminate negotiation and close on integrity, you'll never have to worry about haggling with this customer on repeat orders. Of course, if your company does not establish its integrity, and if your product turns out to be inferior, repeat business won't be a problem. There won't be any.

As a rule of thumb, Integrity Close Number One works well with buyers who have a high need for self-approval and approval of others. Identity and power buyers like Jerald H. Maxwell are excellent targets. Buyers like Dan Moran are even more vulnerable. If you recall, Dan was the company rationalizer who would wrap a devious or destructive alternative in a cloak of self-righteousness and justify it to his victim as he rammed it down his throat with a smile. Dan sold integrity and self-righteousness, so Dan was naturally susceptible to anything that smacked of it. Dan's mentor, the chairman, had built a whole company around a product that was extremely expensive, difficult to implement, and impossible to measure in results. So, like the snake oil salesmanship of the past, a lot of integrity had to be sold before prospects would believe his company could help them.

So with Dan Moran and his chairman, Jerald H. Maxwell, and the thousands of other buyers like them, Integrity Close Number One will always work because it reinforces what they want to believe about themselves and what they want others to believe about them. The Integrity Close knows no barriers. The buyer on which it works can be a Doer, a Waiter, or a Watcher. Your best clue for when to use it is your own evaluation of the customer's personality based upon his conversation. If he is stuffy and pompous and talks platitudinally, you've got yourself a buyer who will respond to the Integrity Close. But make sure that you distinguish the hawks from the pigeons. If you use the Integrity Close on a buyer who is not impressed by you, your company, your product, or your pitch, he's going to laugh at you. Talk about rejection! It's bad enough for a buyer to say no, but if he laughs while he's saying it, it's time to change your act.

Integrity Close Number Two

Integrity Close Number Two is not as much fun as Integrity Close Number One because it puts the salesman in an apparently servile position. Doers and Need Salesmen do not like Integrity Close Number Two, since it reflects badly on their self-image. However, Advocate Salesmen use it and use it very effectively. If, by his own dress, demeanor, and bearing, the salesman presents himself as a person of substance worthy of respect and then subordinates himself to the buyer, the buyer is doubly flattered. After all, one king bowing to another king is much more impressive than the bent knees of 100,000 peasants. With Integrity Close Number Two, the salesman makes a point that the customer doesn't necessarily want to accept, but phrases it in such flattering terms (which the buyer does want to accept) that it cannot be totally rejected.

"Certainly a man who spends as much time as you do with his family, Mr. Jones, and cares for them as you must, would want them to enjoy the creature comforts featured in our Comfort Camper 6000."

"A man like you, Mr. Van Steelant, who is smart enough to have risen to the top executive rank in one of the Fortune 500 companies would want to have his second home by the lake reflect the benefits of his diligence and hard work. Certainly a home like this would be greatly appreciated by your family and friends, all of whom probably wish that you had more time to spend with them. This home can serve as your retreat."

"I can appreciate your company's position, Mrs. Abrams, and I know how demeaning it must be to someone like you to be forced to negotiate price when it's obvious that your company needs our products and no discounts are possible."

"Mr. Chairman, I know that a company like Sycon Oil would want its officers, directors, and shareholders protected by the service, integrity, and worldwide facilities of only the very best and most highly reputable accounting firm."

"I can see, madam, that a woman like you would want her baby to have the very best things that money can buy."

"In reality, sir, only a person who has achieved great stature in life can appreciate a boat of this quality."

Each of the above is a solid opener for an Integrity Close Number Two on a variety of products. Big law firms and big accounting firms are hidebound in using Integrity Close Number Two because it reflects upon their self-created, self-perpetuated integrity and impeccable reputation. They would be well advised to learn a few other closes to combine with integrity, because no Advocate Salesman or organization aggressively soliciting business should be hidebound in using any type of close. Integrity Close Number Two appeals to people's need for approval of others and self-approval. It is the antithesis of rejection. The seller is unequivocally and wholeheartedly accepting the buyer. In fact, the seller is displaying envy of the buyer as well as respect.

The expression "Flattery will get you everywhere" is a truism. But beware of the steely-eyed buyer who has learned to curb his narcissistic instincts. Undue flattery waves a red flag in front of this bull. The key to the choice of a close is to know your buyer's receptivity. Not everyone responds to flattery. But when you find a buyer upon whom Integrity Close Number Two works once, be advised that it will work again and again—and again!

Dan Moran, regardless of his motives, capitalized on being able to sell his chairman internal policies and projects Dan was sponsoring. He did this by utilizing Integrity Close Number Two quite effectively. What brought on Dan's demise was the fact that his credibility with the chairman waned, so his flattering praise was no longer flattering. For praise to be believable, it must come from aristocrats and peers. The great unwashed will receive nothing in return for their adoration, because the king considers their adoration his due. However, aristocrats and peers who heap praise upon the king are invariably rewarded for their efforts.

So if your buyer exhibits a strong need for power, self-approval, and approval of others—or if he just sits in his chair like it's a throne and runs his fiefdom accordingly—it's a good bet that he's an excellent candidate for Integrity Close Number Two. Just don't try it if you look and smell like the great unwashed!

The Service Close

The Service Close is a defensive close. But it is a good one because buyers respond to it. Every product is made up of hardware, software, and service. That goes for everything, not just mainframe data processing equipment. When a woman buys a Cuisinart she's buying three things. She's buying the hardware, or the Cuisinart itself. She's also buying the instructions on how to use it. That's the software. And of course she wants to be able to instantly pick up her telephone and call her local authorized Cuisinart dealer to come over and fix it after she's shredded a spoon along with the carrots. That's the service.

The Service Close is effective when a buyer is on the fence and can't quite make up his mind whether to buy. "You needn't worry about this oven ever breaking down, Mrs. Habercork. Our microwaves are guaranteed for three years and we have a service contract that will provide free parts and free labor that is built into the price of the unit."

"I can appreciate that you feel our unit cost for your automobile fleet is somewhat high, but if you'll sign right here, sir, I'll guarantee that my company will, at no charge to you, provide free labor and cost only on parts for all tune-ups and minor repairs for the length of the contract. Major components, of course, are covered by factory warranty."

The Service Close is defensive because it can be used as a substitute for a reduction in price, thereby maintaining a surface continuity of prices among all customers. This can be extremely important in protecting against continued inflation.

Salesmen who do not have leeway on price concessions in a price-sensitive market should be instructed in how to compute the actual cost of services that are bargained for with the customer. Service is a salable commodity. The alternative is price reduction on a large scale. And large-scale price reductions can have the effect of reducing inflation, thus forcing companies to pay back loans in dollars that have the same value as those originally borrowed. Horrible thought, isn't it?

When the large mainframe computer manufacturers got started, they were creating need for a new product. So they packaged the hardware, software, and service together and included it in the original cost of the sale. This was true until the need for data processing equipment became institutionalized in the minds of American businessmen. Then the mainframe suppliers began a process known as "unbundling"—that is, charging the customer separately for each item used. Today if you buy a mainframe computer you have to buy the software from a service bureau and also pay the engineer to make repairs when the computer breaks down. Most smaller companies have not reached that degree of sophistication. Nor do they have such a lock on their market. Therefore their representatives can still trade service for price and use the Service Close quite profitably for everyone concerned.

When Pete Abbott was unloading Thermacon's $25 million in outdated inventory, he motivated his buyers to buy the Thermacon-A by raising the safety issue of proven versus unproven technology. As you can well imagine, his hooker was the Service Close. Thermacon-Frigacon had a nationwide network of service engineers, something its new competitor could not yet afford.

Relationship Salesmen are very effective at using the Service Close because they are giving the customer something that will please him. The danger is that they will give away the store and get nothing in return. An Advocate Salesman selling need will avoid that pitfall. The Service Close and the motivation of safety have a direct correlation, as Pete Abbott clearly demonstrated. The Service Close is also quite effective when your buyer's motivation is greed. If you throw in a little bit of service at no extra cost, he will jump at it. He can't resist getting something for nothing.

Al Thomas used the Service Close very effectively. His looseleaf legal services had one major drawback. Once a week a handsomely paid legal secretary was required to open these ring-bound tomes, take out the old pages, and put in the new ones—a very expensive task for the firm and very boring work for the secretary. Al figured out that the size of a law library had nothing to do with its initial expense. Books are to lawyers as dope is to addicts. There is never enough. It was the indirect expense and motivational problem of having a high-priced secretary perform a mind-numbing task that limited the number of services his customers would buy. So Al dreamed up a solution that pleased his customers, made him a great deal of money, and beat the pants off his competitors.

Al offered to do the filing himself each week if the customer would expand his law library to a size that justified the service. Tickled to death but skeptical that Al could fulfill such a promise, most of Al's customers complied nevertheless. He had always delivered before. Al soon found himself filing instead of selling, but he had prepared for that. After speaking to guidance counselors at the local high school, Al mustered an army of eager-to-work students to file the services after school. Al's bonus and commission on new sales were more than enough to cover the cost for the first year. The next year Al told his customers that he would have to pass the cost of filing the services on to the firm. A few canceled, but most did not. After all, Al had sold them books they needed, and the student's wages were so low compared with the wages of legal secretaries that the cost went almost unnoticed. Al continued to provide the filing service free to new customers because his commission plan had a high yield for newly acquired business. But remember, Al first had to sell the need for the specific services that he sold. The filing service was simply the close.

The Safety Close

The Safety Close resembles the Service Close, but only in application. Safety is considerably different from service. As with any close, need must be sold first and the close used to tie up the sale.

Every sale involves some concern about safety. It can take the form of safety from injury, safety from excessive repair bills, safety from malfunctions, inferior quality, missed delivery dates, misrepresentation, and so on. The smart Advocate Salesman first recognizes where his buyer's area of concern is. Then he covers that base with as many insurances and guarantees as he can. In 1981 Chrysler's host of dealer salesmen began to turn their sick company around by selling cars with an extended warranty of five years. The fact that Chrysler might not be around in five years to make the warranty good never seemed to cross anyone's mind. Chairman Lee Iacocca was in fact combining the Safety Close with the Service Close. When a warranty is used as a close, it is safety that people are buying. Chrysler's salesmen used the Safety Close very effectively. Safety can also be mated effectively with integrity. The buyer's fear of misrepresentation or a below-quality product can be relieved by combining the Safety Close and Integrity Close Number One.

"You know our company, Mr. Zimmerman, and you know me. I can guarantee you that each of the pinnings will be to your exact tolerance and delivered on time. If you'll sign right here and let me borrow your secretary for a few minutes, I'll dictate an amendment to this contract that provides for a penalty clause to our company if we don't keep our word."

The trick in using the Safety Close is to find out what your customer is afraid of and then give him whatever reassurance or guarantees it takes to close the sale. But be careful to stay away from guarantees that you can't fulfill. If a man is afraid that his wife won't like the color of the automobile you are trying to sell him, it's awfully hard to guarantee him she will and still maintain credibility.

The concerns that lend themselves to the Safety Close are ones that are measurable—delivery date, quality of product, and the like. Thus you can use representations and guarantees of specific quality and specific dates to close the sale. Guarantees of increased productivity from new equipment are dangerous, because the competence of the operator is the determining factor, regardless of how good the equipment is. The customer is aware of that if he's half awake. So when you use the Safety Close, remember that the primary element must be the believability of your guarantees.

The Substitution Close

The Substitution Close is known in the district attorney's office as the old "bait and switch" technique. For years con artists have baited people with a valuable product and switched them to a worthless one at the time of delivery. So the Substitution Close has a bad reputation. But a legitimate application of the Substitution Close is to nail down the sale by giving the buyer *more* than he asked for. This is "bait and switch" in reverse.

"If you will agree to my proposal, Mr. Hemphil, I will substitute an ad that specifically features your stores for our normal advertising in the Eastern Region during the three months preceding the Christmas season."

One enterprising Advocate Salesman for a major seminar company sold his buyers on the need for a certain type of training without ever mentioning who would lead the seminar. The salesman was selling need, not the seminar leader's personality. When an ambivalent buyer was moving toward positive action, the salesman would try to hurry the process by telling the buyer that if he would block out a certain week for the seminar, he could guarantee that the Old Man himself would lead it. Naturally the salesman checked on the chairman's availability before making the commitment. To be effective, the Substitution Close must always offer some benefit to the customer.

The Substitution Close is basically holding the best for last, giving something to the customer you had planned on giving him anyway, but that he didn't expect. And remember, if you wrap up the sale early on another close, you don't have to give the customer your goody unless you really want to.

The Substitution Close always appeals to a buyer motivated by need or a buyer motivated by greed. The former is always pleasantly surprised to receive something he needs or can use as an unexpected gift. The latter is always pleasantly surprised to receive any gift whether he needs it or not. Money-driven buyers are particularly vulnerable to the Substitution Close. Identity and power-driven buyers are not, unless the substitution somehow satisfies their need for identity and power. If the substitution brings self-approval, approval of others, or safety to a buyer who is so motivated, it will work. Make sure that your substitution has a benefit that appeals to your buyer's particular motivation.

One salesman learned this lesson the hard way. He attempted to close his sale by offering to package his products to a wholesaler in a particularly attractive and expensive layout that had a proven ability to stand out on display and attract customers. After his close flopped, he learned that his buyer intended to sell his product by direct mail and would probably have to take the product out of the package before shipping to hold down delivery costs. However, a nice thing about the Substitution Close is that "it's the thought that counts." Even though the wholesaler could not use the package the salesman was offering, he appreciated the offer. In fact, this new information allowed the salesman to find the right Substitution Close—after a quick call to his home office. The wholesaler's product could indeed be packaged in a lightweight but durable container that lent itself to postal delivery. So the salesman recovered his earlier failure by finding something that had real benefit for his buyer.

The Personal Greed Close

The Personal Greed Close shares many of the same elements as other closes that rely on greed as a motivator. But there is a subtle and important difference. Professional managers of corporations spend millions of dollars to satisfy the need and sometimes greed of the corporation they serve. Yet there is nothing really in it for them. What can a salesman offer to benefit the manager personally? We're not talking here about favors under the table. Nor are we talking about tickets to the ballgame or a paid vacation for the buyer's family. These are nothing more than socially acceptable forms of bribery. We're talking about finding some benefit that can *legitimately* be tied to the sale for your particular buyer.

One manufacturer whose plant was located in the Sun Belt annually held a two-day workshop that covered all the product engineering designs and changes plus a demonstration of future technology. The company picked up the tab for the airfare and hotel and conveniently scheduled the meeting for Thursday and Friday. Any buyer who chose to remain over the weekend paid his own out-of-pocket expenses. Most did. The airfare and hotel charge were legitimate expenses for the manufacturer. By accepting the offer to attend the workshop, the buyers were acknowledging a special relationship with this manufacturer. The company now had a two-day captive audience to sell, sell, sell. And the buyers had every opportunity to ask the design and engineering people the penetrating technical questions the salesmen usually cannot answer. The buyers had a superb opportunity to put the manufacturer's products under close scrutiny, which was a legitimate benefit to their employer. That's the key to using the Personal Greed Close. Make sure that your *buyer* wins, make sure that *his employer* wins, and make sure that *you* win. If only your buyer wins, what you've offered is probably nothing more than a bribe. And it's absolutely a bribe if his employer loses as a result of the transaction you've closed.

One enterprising tire dealer was trying to gain the replacement business of a major corporation with a fleet of over 300 company cars. He finally closed the deal by making a bet with the purchaser. If the dealer could *prove* that his tires achieved a minimum of 25 percent less wear, would the buyer give him the business? The buyer agreed. As a measurement vehicle, the dealer offered to mount tires on the buyer's car and on three automobiles in the fleet that were driven the most for a period of six months. He would do this for free. The test was on. At the end of six months the dealer got the order. If he had simply tried to bribe his buyer with a new set of tires, he probably would have been thrown out of the building. Again, in this case the buyer won, his employer won, and the dealer won a major account. The Personal Greed Close is the only close that must have a win for everybody in order to be ethical.

The Hero Close

Like the Personal Greed Close, the Hero Close assumes that a lot of professional managers are working diligently making purchases for the corporation in return for simply a paycheck. It's the wise salesman who can add to the manager's rewards. Not financially—just make a hero out of him so he can get a deserving pat on the head! That's what he is really working for. Otherwise he'd be in business for himself.

When George Bordeaux closed a deal for an institutional food service contract, he would invariably schedule a dinner at his company's expense for all the top executives of his new client. He would hold it in the executive dining room. When he had everybody's attention, George would run through a list of all the problems, dangers, and concerns that were associated with implementing this fine new food service. All of this after an excellent meal. George purposely picked some areas of risk that only he knew about, so he gained everybody's attention immediately. He then told them about some risks they had taken that they didn't know about.

George, quite legitimately, went on to give credit for the solution to these problems to the buyer who had worked the hardest for him as an internal sponsor. Sometimes the buyer himself was not fully aware of the impact of the risks that he and George had taken, but that didn't matter now. George was careful to give him credit only for the problems that he actually solved. The man's esteem with his colleagues naturally went up, and George had nothing to lose. Had something gone awry during the implementation of the new system, George would have taken the responsibility himself and not blamed his sponsor. But now that the plan had gone right and George had his commission in his pocket, it didn't hurt anyone a bit to give credit where credit was due. Situations like that can be structured beforehand. More important, once word got around about George's generosity in sharing the glory, other buyers in other plants began to call his company and ask specifically for George to call them back.

To be effective, the Hero Close must place the buyer in a situation where he has a chance to look good. If there are risks involved, the customer should be told about them. But remember, the risks should not be stressed any more than the benefits. The buyer is a big boy too.

One worldwide organizational development and training firm with its headquarters in Europe decided to put a lid on its soaring payroll costs by licensing the delivery of its program to someone from the customer's Training Department. This was considerably cheaper than maintaining a large salaried staff to deliver the program. "Slack time" would be paid by the customer.

This initiative was a total flop at first. But then it took off like a rocket. What changed was that the company's enterprising sales force turned what at first appeared to be a disadvantage to the customer's Training Department into an advantage by selling the fact that the selected course leader would be a very "special" person. He would receive special training. By virtue of the fact that he was teaching management development to the customer's top people, the course leader would have intimate exposure to solving the problems of top brass. In addition, the course leader would serve as a consultant for special problems that were within the expertise of the management development company. What had originally been perceived by training personnel as an additional workload was now perceived as an opportunity to shortcut that long, hard path to success.

As a result of the adroit use of the Hero Close, this firm was able to maintain an artificially high price for the training of licensed instructors. In a few short years it had over 2,000 instructors worldwide who were, in effect, working for them but who were on their customers' payroll. All the organizational development firm had to do now was ship the licensed instructor his materials. Because the instructor's own career was intertwined with the licensing firm, he made sure that his program was the very last one cut from the budget in hard times. With such a captive audience, the licensing firm was able to increase the cost of materials regularly and to package them in minimum-purchase units. Not a bad end result from the mere application of the Hero Close. The Advocate Salesman who got the licensing alternative moving in the first place knew that his buyers were going to spend their training budget somewhere, and he knew that his company's program was very well respected. So once need for his company's program was clearly established with his Economic and Feasibility Buyers, he simply closed each deal by showing his Implementive Buyer how he and his department could become heroes.

In another application of the Hero Close, an adroit Advocate Salesman landed a deal with a major Fortune 500 company to assess its telephone bills over the last five years and recover any overpayments he could find. He did this by showing his buyer copies of successes he had achieved for other companies of equal size that had been written up in the companies' internal newsletters. Naturally, each article included substantial mention of his buyer's wisdom, guidance, and contribution to the success of the project.

These newsletter reprints were very potent. First of all, they gave the salesman's story credibility. Second, they helped the salesman close the deal since the implication was that new buyers would be given similar credits.

Interestingly enough, it took very little effort and even less time to have those stories printed. Almost every company has an internal newsletter. Every Personnel Department is responsible for it. It is often dull. Its one saving grace is that the chairman reads it. Personnel is a world of Waiters and Watchers. As a consequence, when the salesman approached these people with a success story that had real, solid meat in it—and also agreed to write most of it for them—they jumped at the chance and returned the favor by displaying the article prominently on the front page of the newsletter. There was something in it for everybody, including the chairman. He got to read something interesting for a change.

The Imminent Change Close

The Imminent Change is a cute little close. It is particularly effective when a buyer is recalcitrant. You know he wants what you are selling but you just can't force a yes out of his mouth. By describing a change that is imminent which will negatively affect either the deal you are talking about or the results it is designed to achieve, you can force a time frame for action on a natural procrastinator.

Product design and technology change all the time. An imminent change in your product that will eliminate or change benefits and features may be all that it takes to motivate your buyer. Remember, people resist change even when they aren't happy with the way things are. Fear of the unknown works very well with the Imminent Change Close. Delivery time and shipment costs are rapidly changing variables that a salesman has to contend with during a sale. A quick check with the home office will allow you to truthfully tell a customer that a longer delivery time is anticipated for orders not in by the end of the quarter.

The Imminent Change Close is also useful for selling future deliveries. One freshman salesman learned the hard way that his company always limited production runs on new products. In his second year, he was the first to book advanced orders for these introductory products. He would truthfully explain to his customers that when the product was formally announced, they probably wouldn't be able to receive shipment until after the second production run—months into the future. He didn't tell them, nor was he ethically required to tell them, that the reason they probably wouldn't be able to obtain any of the new products if they waited for the formal announcement was that he had successfully presold a backlog of the entire first run's production. The funny thing was that it took years for his own company to catch on and increase the size of the first run, in spite of the fact that he had made that recommendation hundreds of times to everyone who would listen. Manufacturing ruled in his company.

The secret of using the Imminent Change Close successfully is to recognize that people resist change. Whenever you so much as mention the word "change"—and be sure that you do when making the close—you will have people's attention. Before the crash of the 1980s real estate salesmen used the Imminent Change Close with great glee and satisfaction. "If you don't want to put a binder on the house, I can't guarantee that it will be available tomorrow because I have two other people interested in making an offer." The buyer now fears he will suffer a loss. He doesn't yet possess the house but he thinks he would like to. Therefore the house is three-quarters his in his mind. The threat of somebody else buying his house is almost an insult and an invasion. His impulses say "buy," and he reacts.

The retail salesman who closes a deal for an expensive suit by truthfully explaining that the fitter will be taking his vacation shortly is applying the same kind of pressure. The impending absence of the fitter causes the customer to feel a sense of loss at not being able to get his suit right away, which goes back to that primeval instinct of possession. Once we acquire something it becomes ours. Once it is ours, we want possession of it instantly. An impending event that would deny us possession of something rightfully ours stirs action cells in the old part of our brain that recalls images of scavengers stealing away with our hard-won prey.

There can be only one summary to this chapter: Use each of these closes wisely!

CONCEPT 12

Controlling the Buyer's Decision

Executive decision making has been a subject of endless research. The great risk of making a bad decision in the world of huge corporate expenditures has given the behavioralists a fertile laboratory for their studies. Ever since the Japanese began beating the pants off American businessmen in the 1970s with their "quality circles," no new breakthrough texts on the subject have been written. But for the dedicated student, some of the original works are still available.*

Remember, such lofty research into the fine tuning that supposedly goes on in a potential buyer's mind is useful only to the Pavlovians who wish to experiment and then criticize each other's reports in depth. Nowadays the gurus are all learning to read Japanese! Yet they still refuse to admit that selling involves managing the buyer's *emotional process*, not his *logical process*. That's why selling is still an art. It's also why salesmen tend to refer to gurus as goofies. Oh well!

Opinions aside, a sale does ask for some decision, so the decision-making process cannot be ignored. Unfortunately, the behavioralists have limited their analysis of the decision-making process to one used by the buyer to evaluate product alternatives. They have not yet formally devised one for the salesman who seeks to control the buyer's decision! Of the lot, Kepner-Tregoe, Inc. (Princeton, New Jersey) has possibly the best practical decision-making process that can be adapted

* For example, *New Decision Making Tools for Managers*, Edward C. Bursk and John F. Chapman, eds. Cambridge, Mass.: Harvard University Press, 1963.

by a hotshot Advocate Salesman who is interested in commissions rather than academic theory.

Kepner-Tregoe's system dictates that the buyer making a decision should first distinguish the objectives of the decision from the results to be produced and the resources to be used. The second step is to classify those objectives into what he must have (delivery within 10 days) and wants to have (delivery in less than 10 days). From there the buyer generates alternatives, courses of action, and/or products that meet those objectives. The third step is setting up a complicated "compare and choose" matrix, and assigning weights to the various alternatives.

This system is all well and good for the purchasing agent whose life is dedicated to buying something, but it is totally unnecessary for the salesman who is trying to sell something. The salesman has only one alternative—his product! Therefore he needs to pay attention only to the objective-setting portion of his buyer's decision-making process—and to a concept called adverse consequences, as we will see below.

Why help the customer set his objectives? Because in doing so you are helping him build a set of specifications that will directly benefit your sale. A product is an alternative to achieve a set of objectives. If you help him build the specs, you can bet that your alternative is going to be the one chosen. Your product will be the only one that fits the specifications.

What results does the buyer want to achieve from your product? What is the gain to him? What is the benefit to his organization? What problems does it correct? How soon *can* he expect results? How soon *must* he expect results? How is he going to justify altering the status quo? These are all *result objectives*.

Your product costs money and will alter the status quo. Thus the buyer must consider the impact of buying your product on his resources. What will his return on investment be? How does the cost affect his cash flow? What impact will buying your product have on his employees, his facilities, his equipment? How much time will it take to integrate the product or service you are trying to sell into the organization?

A practical application of this type of analysis is given below. It is followed by an expert's detailed description of how one organization built a formidable and highly successful worldwide sales force by melding the concepts of advocate selling with those of management decision analysis.

George Bordeaux was a salesman in the industrial food service business. George learned that most of his competitors were Relationship Salesmen who would gladhand the personnel director in charge of the plant's food catering service and reiterate over and over how much money it was costing their company to produce such high-quality food at such a low cost. They expected that cost and their winning personality would be justification enough for retaining the contract.

After selling an appointment with the plant manager (the Economic Buyer), who controlled the division's resources, George asked him simply what benefit he would most like to receive from George's industrial food catering service. The plant manager unequivocally replied that he would like to see a service in his plant that the union did not complain about. Noting that, George asked for permission to see the vice president of labor relations (the Feasibility Buyer). The plant manager gladly agreed.

George repeated his conversation with the plant manager to the VP of labor relations. (Note, of course, that he now had the motivators of both safety and the approval of others going for him as a result of his introduction by the plant manager.) Shrewdly, he pursued the VP's own objectives rather than try to close the sale then and there. Why? Because a new food service is a change of major impact and requires a consensus among the chain of beneficiaries. George used a minisale to close each buyer against his own set of objectives and to set the stage for a "next step" minisale.

When George asked the vice president of labor relations the same question about benefits that he had asked the plant manager, the VP cited very specific objectives. He wanted an industrial food service that "kept prices reasonable rather than low, but offered flexibility to provide the same service on all three shifts."

With that ammunition, George asked the vice president of labor relations to have the director of personnel (who would have to live with any change directly, as the Implementive Buyer) arrange a meeting with the union steward (the end user) at the plant. He politely explained to the VP that the request would have more impact if it came from him. George added that he would first like to meet with the personnel director to ascertain his objectives before meeting with the union.

He successfully closed on the next step, and the vice president picked up the phone.

The meeting went smoothly. After all, the personnel director was well aware that his boss and his boss's boss had an interest in change. Personnel's specific objectives were to make sure that the company's rebate from gross vending sales was enough to maintain the Christmas party and employees' bowling league, both under his direct control. George was a pro. He tantalized the director by suggesting that a summer picnic might also be feasible, so now there was something for everybody. But the union, as the end user of the service, had different ideas.

The union, it turned out, didn't care about the Christmas party or a picnic. What it was primarily interested in was 24-hour-a-day service and high-quality food. Some lip service was paid toward the price of food, but much to the surprise of the director of personnel (but not the vice president of labor relations) the union recognized the need to give on price if quality was assured and the service was equal across all three shifts.

George's next minisale was to set up a meeting with management to review a preliminary proposal. He then set up a meeting with management and labor representatives to review a final, formal proposal. By keeping his buyers focused on objectives, and by helping them build their own set of specifications, George was able to say later that no one at any time ever brought up the subject of a bid, which is the way most food service contracts are let.

Essentially what George Bordeaux did was to establish everybody's individual objectives, package them, and present them to the group. The plant manager wanted a service about which the union did not complain. A service that generates no complaints is a very general objective, but the union is a very specific target. More important, the objective is measurable. The plant manager wasn't really concerned whether anybody else complained. He just wanted the union happy.

As George progressed further down the chain of beneficiaries, the objectives became more specific. The vice president of labor relations agreed with the plant manager's objectives. But he also had the specific objective of keeping prices reasonable rather than low in order to make equal service available on all three shifts.

"Reasonable" and "low" are relative and unmeasurable terms. As noted earlier, right is always relative to a particular point of view and usually sides with the victor after the fact. However, the vice president of labor relations did give George one very measurable objective. He wanted the same service on all three shifts.

The union was not a buyer of George's services. But as a *very* powerful end user, it might well have been. The only reason the union was not allowed to pick and choose the food service it wanted was that management stubbornly refused to relinquish control of anything to the union unless it was forced to. The plant manager (George's Economic Buyer) had been right, as had the VP of labor relations (George's Feasibility Buyer). The union people were interested in a high-quality food service—and they meant *equal quality* across all shifts. So when George analyzed the different objectives of his main buyers and other critical links in the chain of beneficiaries, he found a common ground—for everyone except the director of personnel (George's Implementive Buyer).

George knew that most of his Relationship Salesmen competitors had been wining and dining the director of personnel. As the person in charge of implementing food service in the plant, he was the pivot man and a target for all his competitors' wooing. George was almost certain he had the contract sewed up anyway. But he was too smart a player to count his money while he was still at the table. George knew that something could go wrong. Instead of barreling along as his competitors might have done in his place, George put all the horsepower he could muster into anticipating objections, second thoughts, and problems that could be raised by buyers in the chain of beneficiaries. George knew, for example, that the director of personnel wasn't really neutral at all, although he pretended to be.

George spent many days putting himself in the place of his buyers and asking himself, "If I were any one of them, what would be my concern about changing industrial food services? What could go wrong?"

Selling "What Can Go Wrong"

The last and possibly most useful selling tool in Kepner-Tregoe's decision-making process is the concept of adverse consequences. In the nonacademic world, it's called selling "what can go wrong."

Assessing adverse consequences involves anticipating what can go wrong and taking two types of action: preventive or contingent. Fire hydrants are not preventive. They are contingent. They need a fire before they are useful. The same with fire insurance. On the other hand, "No Smoking" signs, fireproof materials, and low oxygen levels are all preventive factors. The idea behind selling is to anticipate basic customer objections and what can go wrong, and then provide the rebuttal to each objection in your main presentation. By raising problem questions and answering them rhetorically, you will preempt the nay-sayers.

Another name for this concept is risk analysis. Assessing the danger of proceeding with a particular decision minimizes the second-guessing that is bound to occur in any sale. The most successful salesman may think he has everybody thinking positively, but he can count on the fact that at some time during a meeting some nay-sayer within the organization will raise his hand and start asking "what if" questions. The nay-sayer is wrong 90 percent of the time, but the 10 percent of the time he's right guarantees his job. Remember the Edsel? The guy who said "It won't fly" is the only one who still has his job.

Using "what can go wrong" as a selling tool assumes that, left to their own devices, buyers will sooner or later get together to shoot holes in your proposal. Armed with this knowledge, you can control the situation. You should, in fact, be the one to insist that such a meeting occur. Then it's time for the reverse sell and close.

"Before I let you change food service contracts," George Bordeaux told his surprised buyers, "and possibly get us all in a mess, let's take a look at what could go wrong."

George had been helping his buyers set objectives for an industrial food catering service. As a minisale, George had previously set up a meeting for management to review what amounted to an *informal* proposal for change in the plant food service. In fact, he had spent long hours on this proposal, which most salesmen would have made as their *formal* presentation, skipping the risk analysis step. But then most salesmen aren't nearly as successful as George. Using "what can go wrong" to assess risk is one of the primary reasons why.

George paid close attention to the management people in

attendance. The Doers tended to be positive. It was the Waiters and Watchers he was concerned about. The vice president of labor relations was more of a Waiter than a Doer, and this was quite natural. His job was reactive. As long as things went well, his job was a breeze. The director of personnel was a real worry. He was a Watcher. In addition, there were three new people present from the personnel staff whom George had never met.

Small talk allowed George to evaluate the newcomers. He began the meeting by reviewing all the objectives he had gathered from the plant manager, the vice president of labor relations, and the personnel director. But instead of going on, he asked each of the three newcomers from personnel what benefits they would like to see accrue from a change in the industrial food service. They had nothing new to add (particularly in view of their high-powered surroundings). Nonetheless, George was sharp enough to recognize that "everybody likes to be asked." He thereby folded them right into the decision-making process he had already established.

The meeting went smoothly except for one issue—price. It was a major concern to all the attendees. Although the union steward had indicated that "reasonable" prices would be acceptable, nobody had any idea of what "reasonable" meant in real dollars. This led George to formulate a new minisale that he hadn't planned on. George asked permission to check food prices at various restaurants and diners surrounding the plant. From these data he would prepare a price comparison of restaurant food versus plant cafeteria food for the formal presentation scheduled for the following week.

George didn't really have to obtain permission to check prices at surrounding restaurants. But as a salesman aware that a consensus was needed to close his sale, George simply wanted to involve everybody in the decision and to *keep control* of everything that was critical.

With everybody on board, the formal meeting was a total success. In fact, George found that the union was more than willing to trade off increased prices for real increased service, so he never even had to use his comparative price chart. All the union really wanted was to make enough noise to assure that everybody understood quality of service was the primary issue and was not to be compromised.

In formulating his sales strategy, George had correctly identified the director of personnel as his enemy. It was not surprising that the director tried to load the meeting with three new people from his department in an attempt to overcome his one-voice, one-vote position. He knew he was in the minority. George's proposal was looked on favorably by everybody else. By anticipating this problem and by anticipating the way his antagonists might present their objections, George was able to defuse the bomb before it went off. In fact, George's tactic of involving everybody in the decision-making process, including the newcomers from personnel, won them to his side. Let's face it, it was their boss, the director of personnel, who had been going out to lunch with George's competitors. They had slaved away doing both their job and his while he was absent. George had isolated his enemy and left him stranded. The director had no choice but to go along.

There are people in the world who have raised selling to a fine art by melding advocate selling with decision analysis. Alan Jay Weiss is one of those people. Alan is currently vice president of Kepner-Tregoe, Inc., the high priests of executive decision making. Previously Alan was responsible for sales in North America and contributed to maintaining Kepner-Tregoe's highly effective, highly successful worldwide sales organization. His analysis of the process follows.

Using the Decision-making Process in Selling

Once upon a time a famous dog food company decided to increase its market share through the addition of a new product. The new product was introduced and disseminated with all the care and fanfare one would expect from a high-powered, product-driven company. Three months after release, the new product had not caught on. In fact, it had actually eroded the market share of the company.

The chairman of the dog food company was a crusty, shoot-from-the-hip, torpedoes-be-damned kind of guy. He convened a meeting of his top managers and aides to find out what had gone wrong. A group of management interns attended this top-level session as part of their training.

"All right, who has some answers?" roared the chairman. As might be expected, he immediately lost eye contact with everyone. So again he bellowed, "How did this happen?"

After a deathly silence that seemed to take years but actually lasted just 30 seconds, the vice president of advertising got to his feet. He was married to the chairman's niece, and thus figured he had slightly more job security than the others. "J.B.," he stammered, "this ad campaign was a work of art. It won awards in the advertising community for its inventiveness and consumer orientation. Whatever the problem, it was not the advertising."

Emotionally spent, the ad VP dropped to his seat. Taking his cue, the marketing executive took the floor. "We spent $400,000 on preliminary research for the new food," he explained. "Every independent source, every retailer, and all our own people felt it was the right food at the right time. The demographics were perfect. Marketing could not have been at fault."

Seeing the guns firing around him, the product manager stood up. "May I add, sir, that we employed 16 scientists, 11 nutritionists, and 6 biochemists for six months on the development of our new food? It met and exceeded every government requirement for dog food and contained not a single harmful element. It is hard to see," he concluded, "how the product is at fault."

"Well, fine. If it's not the product, nor its marketing, nor its promotion," implored the chairman, "what exactly *is* the problem?"

With that, a hand waved unsteadily aloft along the far wall. Attached to it was a frail management intern, with the company for three weeks, who now appeared to wither under the chairman's glare.

"Yes, what is it?" yelled the chairman, as if expecting a request to use the rest room.

"I believe I know the reason for the lack of sales of the new food," whispered the youngster.

"At last," shouted the chairman. "Well, come on, what is it?"

"Well, sir," the intern explained, "the dogs just won't eat the stuff."

Tailoring Alternatives

Apocryphal? Not really. The same thing is going on every day in companies large and small, and among salespeople selling everything from earth movers to erasers. The company in this story had sold itself. It had made a decision *as if it were the buyer.* It never really looked at the actual buyer's main concern: Will my dog eat this stuff? No matter what the price, no matter what the nutrition, no matter how conveniently it is packaged, and no matter how many ads besiege the buyer, the product is doomed if the dog won't eat it.

In any sales situation, there is a strong tendency to sell yourself on the benefits of your alternative and assume that the buyer's objectives will be the same as yours. Ford did it with the Edsel. GE did it with computers. NBC did it with *My Mother, The Car.* Braniff did it with a proliferating route structure. These companies, and hundreds of others like them, had fine talent and superb brains on board. If they can make such mistakes, can't you? In a minute!

When you take an advocacy position, it is paramount to make your alternative fit the buyer's objectives. And make no mistake about it, as much as you feel you are selling to need, you are selling to a very sharply defined, highly discrete need: the need that can be answered with *your* product or service. How many salespeople sell purely to need without application and then eventually have to back off? "Sorry, Mr. Davis, but as I've drawn out your need I've begun to see that nothing in my particular bag of tricks will meet it. So rather than have you buy something that won't really do the job, why don't we end it right here? Thanks for your time." You can count on one knuckle the number of successful people who do this. They've already qualified the prospect sufficiently to know that there's a fit of some kind between the customer's inevitable needs and the alternative being espoused. And that's enough.

So the trick is to "manage" the prospect so that he recognizes and verbalizes needs that you know are perfect for one of your alternatives. Perhaps an historical example is in order.

During the Civil War, a brash young Napolecn of a general shot into the sky like a comet. His name was George B. McClellan. (In 1864 he was to run for President against Lincoln.) He rose to become Commander-in-Chief of the Army of the Potomac, the largest Union force in the war, and the one facing Robert E. Lee. Yet McClellan had no substantial military achievements. He had never led large numbers of troops in battle. He had not even served with distinction in previous Civil War battles. But McClellan did have one strong ability: He understood what he had to offer and was able to convince Abraham Lincoln that this was exactly what the President needed. George B. McClellan was superb at knowing how to make up the other guy's mind. McClellan was an excellent salesman, even though he didn't have much of a product.

At the time, the Union had suffered a string of unbroken defeats. Lincoln had gone through several inept generals in search of someone who could, quite simply, take the Union forces and do what needed to be done—defeat Lee's Army of Northern Virginia. McClellan had no real plan to do that. But he did have assets to sell. He sold himself as the master of military strategy and discipline. He quoted Clausewitz. He cited Frederick the Great. He held maneuvers. He dressed his troops like soldiers and developed them until they were spit-and-polish proficient on the drill field. He postured. He paraded. He accepted the repeated huzzahs of his men.

McClellan finally sold Lincoln—who, to say the least, was a pre-eminent authority on which people you can fool how much of the time—on the idea that what Lincoln needed was a professional soldier. And, of course, who was better suited for that than George B. McClellan? Lincoln never realized that his objectives had *changed* somewhat to fit this alternative. That was McClellan's real feat. McClellan made Lincoln lose sight of this. Rather, he focused Lincoln on the need for a "professional" soldier. He *sold* Lincoln that *need*. Lincoln thought he was buying what he wanted.

Events were to prove otherwise. McClellan was a disaster as a field leader. Not only did he sell Lincoln, he also sold himself on the idea that a professional soldier was sufficient to solve the problem. It took several more generals to fail in that position before Lincoln finally turned to Ulysses S. Grant, who had been winning battles almost from the outset in the West. Grant was a drinker off the field of battle, dressed like a prisoner of war, left discipline to others, and half the time enjoyed his greatest victories only after the enemy had completely surprised his forces. But, never mind, he knew how to use the strengths of the Union forces to defeat the Confederacy.

You know that when you meet a prospect, you have some alternatives to offer, one or more of which must be sold if you are to be successful. It is all well and good to speak of win/win situations for the seller and the prospective buyer, but the inescapable fact is that the salesman will either make the sale (win) or not make it (lose)! To put it another way, for the prospect to win, you must win first. Your alternative might be a line of cars, computer software, insurance, photography, or vacation sites, but it is something that is quite tangible for you and, presumably, something that you can support in words, pictures, and examples. In other words, you have sold *yourself* sufficiently to want to sell *others*.

Now the question arises of how to evaluate the buyers. What objectives are attractive to them? What needs do they want filled? If they've come to see you in the auto showroom, you know some of this. If you're pursuing them to sell insurance, you're not certain of anything. Moreover, you need to determine which of those needs and objectives you want to emphasize because they are appropriate for your alternative. A buyer might be seeking to enhance his self-image with a new car, but all you happen to sell are soft and cuddly fuel-efficient things that go from 0 to 60 in two days. Or a buyer might want to improve his disability insurance protection while you carry only life and casualty lines. So you need to unearth two sets of facts: (1) what objectives and needs your prospect wants met and (2) which of these needs you can fill with your alternative—or, how you might restate these needs so that your alternative becomes attractive. To do this, you must evaluate your buyer, and it is to that procedure that we will now turn.

A prospective buyer will be motivated to make a purchase by one of three things. That's right, three things. No mirrors, no tricks, no "ten secrets to million-dollar sales." Three things.

Motivation Number One: Rational Self-Interest
People will buy something because they honestly think that it will help them. This is the most effective motivation for buying because it

is internally generated, is usually long-lived (not dependent upon keeping a certain message or presence in front of the buyer), and is self-reinforcing if the purchase meets the buyer's expectations. People buy ice cream cones because they think they will like the taste. They did so in the past and liked the experience, so they feel the pleasure is worth the $1.25 it now requires.

In some cases the buyer has recognized this self-interest and is pursuing its fulfillment: "I need a fuel-efficient car to reduce my auto expenses and that's what's brought me into a place like yours. I'm going to buy the one that best meets this need."

In other cases, the buyer needs to be made aware of the need, and only then buys into it with a vengeance: "You mean an attic fan will actually keep my house cooler and allow me to reduce the air conditioning? If that's true, I'd certainly be interested. Let me see that *Consumer Reports* article you're citing."

People buying in light of their own perceived rational self-interest, whether for themselves or for their organizations, are usually direct and unequivocal. They like to examine ancillary benefits (since the primary one is so obvious). "Your car gets 36 miles per gallon and the tests I've seen validate that. Now tell me about its repair frequency. Can it pull a light trailer if required? Does it come with air bags?"

If a buyer comes to you, you can be pretty sure you're dealing with a rational self-interest buyer (though this can be deceptive—see Motivation Number Two). If you're not sure, you can evaluate whether your prospect is in this mode by asking a few questions:

"Have you ever thought of making such a purchase before? Why?"

"At this point, what advantages begin to emerge about this product or service?"

"How important is this purchase to you?"

"Have you had good experiences in this area in the past?"

Rational self-interest can also be created. However, it must be done properly. Telling a buyer that "everyone in your position has one" is not an appeal to rational self-interest. Telling him how your alternative will make his life better, as though you've been there yourself, *is* a good way. Many's the Advocate Salesman who, in his quest to determine what constitutes rational self-interest, says, "I don't know if you're like me, but I know that when I choose an investment vehicle I like to be as liquid as possible." If the answer is "Right," then you've discovered something. If the answer is, "My liquidity is well taken care of elsewhere," then regroup and seek self-interest in other areas. The phrase "if you're like me" is an ageless device for evoking honest replies about what really constitutes self-interest.

Motivation Number Two: Conformative Pressure

People often have an urge to buy because they want to belong to a certain group or to conform to a certain norm. A large portion of advertising is based on conformative pressure. Be part of the Pepsi generation. Be a Marlboro man. In general, be part of that "in" crowd that has determined the truly blessed qualities of Aunt Sophie's Marshmallow Soda. Everyone who drinks it looks fabulous, sings well, enjoys a great sex life, and bets the right way on the Superbowl.

A sale that features a lottery appeals to rational self-interest ("Maybe I can win money—I recall feeling pleasure in that experience"), but one that relies on "everybody doing it" brings the full weight of conformative pressure to bear. Adidas sporting goods comes to mind, as do most jeans commercials.

Conformative pressure is powerful but fickle. It lasts only as long as it lasts. If something goes out of style, or a more substantial conformative pressure is introduced, the original pressure will die. There is conformative pressure to drive a fairly new car, irrespective of self-interest objectives like mileage, safety, and muscle. But there is no conformative pressure to have vast amounts of insurance coverage.

Conformative buyers give themselves away when they ask questions like these:

"Is this the same one that others are using?"

"Is this the one I've heard about?"

"I'm interested in the one I've seen. . . ."

"What other kinds of people use this?"

Given the conformative buyers' objectives, the sales presentation should concentrate on the widespread popularity of the alternative. What, your alternative isn't widespread yet? Then position it as the coming thing, the wave of the future, the alternative that most bright, farsighted people are already exploring. Young people are usually more prone to be conformative buyers than older people, but don't be surprised at the high-powered executive who wants to know if it is *really* what they're using at IBM.

Reference selling and third-party endorsement can appeal to both the rational self-interest buyer and the conformative buyer. You can't be sure what the appeal really is until you test by making a sale or failing. And it's dangerous to assume that it is naturally one or the other.

There are those who argue that conformative buying is really a rational self-interest response, since the buyer is merely fulfilling a deep need by being part of the larger group. Stuff and nonsense. The real conformative buyer will often ignore his self-interest *to be part of the group.* Women who wear strappy sandals with thin, spiked heels bear silent and painful testimony to this fact. So do men who insist on having a boring, miserable time in the hotel bar rather than enjoying a good book alone in a room.

So if you find conformative pressure to buy, go for it. Remember that you need to create an identification with the group with which the individual wants to be a member. But also remember that conformative pressure is transitory, and you should act quickly and test the water each time. People stopped buying hoola hoops but they still buy frisbees. A case of one fad being inexplicably longer-lived than the other? Not on your life. The frisbee transcended the conformative pressure to own one and appealed to a genuine rational self-interest—it's damned fun to play with. Not so for the bizarre hoop.

Motivation Number Three: Coercion and Fear

As noted at the outset, there are only three things that motivate a potential buyer to become an actual buyer. The third thing is fear. Of course people will buy if they're bullied, intimidated, harassed, and hounded. But that's not what I'm talking about (though more and more lawyers are making a good living talking about it to the judge, so watch out). Rather, I'm referring to the fear of missing a good thing, the fear of *not* taking action, and the fear of rejecting something and being rejected in return.

The person who is buying out of fear often sounds like this:

"Are you sure this will take care of the problem?"

"I'll need some kind of guarantee."

"Oh, I think this is just what *they* are looking for."

"Will you show this to some other people for me?"

This person is not trying to choose an alternative for self-interest or to be part of the "in" crowd. Rather this person is afraid and is seeking assurance, protection, the ironclad thing. He might perceive his job to be on the line, he might know his self-esteem is on the line (again), or he might be unable to reject anyone with whom he has established a relationship—even a salesperson.

Fear buyers should be treated gingerly. They will either buy too quickly or not buy at all, because they tend to view everything in black and white. This is the solution, or it isn't.

Fear buyers have generally been ordered to secure something. Even if the order is only a mild request, they perceive it as an order. They are insecure about performing the deed. The request could have come from a superior, peer, social acquaintance, or spouse. Their motivation for buying can be fear of letting others down, fear of being mocked or ridiculed for the choice, fear of the seller, or fear of succeeding and being asked to "do this" repeatedly.

Compared to the other two types, fear buyers are the least common, but that is not to say they are uncommon. They can be encountered at any level in an organization. In dealing with a fear buyer, be careful not to intimidate the buyer. Many a quick sale is reversed when the face-to-face confrontation is over and a letter or secretary cancels the order. Instead, offer guarantees: "If anything goes wrong—not that it will—I'll personally help you with the installation. Moreover, here's our hot line, manned 24 hours a day by service people. It's almost a fail-safe system." Or: "Every small business of your type in this state is using these. Here's a list of the ones in your county alone. Who would dare question your purchasing a system used so widely in your industry?"

Attitudes, Knowledge, and Skills
Rational self-interest, conformative pressure, and fear. How do you position yourself to understand what is motivating a particular buyer? The following questions can help you make this determination:

QUESTION   Why are you looking into this kind of purchase?
Self-Interest: "Because I feel that I need it to improve my operation."
Conformative: "Because I've seen so many people using it."
Fear: "I was told that it would probably make sense for us to use this."

QUESTION   How will the final decision be made?
Self-Interest: "I'll make it, based on the way the alternatives meet my objectives."
Conformative: "I'll make it after I check with some people I trust."
Fear: "There will be several of us involved."

QUESTION   What is the most important quality you're seeking?
Self-Interest: "Return on my investment."
Conformative: "Acceptance of those who will deal with it."
Fear: "A guarantee of reliability."

QUESTION   How important is price?
Self-Interest: "That depends on the value I receive for a given price."
Conformative: "It would be the deciding factor if we agreed that all other aspects are equal."
Fear: "I'm not sure, though I don't think we'd want anything too extravagant."

QUESTION   How soon are you ready to act, especially if I can offer inducements for acting fast?
Self-Interest: "Immediately."
Conformative: "Fairly quickly—it will depend on a few schedules."
Fear: "Don't rush me—this is not the kind of thing that should be hurried."

QUESTION   Under what conditions might you delegate this decision?
Self-Interest: "If the alternatives are clear, I would give them, along with my objectives, to a trusted subordinate."

Conformative: "I would delegate to someone who knows me and what the team is looking for."

Fear: "It's already been delegated to me and I feel that I am now responsible for it."

QUESTION   If you bought my alternative, how would you know you had made the right choice?

Self-Interest: "If my operation were improved to the extent I expected over the time frame I had allowed."

Conformative: "If the feedback from the people using it was favorable and supportive."

Fear: "If there were no complaints and a minimum of disruption."

QUESTION   How would you prefer I make my presentation?

Self-Interest: "Keep it brief, concentrate on what you can do for me, and don't overwhelm me with trivial facts."

Conformative: "Let's get to know each other a bit, then we can talk over lunch. I'll need literature to circulate to others."

Fear: "I'd like a very thorough description of your work, then I'd like to talk on the phone after I've developed some questions."

Naturally, these responses may vary, and you may have more and better questions to ask. The questions should be worked into the conversation fairly early—perhaps even into the preliminary qualifying conversation—so that you can get a feel for the type of buyer you are facing.

Most important, you must make it a habit to build this effort into your initial sales contact. Then develop the skills for dealing with each type of buyer. After you do this repeatedly you will internalize the process and gain that "sixth sense" or "gut feel" about which many speak. *Remember, though, that no successful salesperson works by gut feel.* Such a salesman would soon die of starvation. However, there are salespeople who have internalized this process to the point where they "automatically" check for the buyer's motivation and adapt their presentation accordingly. These salesmen don't do it by magic. They have worked hard to learn where the buyer is *before* launching into an inflexible sales pitch. It's called strategizing the sale and choosing the best tactic.

If you accept the fact that salespeople can be classified into three categories—Need Salespeople, Relationship Salespeople, and Order Takers—you can begin to see the possibilities for success and failure, win and lose, with each of the buyers described above.

Need Salesmen who develop the skills of soliciting and "shaping" need early will have the best chance of success with the rational self-interest buyer *and* the fear buyer, since their needs are usually clear (albeit totally different). They will have the most trouble with the conformative buyer, whose need to belong is clear but whose need for a particular purchase is often vague. Also, Need Salesmen tend to be all business, zeroing in on need and responding to it. The conformative buyer usually needs to be coddled, and needs to *like* the salesperson. This takes time. But overall the Need Salesman is in good shape, especially if he keeps in mind that these different buyers are going to require substantially different time frames.

The Relationship Salesman is in the opposite position. He will readily establish rapport with the conformative buyer, since both are seeking comfortable, warm relationships. Many times this develops into the proverbial "drinking buddy" relationship, where the importance of retaining the relationship on *both* sides overshadows the quality of the product being sold and/or the payment terms of the buyer. Such relationships are not possible with the self-interest and fear buyers.

The Order Taker, of course, is in the worst shape of all. His best chance is with the self-interest buyer, because if the product is good enough the order will be "given." However, a more aggressive salesperson with an equal product will probably take the business, since this buyer wants to make a quick decision. Since no relationship is attempted, the conformative buyer won't see any payoff in dealing with the Order Taker, and the fear buyer seldom takes the initiative to contact an Order Taker to place an order. This requires much too much risk for the fear buyer to accept.

Risk

In considering the decision-making process of the buyer, be careful not to assume that you understand that process simply because you have sold yourself on the benefits of your product.

Life is a series of trade-offs and no alternatives are perfect. Even sliced bread leaves crumbs. The Garden of Eden probably had some rough spots too. So the odds are that your alternative isn't perfect either. No one will point that out to you more quickly than the prospective buyer. Therefore *you* should be even quicker. Never mention a benefit or attraction unless you are also aware of potential drawbacks, no matter how farfetched, and are prepared to offer mitigating actions. If you are trying to sell whole life insurance, for example, you know that the prospect will say that it's a poor savings device. You can successfully deal with this by pointing out in advance that the alternative isn't meant to be a savings device at all, but rather is meant to provide noncancelable, high-value insurance while also providing the owner with a loan option should events necessitate it. If you're selling swimming pools, you know that the prospect will raise the issue of maintaining it. You can counter this by pointing out that it's the perfect job for the buyer's teen-aged children, or by throwing in a maintenance contract "free."

These are the types of concerns which surface when the buyer is close to a buying decision and is seeking to stall or reject the purchase. You know you've done your homework well when the buyer says, "Gee, I can't think of anything else that would concern me."

Suppose that I'm trying to sell you a car. In my conversation I mention the points listed below. What possible objections am I attempting to defuse with these statements? (Answers appear below.)

Statements

"At 36 miles per gallon, it has a cruising range of better than 525 miles."

"The small spare is easier to handle, allows for more trunk room and better gas mileage."

"Are these your two children? This car will transport the four of you in comfort with great economy."

"The vinyl interior is almost impervious to stain and is washable with commercial detergents."

"You are seeing more and more of these on the road today, as people come to appreciate the compactness and economy."

"It adheres to every federal emission and safety standard and exceeds most. Like every other car you'll look at, it sacrifices some performance because of that."

Potential Objections Defused

"It has only a 15-gallon tank. Will that require excessive fuel stops?"

"I'm used to a full-sized spare tire. Is this dinky thing sufficient?"

"The back seat is clearly too small to transport adults for long periods. How often will this pose a problem?"

"The interior looks drab. How will I feel without leather or fabric on the seats?"

"The car is not very distinguished. What about my image—will I feel good about myself in this car?"

"The acceleration must be pretty bad. Can I live with that?"

Every buyer uses a similar decision-making process, though the objectives will vary and the alternatives will have different value to each individual buyer. Graphically, the system resembles a huge funnel, with which the buyer tries to eliminate alternatives that won't meet his needs.

The Decision-making Funnel

ALTERNATIVES

CRITICAL NEEDS

DESIRES

RISK

OBJECTIVES

Alternatives
discarded
due to:

Critical needs
not met

Critical needs met but
too few additional
benefits perceived by
buyer

Critical needs met and additional
benefits plentiful, but adverse
consequences outweigh benefits

The alternative with maximum
benefit *within* acceptable
risk limits

   The key steps, for you as the salesperson, are to (1) recognize that you have one of the alternatives about to enter the funnel; (2) position it so that it meets the prospect's critical needs; (3) inform the prospect of the additional benefits; and (4) anticipate and counter the risks perceived by the prospect.
   If you can do this you will be far ahead of the other salespeople

whose alternatives are also entering the funnel. And you can do it if you recognize what is motivating your buyer so that you can escort him through the decision-making process. This is advocate selling at its best. This is how to make up the other guy's mind. This is a sale.

Summing Up

The concepts of advocate selling are immensely flexible. This book describes various advocate concepts in detail. Mr. Weiss's application for his sales force focuses on three areas of motivation that are critical to the organizational development services that Kepner-Tregoe sells: (1) self-interest, (2) conformity, and (3) fear. These buying motivators are derived from (1) need, (2) approval of others, and (3) a combination of safety and fear—buying motivators identified earlier in the advocate selling process. They also accurately reflect the motivation of Doers, Waiters, and Watchers.

Every company has an established process for selling its product—otherwise it wouldn't be in business. Advocate selling is not designed to replace that process. On the contrary, it is designed to be melded into the selling process that an organization already sucessfully uses. The company's salesmen can continue to do well what they already do well. But they now have a set of additional tools that will enable them to produce those spectacular increases in sales that generate the commissions necessary to fulfill the great American dream: gaining a bigger piece of the pie. That's also the name of the game.

CONCEPT 13

Sales Strategy: What It Is and What It Means

Everybody talks about sales strategy and everybody talks about sales tactics. Nobody seems to know what a sales strategy is. Nobody seems to know what a sales tactic is. When you ask someone to define or compare and contrast the two, you are rewarded with embarrassed blank stares for your trouble. So before we get too deep into the differences between management strategy and sales strategy, let's go back to basics. According to the *Random House Dictionary*, "strategy" is defined as follows:

Strategy
1. generalship, the science or art of combining and employing the means of war in planning and directing large military movements and operations;
2. the use or an instance of using this science or art;
3. skillful use of a stratagem;
4. a plan, method, or series of maneuvers or stratagems for obtaining a specific goal or result: *a strategy for getting ahead in the world.*

General Patton worked for Eisenhower. He and Montgomery had a strategy for conquering North Africa. Eisenhower worked for Roosevelt and Churchill. He had a strategy for conquering Europe. Roosevelt and Churchill had a strategy for freeing the world. One man's strategy is merely a tactic for others on a higher conceptual level.

The definition of "tactics" is as follows:

Tactics
1. the art or science of disposing military or naval forces for battle and maneuvering them in battle;
2. the maneuvers themselves;
3. mode of procedure for gaining advantage or success.

Thank you again, academia. In the adversary arena in which we live, love, and function, the definition of a Sales Strategy is *what you are trying to achieve*. The definition of a Sales Tactic is *how well you do the things necessary to accomplish what you've set out to achieve*.

It would be very easy to dictate a whole list of recipe strategies that have no real meaning unless cause and effect is clearly understood. Recipe strategies are formulas. If the reason behind them is not clear, they would fail as soon as the environment in which they are designed to be used changed. So it is necessary for a salesman to understand why he must formulate a sales strategy in the first place. The reason is that companies themselves formulate management strategies and implement them. Some do it well. Some do it badly, but they all do it with boring regularity. Being able to understand how a buyer's management strategy is formulated will enable the Advocate Salesman to observe and deduce what that strategy is. The advantage of this priceless knowledge is that the salesman can gear his sales strategy in such a way that it does not come into conflict with his customer's management strategy. In fact, he can enhance his customer's management strategy if he perceives it correctly. Otherwise he may find himself in the ridiculous position of selling contrary to need. One salesman attempted to lease an automobile fleet to a major distribution company at a point when it was attempting to build assets and net worth by owning capital equipment. A few questions and a good guess would have saved that salesman time and embarrassment.

One reason corporate management strategy is vitally important to an Advocate Salesman is that every buyer is committed to it, whether he agrees with it or not. Corporate strategy is corporate policy. If your product or service conflicts, your presentation will be deflected as easily as a .22-caliber bullet off the turret of an M-60 tank. In order to formulate a sales strategy that will successfully penetrate corporate defenses, you must first understand how corporations formulate their own management strategies. This will help you understand how to approach the individual buyers whose approval is necessary within the organization you are trying to sell.

So before we examine the process of formulating sales strategy, let's examine how corporate buyers formulate their management strategy.

While Kepner-Tregoe has not made any changes in its basic process of rational problem solving, decision making, and planning, Dr. Benjamin B. Tregoe and his associate, John W. Zimmerman, have made significant strides in reducing the Kepner-Tregoe management strategy formulation to an easy-to-understand matrix that may standardize the process in American business and industry.* Tregoe and Zimmerman first invite members of top management to test their strategic IQ. The quiz is designed as a failure exercise to shock top executives and capture their attention. The questions provide an insight into the kinds of problems that Economic Buyers of any type or size of business are faced with on a day-to-day basis. This is critical for an Advocate Salesman to understand if he is to present Economic Buyers with solutions to problems at the correct conceptual level.

As you read each of the following questions, put yourself in the role of the Economic Buyer of your best account and try to answer the questions as he would. The best practice in the world is to begin thinking like your buyer. If you can think like him, you can anticipate him. If you can anticipate him, you can sell him.

Testing Your Strategic IQ

- Has top management consciously determined what it wants the organization to be—the nature and direction of the business—over the next few years?
- Do you know the details of your organization's strategy?
- Would each of the other key managers share the same vision of your organization's future strategic direction?
- Is your strategy sufficiently clear so you and the key managers around you can readily agree on what new products and markets your current strategy would include and exclude?
- Is your strategy used for making future product and market choices

* See Benjamin Tregoe and John Zimmerman, *Top Management Strategy: What Is It and How to Make It Work* (New York: Simon & Schuster, 1980).

(as opposed to making such choices solely on the basis of cost/
return analysis, manpower availability, skills required, and the
like)?
* Are your strategic deliberations held separately from your long-
range planning efforts?
* Is your future strategy clearly determining what you plan, project,
and budget (as opposed to your plans, projections, and budgets
determining your strategy)?
* Are your assumptions about the business environment used for setting strategy (as opposed to their being used mainly as a basis for
long-range planning projections)?
* Is your future strategy clearly determining your decisions relating
to acquisitions, capital appropriations, and new systems (as opposed
to such decisions determining your strategy)?
* Do your line divisions or business units have clear, stated strategies?
* Do these business-unit strategies state precisely how they support
your corporate strategy?
* Do your key staff departments have clear strategies and do they
state precisely how they support your corporate strategy?
* Do these staff department strategies fully support corporate and
business-unit strategies?
* Is the overall performance of your organization and its business
units reviewed on both strategic accomplishment and operating results?

The more questions to which you answered no, or could not firmly
answer yes, the more your company's strategy is in trouble. If you answered no to all, then you can probably hold last rites for strategy in
your organization. It is officially deceased.

You now have a little bit of knowledge about the kinds of
strategic management problems your buyers and prospects are
faced with. Whether your customer is Mitsubishi trying to accurately estimate the breadth and scope of the American market or the owner of three printing shops trying to decide
whether he should expand or contract his business in the near
economic future, the problems are the same.

But as someone once said, "A little bit of knowledge is dangerous." Knowing the kinds of questions your buyer is asking
himself in order to formulate strategy is not enough. You need
to know if he plans to do something with the answers. If he
does, you need to know what that something is.

Tregoe and Zimmerman go on to explain why a company
must do something about its management strategy. More im-

portant, they draw a very clear distinction between that much misused term "corporate planning" and the real formulation of management strategy. That definition will help you understand exactly how and where a successful sales strategy must interlock with a corporate management strategy in order to produce sales.

Strategic Thinking:
Key to Corporate Survival

Most companies face the future unprepared. Though long-range planning has saturated our corporate environment, it does not guarantee success. In our constantly changing environment, the key to corporate survival lies not so much in the quality of our long-range planning as in the clarity of our strategic thinking. To survive and flourish, organizations must face the future knowing *what* they want to be— strategic planning—as well as *how* to get there—long-range planning and operational decision making.

It is our thesis that strategy should provide a picture of the organization as it wants to look in the future. Strategy is vision. It is totally directed at what the organization *should* be rather than *how* the organization will get there. Unfortunately, the word "strategy" has been used rather casually in both management literature and the marketplace. In fact, it has assumed a variety of meanings, some of which confuse the "what" and "how" dimensions.

For example, strategy is sometimes called "strategic planning" and then is used indiscriminately with "long-range planning." Executives talk frequently about a "market strategy" or a "pricing strategy" when they really mean a plan to penetrate a market or a plan to keep prices competitive. Such "strategies" are really major operational decision points that presume an overall corporate or divisional strategy.

While not interested in legislating the meaning of the word strategy, we are interested in avoiding the confusion we have observed. For us, strategy has a very precise meaning, which we define as a *framework that guides those choices that determine the nature and direction of an organization.* These "choices" confront an organization every day. They include choices about an organization's products or services, the geographical markets and customer groups the organization serves, the organization's capabilities of supporting those products and markets, its growth and return, and its allocation of resources.

How these choices are made determines the nature of an organization. If they are made within the context of a strategic framework, the organization's direction is clearly under the control of the managers who develop that framework. If these choices are made in the absence of a strategic framework, you abdicate that control and run the risk of having a direction that is uncoordinated and in the hands of whoever is making these choices.

Since strategy sets direction, it must be formulated prior to long-range planning and the day-to-day decision making that flows from such planning. Failure to separate strategy formulation from planning and operations compromises corporate strategic thinking.

Clear strategy and effective operations are a winning combination, but with unclear strategy and ineffective operations, you are bound to be a loser. If strategy is clear but operations are ineffective, the result is uncertain—you may still win, but winning depends almost totally on your ability to predict and then be carried by the kindness of external forces such as the economy and competition, forces not generally known for their beneficence. Similarly, if operations are effective but the strategy is unclear, you may survive by being swept forward efficiently—but for how long?

The late W. T. Grant Company was a loser because it did not have a clear idea of what it should be in the future and had inadequate operational plans. The following commentaries from *Business Week* attest to Grant's lack of direction:

> Worse yet, early on Grant seemingly could not make up its mind what kind of store it was. "There was a lot of dissension within the company whether we should go the K Mart route or go after the Ward and Penney position," says a former executive. "Ed Staley and Lou Lustenberger were at loggerheads over the issue, with the upshot being we took a position between the two and that consequently stood for nothing."

In addition to its lack of direction, Grant's day-to-day results suffered from ineffective operations:

> From 1963 to 1973 Grant opened 612 stores and expanded 91 others, with the bulk of the increase starting in 1968 under the guidance of President Richard W. Mayer and Chairman Edward Staley. "The expansion program placed a great strain on the physical and human capability of the company to cope with the program," says Chairman James G. Kendrick. "These were 11 large stores—6 million to 7 million square feet per year—and the expansion of our management organization just did not match the expansion of our stores." Adds a former operations executive: "Our training program couldn't keep up with the explosion of stores, and it didn't take long for the mediocrity to begin to show."

On the other hand, Sears, Roebuck & Company is typical of a "winner." With a clear image of what it should be in the future, it has also been eminently successful in its operations. While Sears has had its share of trouble recently, over the years it has consistently demonstrated the ability to anticipate needed changes in direction and to organize quickly and efficiently in order to make those changes.

The majority of organizations probably fit in the middle. For example, many conglomerates are characterized by well-defined growth and financial objectives and ineffective operations. Such organizations tend to see themselves as diverse giants that provide a wide range of products and services. However, the carefully thought-out grand scheme has often been marred by poor operational planning, with resultant overexpansion and inability to manage.

The Swiss watch industry is typical. Superbly efficient at producing and marketing, the industry was overtaken by changes in technology. The Swiss watchmakers' strategy was inadequate to help them anticipate external threats to their survival.

In the United States, strong operations historically have been more important than clear strategic thinking. In the past, many U.S. organizations survived even when they lacked a clear sense of strategic direction. After all, with unlimited resources, skilled labor, and a large, homogeneous market, who needed to think much about what kind of a business they wanted to be in the future?

Now, however, with diminishing resources, world competition, and rising costs, even the most efficient operations may no longer survive the handicap of operating without a clear, strategic direction. Today's company must formulate a clear strategy from which effective operations flow.

Tregoe and Zimmerman clearly delineate the difference between long-range planning and true management strategy. They also show what can happen to organizations that mix the two. Tregoe and Zimmerman go on to explain several examples of their methodology that make the following questions self-evident. What is the *real* strategy of the organization? Therefore what specific actions should it take? What products should it buy? What products shouldn't it buy? What moves should it make? What moves shouldn't it make? Knowing the answers to these questions is very valuable sales intelligence. It allows you to anticipate your buyer and be in tune with him rather than mucking around trying to sell needs and objectives that fly in the face of the direction he has chosen or been told he will take. Remember, if your target company does have a management strategy, your buyer will have knowledge of what it is—at least the part that pertains to him. Well-formulated questions will elicit the answers you need. But in order to formulate the right questions, you need a better understanding of the management strategy formulation process. In the following, Tregoe and Zimmerman go into detail.

The "Driving Force": Key to Strategy

The key to developing a simple, clear, and useful statement of strategy lies in the concept of the "driving force." Our research has identified nine strategic areas that impact and influence the nature and direction of any organization. These nine areas can be grouped into three basic categories:

1. *Products/markets*
   Strategic area:
      Products offered
      Market needs
2. *Capabilities*
   Strategic area:
      Technology
      Production capability
      Method of sale
      Method of distribution
      Natural resources
3. *Results*
   Strategic area:
      Size/growth
      Return/profit

In every one of the 75 major organizations with which we have worked, we have found that one of the above nine areas can be identified as the *driving force*—the strategic area that is the primary determinant of the organization's products and markets. The driving force also determines the requirements of the organization's other strategic areas.

The following examples, taken from observations of the product and market actions of companies in various industries, further illustrate the concept of the driving force.

1. *Products offered.* The organization with products offered as its driving force will continue to produce products similar to those it has. New products will tend to be very similar to current products, and the organization will seek new markets where there is a need for its existing product line. Its capabilities will be directed toward the support of its basic products. For example, research and engineering would be devoted to product improvements rather than to the development of different kinds of products. The actions of the major automobile companies suggest that their driving force is "products offered."

2. *Market needs.* The organization whose driving force is market needs determines its products or services from needs in the markets

or market segments it serves. This organization will constantly look for new and different products to fill these market needs. It will also search for new or emerging needs in these markets. While its capabilities are directed to the support of its current markets and products, it is perfectly willing to acquire very different capabilities to introduce new kinds of products. The actions of major consumer products companies, such as Procter & Gamble, suggest that their driving force is "market needs."

3. *Production capability.* An organization is driven by production capability when it offers products or services that can be performed using its production know-how, equipment, and processes. Looking for economies of scale, it will focus on efficiencies in production, and any new products will utilize the same production know-how, equipment, and processes that produced the original products. The actions of commodity-based companies, such as many of those in the paper industry, suggest that their driving force is (or was) "production capability."

4. *Return/profit.* An organization driven by return/profit will have very specific return/profit targets that may be quite different from its current level of performance. These targets are the basis for developing or acquiring future products and/or markets. Such a driving force will frequently lead this organization into very different and unrelated products or markets as a means of achieving these return/profit objectives over time. The actions of certain conglomerates, such as ITT World Communications, suggest that their driving force is "return/profit."

On first thought many top managers see return/profit as their driving force because profit is equated with survival and is the key measure of continued success. Thus all companies have profit objectives by which to measure operations. Profit, however, is a driving force only if it is the primary determinant of the kinds of future products and markets that characterize an organization. But this is the case in very few companies.

There is no implication in the above examples that the driving force remains fixed. Changes in external events or the desires of top management can change an organization's driving force. A typical pattern of change is from "products offered" to "market needs." For example, this pattern is true for many of the consumer goods and services companies, such as Procter & Gamble, Gillette, Playboy Enterprises, and Merrill Lynch, Pierce, Fenner & Smith Inc.

Another common pattern is to shift from "production capability" to "products offered," a change that has characterized such companies as Kimberly-Clark and International Multifoods (formerly International Milling Company).

Four key reasons explain why the concept of driving force is critical to setting strategy:

- The essential nature of an organization is reflected in its products or services, the markets or customers it services, its capabilities to support these products and markets, and its growth and return. The driving force is the focal point for describing and integrating these key strategic elements.
- Top management discussions to arrive at a driving force bring to the surface issues that must be resolved if an organization is going to arrive at an effective strategy statement. An approach that allows top management to stop short of this will facilitate agreement, but will also result in a general statement of strategy that is no more useful than those previously illustrated.
- Every organization has a momentum that carries it in a certain direction. This momentum is generated by the driving force. Unless the driving force is recognized, attempts to change this direction will be futile. You must know *from what* you are changing. The driving force provides the basic means for thinking about alternative futures and what each might mean in terms of products, markets, capabilities, and return.
- The concept of driving force also has great value in tracking the competition. Since there generally is no way to know the stated strategy of your competitors, assuming they have one, simply observe their actions to determine their driving force and then project what their future courses of action might be.

Sales strategy is different from management strategy as defined by Tregoe and Zimmerman. There is no driving force in a sales strategy except to make the sale (that is, there is no strategic need to maintain any account relationship except to make a sale). Companies need to define themselves in order to know where to search for the business that fuels the organization. They need to know whether the organization will run smoothly on a particular type of business terrain. However, companies have the ability to change their nature and change their direction. They can also find different businesses with which to fuel themselves. Therefore they can make themselves an entirely different animal with the same logo. That's why companies diversify and mergers and conglomerates occur.

However, salesmen do not have that same luxury unless they change jobs or represent a different product line. So sales strategy is one conceptual level lower than the top management strategy outlined by Tregoe and Zimmerman. However, knowing or being able to guess the management strategy of a potential customer is invaluable to the salesman who is gathering data to formulate his own successful sales strategy in order to penetrate the organization and develop a lucrative customer relationship.

As easy, logical, and simple as Tregoe and Zimmerman's process sounds, it is important to note that the reason their book *Top Management Strategy* has been so well received in the marketplace is because most companies have a weak or incorrect process for formulating management strategy. That's why Tregoe and Zimmerman are in business. Some companies do not rigidly follow their management strategy. Many have a management strategy that is purposely reactive and flexible to take advantage of sudden opportunities—it is more of an operational plan that a strategy. The worst have a management strategy framed on the wall under the rubric "Basic Corporate Beliefs." Every two years someone reads it.

However, it is critical that the salesman understand the strategy of the organization *even if that strategy is squirrelly or incorrect.* It is not the salesman's job to pass judgment on the validity of a customer's management strategy. His job is to correctly ascertain what it is. Remember Dan Moran's boss? The old chairman had built one of the most powerful and successful sales forces in his industry. It was smooth, it was operational, and it was *very* profitable. However, the chairman maintained (with an iron fist, if need be) that his company's driving force was technology. The fact that no new technology had been developed for 25 years was beside the point. He insisted that his company's strategy was driven by its technological capabilities. In point of fact, the chairman was confusing real capabilities with potential capabilities. But like the 800-pound ape, he could confuse anything he wanted to, anywhere he pleased. His company's real capabilities were in selling and distributing a high-ticket intangible service. But anyone selling the chairman had a much better chance if he presented his product in a way that reinforced the chairman's legislated strategy that his company's driving force was technology.

Dan Moran was a master at telling the chairman what he wanted to hear. But Dan was a destructive internal salesman. There is absolutely no reason for an Advocate Salesman to misrepresent what his proposal will accomplish in order to make it more attractive. If his product does have particular benefits that relate directly to the company's strategy, those benefits should most certainly be highlighted even if they make up only a small portion of the total. Let's face it, once people make a decision,

they embrace everything and everybody who reinforces that decision. They also reject everything and everybody who contra-
dicts it, sometimes to the point of their own detriment. But
that's not the business of an Advocate Salesman trying to close
a sale.

The chairman truly believed that his company's driving
force lay in the area of technology. As a result, he diverted
much-needed resources away from developing and maintaining
the keen edge of his corporate sales force, his company's real
capability. His true driving force was "method of sale." Nevertheless, commission plans were eliminated and the sales force
deteriorated, and because no new technology was ever developed, the company's product rights fell into the public domain.
Competitors who recognized that the best driving force was
either "method of sale" or "method of distribution" began
cropping up everywhere. The chairman's company declined.

Tregoe and Zimmerman advise top managers to observe
their competitors' actions in order to determine their driving
force and thus anticipate what their competitors' future course
of action will be. Advocate Salesmen, through observation and a
few questions, can also correctly ascertain the driving force of
the organization they are attempting to sell. But be cautious.
Only the *real* driving force will become evident through observation. Top management may choose to delude itself, as Dan
Moran's chairman did. It is not your job, nor will it benefit you,
to pass judgment on the difference. Again, data-gathering
questions will enable you to decide whether to sell to the company's real management strategy or its *perceived* management
strategy. Don't be self-righteous. Yours is not to wonder why;
yours is but to sell or die. If your buyer thinks he's Napoleon,
sell him a tricornered hat so at least he can look like what he
thinks he is. In such cases, accept only cash.

The major distinctions between sales strategy and management strategy lie in scope. Sales strategy is essentially an "attack" strategy. Your target is the company or prospect to whom
you want to sell something. A good strategy devolves into a series of optional approaches, or tactics. Your sales strategy is
directed at the results you want to achieve by selling the account. The tactics you use are the various methods by which
you can achieve these results.

Sales strategy does not have to be limited to major corporations that require the approval of many buyers. Good insurance

salesmen form a strategy for establishing a customer relationship with a single family. One very successful broker makes the best deal he can for his client on any type of insurance: fire and casualty, life insurance, annuities, or whatever. He would throw in his commission to reduce premiums if he could in order to formulate the initial customer relationship. His strategy is to build such confidence in his customers that he winds up with *all* their insurance business. Therefore his tactics for gaining the customer relationship in the first place are aimed at selling that first policy by any method as long as it's moral, legal, and ethical. From there he implements his overall sales strategy and garners as much of that particular customer's insurance business as he possibly can, as profitably as he can, and in the shortest possible time.

Target Your Adversary

In order to formulate a successful sales strategy, you must first identify your buyers. If the primary buyer is an organization rather than an individual or group, the name of the organization should be placed on the top of the page. That is your target!

WHO

Next, identify the individuals within that organization you should be concerned with. The Economic Buyer controls all the resources. Who in the organization is the technician? That's the Feasibility Buyer. Who in the organization is going to be in charge of implementing whatever it is that you're selling? That's the Implementive Buyer. Who are the end users? Who else is going to be involved in or affected by any change the purchase of your product will bring? They are members of the chain of beneficiaries. Do you need or want a sponsor? Who should it be? What will a sponsor do for you? Is a sponsor necessary in the sale or are you simply looking for a sympathetic ear who will listen to your pitch but can't buy a thing? All the above are part of the who questions you must ask yourself in order to accurately identify your buyers.

WHAT

Once you have identified who your buyers are, you've got to address the what questions of sales strategy formulation. What does each of your buyers work for—identity, power, money? What kinds of people are they—Doers, Waiters, Watchers? Do they respond to need or relationships? What link do they fill in the chain of beneficiaries? What is their function within the organization? What will be the impact on them individually and collectively if your product or service is purchased? The above are what questions designed to help you formulate the best strategy for attacking your target and to select the correct tactics for the upcoming miniconfrontations, minisales, and closes which are the critical parts of any selling process.

A critical step at this point is *analysis* of the data you have gathered. First, each buyer should be ranked—the Economic Buyers, Feasibility Buyers, and Implementive Buyers. Then list end users and individuals in the chain of beneficiaries. Start at the top of the hierarchy by (1) function and (2) title. Work down to the janitor, if need be. Where there is more than one Economic, Feasibility, or Implementive Buyer, note the differences among buyers at the same level. Different motivators will probably be called for. Once you've done this, the next step is to compare the similarities among buyers so that common motivators can be applied.

After differences and similarities are established, the buyers, end users, and members of the chain of beneficiaries should be classified as Doers, Waiters, or Watchers. Then a determination must be made as to whether they would react best if need is presented or a relationship is established first.

Now the "how to sell them" part is almost a breeze. Match each buyer with a primary motivator best suited to him, based on the data you have. Be sure to assign several secondary motivators to each buyer. Remember, at least two motivators are necessary to move him from interest to action. And a backup motivator needs to be thought through ahead of time in case your who and what data prove to be only partially correct. You need to react quickly in such a situation, so it's best to be prepared.

HOW

The next set of strategic questions relate to how. How is each buyer motivated? How is each buyer to be sold? Need, greed, fear? Self-approval, approval of others, safety? How can you provide a motivation for each beneficiary so that he or she will react positively to change? How can each buyer's decisions be controlled? Can anything go wrong? How can it be prevented from happening? How will you handle it if it does? How are end users to be motivated? Do they require a different tactic? These are all examples of how questions you need to think through before making the final selection of your sales strategy and tactic.

Using Assumptions

How does anybody find time to acquire all this information, you ask? The answer is on the first call or cold call, you don't. So it is necessary to make certain assumptions. Let's face it. A sales strategy based on logical assumptions is infinitely more desirable than winging it with no strategy at all. Who do you assume your buyers to be? What do you assume their position to be? If you don't have names it's easy to substitute functions: manager of personnel, district supervisor, vice president of marketing, or general manager. The assumption about what function within the organization the buyer has will serve as a temporary substitute for the "who are my buyers" questions so vital to the formulation of a penetrating sales strategy.

But sooner or later all the who and what strategy questions must be completely answered or the how of your sales strategy will prove to be a futile exercise. Untested assumptions are the foundation of canned pitches and canned pitches belong to the dark ages of professional selling. Therefore, your first minisale must be to test your assumptions. Then gather information that will precisely answer the who and what questions in order to formulate the critical how questions. If you find that your assumptions are wrong you can always make an instant correction. Naturally the more complex the sale the more information you must gather to test your strategic assumptions. But remember, never use a tactic *in a main-thrust confrontation* that is based on a strategy full of assumptions. You are putting yourself in a win/lose situation. The whole purpose of developing a sales strategy is to eliminate flip-of-the-coin success patterns. A well-thought-through strategy and a carefully chosen tactic will invariably tilt the odds heavily in your favor.

General Advice About Strategy and Tactics

If your customer's organization is complex enough, you may want to find a sponsor who can shortcut your information-gathering process. Remember Nick Margolis? That was essentially what Jane Bloomingdale told him to do. Nick did it well!

Never think that a sales presentation is you talking and the buyer listening. Advocate Salesmen always listen. They listen because when a buyer talks, he is committing himself to certain premises and beliefs. Whether those beliefs are right or wrong doesn't make any difference. If he believes them, as far as he is concerned they are right. Smart salesmen let the customer test their strategic assumptions for them by listening. When a customer articulates an objection or a basic belief that decimates a strategic sales assumption, the Advocate Salesman can recognize it instantly and adjust his strategy and tactics to accommodate this new information.

A sales strategy is designed to make sales tactics work in the ultimate confrontation of the close. With the single exception of the Confrontation Close, the closing techniques developed earlier are merely subtle ways for the Advocate Salesman to test whether his strategy and tactics are working. He can make this test without risking the final yes/no confrontation from which there is no retreat. Strategic assumptions and tests of those assumptions will allow the Advocate Salesman to formulate mini-sales and closes on the basis of the tactical approach and motivators that he feels are best suited. It will also give the Advocate Salesman an opportunity to evaluate the degree of need to sell priority, and to whom. It will allow him to formulate meaningful objective-setting questions so that he can sell objectives that fit his product alternative and can evaluate how and when to sell what can go wrong. But the key elements of a successful strategy are the who, what, and how data which must be carefully gathered and analyzed. Only from these data can a successful sales strategy be formulated.

There is plenty of help available to the Advocate Salesman to make strategic assumptions in the absence of direct information. If the customer is local, there are people you can ask. Also, read the customer's advertisements. They will tell you much about his basic strategy. Remember Tregoe and Zimmerman's advice: "Observe your competitor closely and you can correctly deduce his strategy." If you observe your potential buyer's advertising it will tell you how he wants others to perceive his business. This is a natural reflection of his strategy. For larger companies there are many outside sources: *Standard & Poor's;* articles from *Newsweek, Business Week,* and *The Wall Street Journal;* and corporate annual financial reports. Dun & Bradstreet will give you not only the functional titles of the major buyers in an organization but will include their names and telephone numbers. Some Advocate Salesmen target a particular company and then, as a strategic first step, compare the target company with a similar company with which they have previously done business—for example, American Can versus Continental Can or International Paper versus Weyerhaeuser. This can make strategy formulation tricky, because there are always major organizational differences between even the closest competitors. Assumptive company comparisons are an alternative of last resort.

The Advocate Salesman who sells best knows the most about his customer before he begins the adversary process of selling. He knows that the tactic he chooses must be appropriate to the situation regardless of whether it is comfortable and compatible with his personality.

Tactics are dictated by strategy, not by the salesman's personality. Advocate Salesmen realize this and train themselves to be comfortable using tactical approaches that were originally difficult for them—like paratroopers learning to leap out of airplanes and move swiftly over rough terrain. A successful sales strategy will not benefit any salesman who is not skilled in using every tactic called for to implement that strategy. Stalking and cornering the game is one thing but you've also got to know how to shoot your arrow and throw your spear.

The strength of any Advocate Salesman rests squarely upon his basic attitude. When a particular tactic is difficult for him to master, he applies himself harder to learn the skill. His attitude will lead him to the knowledge necessary to completely understand the tactic and thereby master the skill necessary to implement it. That's what the sales profession is all about. That's why it's called a profession.

Dennis Lahey has been a sales trainer for advocate selling for years and has developed a series of case studies to help salesmen develop the skills necessary for formulating a sales strategy. The basic premise of the training is that no salesman ever has enough information about a customer whom he is attempting to strategize. Therefore he must work with what information he has! Dennis has found the most critical and most difficult part of formulating a strategy to be the correct identification of (1) real buyers, and (2) those in the chain of beneficiaries who can hurt you even if they can't help you. The first case study below focuses on that set of objectives.

Before you read the solution, take a few minutes to jot down the Economic Buyers, Feasibility Buyers, and Implementive Buyers and other key people in the chain of beneficiaries who can help or hinder the sale. In this situation, the Advocate Salesman has some knowledge about his buyer and has found an internal sponsor.

Case 1: Who Are the Buyers?

At a meeting of the Society of Mechanical Control Engineers, Ian Gallagher was the featured speaker. He was a sales engineer for AMROBI (American Robots, Inc.). He talked about one of the most difficult sales he had ever faced. He called it the backward sale. The top man was sold but everybody else either didn't know about the product or was against the idea. He told the story of the Data Control Products (DCP) sale.

DCP was in trouble. It made components that went into most computers in the personal computer field. It controlled 25 percent of the market; the market was growing and profits were healthy. Things looked rosy to most observers. Tom Stuart, president of DCP, knew better.

His customers, manufacturers of home computers, were in a very competitive marketplace. Pressure to reduce costs of components was heavy. Some of DCP's customers had long-overdue bills, and rumors were flying about some of them going Chapter XI.

His bank was reluctant to extend his line of credit at the same favorable terms originally negotiated. The prime rate had risen. The bank was also concerned that DCP had no long-range plan to increase profits or to adjust to a potentially changing market.

His labor force was agitated. The work required a lot of assembly under magnifying glasses. There was pressure by management for maximum speed to keep unit costs down and to keep up with production schedules. Informal feedback showed high interest in organizing a union.

The members of his board of directors, many of whom were related to the founders of the corporation, were interested in long-term profits. They were continually putting pressure on Tom Stuart to make decisions to increase the value of the stock.

Fortunately, Tom had the answer to all these problems. Robots. Unfortunately, Tom had no idea how to convince everyone involved that robots were the *only* reasonable answer.

That's where Ian Gallagher came in. The particular brand of robot that Ian represented was optically oriented, computer controlled, and highly adaptable. The robots could sort and type incoming component parts. They could position, assemble, and weld parts. They could also quality-check components for electronic reliability. Most important, because of their adaptability, they could handle the manufacture of all the types of components that DCP was considering for the next seven years.

The robots would allow DCP to take a market share of 70 percent, increase production ten times, maintain the same number of employees, and increase profits fivefold.

Tom Stuart saw very few negatives in Ian's proposal, but he knew that others would not share his view. The cost of installing the robots would wipe out profits for 18 months to two years. Installation would not be possible without a huge bank loan or a large stock issue in a down market.

An investment of this magnitude would wipe out any potential for management bonuses for two years. All key managers, including Tom, could plan on no bonuses for those years. Some of the present labor force could not be trained to work with the sophisticated robots and would have to be laid off. A major program of hiring trained technicians would have to be undertaken.

Meanwhile, a Japanese robot manufacturer was going over Tom's head and marketing directly to the board. Its mechanical robots would do the present job at one-third the cost of Ian's computer-controlled robots. However, they could not adapt to even minor changes in the types of components being manufactured.

In spite of all the obstacles, Tom knew the only way to ensure the life of DCP was to convince all the others and install the robots as soon as possible. Ian and Tom decided to plan a strategy to get all the key players on board the AMROBI robot train. It was Ian and the president of DCP, Tom Stuart, against the world. Or so it seemed at the time.

Ian took a few minutes out from his prepared presentation to ask the audience what questions had to be answered and what obstacles had to be overcome. You might use this time to think about what you would do in the situation that Tom and Ian faced.

SOLUTION

Ian and Tom Stuart decided to approach the situation using the *chain-of-beneficiaries* concept. They would look at the various groups of people who were affected by the potential robot sale and analyze each group for its hot buttons, both pro and con. Then they would devise an appealing approach tailored to the needs of each group.

The main buyer groups were (1) the board of directors, (2) the management staff, (3) the workers, and (4) the outside bankers. The approval of all these buyer groups was necessary to complete the sale of the robots that Tom Stuart desperately needed to change the capability of his company. One negative group would kill his chances. Tom Stuart was normally an Economic Buyer in his own right. However, a sale of this magnitude left him without total authority. He knew that in order to avert a strike and the probable failure of his company he had to have labor participate in the decision and agree with the alternative—a classic case of an end user possessing massive veto power.

The management staff was more under Tom's control. He could hire or fire managers at will. But a radical top-management reorganization would weaken his position with labor, and Tom hated to lose good men because he simply hadn't sold them on his alternative. They would be vital in implementing the new production capacity derived from the robots that Ian's company would install. They were the Implementive Buyers. And, as Ian pointed out to Tom, the real Feasibility Buyers in this sale were not the engineers on Tom's staff but the bankers. There are several sides to technical feasibility, in this case the engineering side and the financial side. The bankers held the ace in the hole. Tom was his own Feasibility Buyer when it came to the engineering competence of Ian's production robots. But the bankers had to be convinced, from the company's financial position, that the purchase was technically possible. However, the board of directors was the true Economic Buyer because it had the ultimate control over all the resources, changes, and adaptations necessary to make the purchase. In this instance, Tom Stuart did not.

After Ian and Tom listed and ranked buyers, they labeled them Doers, Waiters, and Watchers. They used their own knowledge and pulled data from others about the basic motives of those buyers—identity, power, money, need, greed, fear, and so on. They paid particular attention to Doers and Waiters. Doers would have to be sold in order to change the corporation on the magnitude that Tom's plan entailed. Waiters would have to be sold because they could stop the sale in midstream by taking the floor and shooting holes in the alternative. They would be contributing to the problem but not the solution. Ian and Tom were not too concerned about Watchers, but they analyzed them anyway in case one decided to become troublesome. Once their strategy was formulated, Tom and Ian paid careful attention to asking questions of and answering questions for the Doers and the Waiters of the group. In general, they described the present situation. They detailed what would happen during the next three years if no changes were made. They explained the impact on each group in graphic terms. They discussed the robot proposal that Ian's company was making. They described the projected benefits to each group in the same graphic terms.

The workers had to face the prospect of losing some jobs and going through a rough retraining program if the robots were brought in. However, they faced the prospect of losing *all* their jobs in a few years if they were not brought in. Tom and Ian explained that the workers would have a very marketable skill once they were trained in the care and feeding of robots. The company would pay for all training and would start to find other work for those employees who chose not to be retrained.

The management staff was dealt with a little more directly. Managers were reminded that even in profitable years bonuses were available only to high performers. Those who stuck with it could look forward to two lean years and then to projected bonuses far above the norm. And yes, Tom would put those promises into writing in their employment contracts. In addition, they should realize that management experience with robot production would make them all the more marketable should they leave in the future.

Surprisingly, the bankers were the easiest of the groups to deal with. Tom and Ian went to them with a revised and detailed business plan, this being the main item with which the banks had been concerned. The rate of interest did go up but at least the loan was granted. One of the main reasons was the adaptability of the AMROBI robots. The bank was able to take title to them on a secured basis. If the worst happened, they felt they could sell them to other manufacturers hungry for robots. The mechanical robots from Japan would not have qualified as collateral since they lacked that basic flexibility.

The board of directors was not happy at the prospect of lower earnings for two years. Fortunately, DCP was a closely held company. It did project a good deal of public selling, which would drive the price lower. Tom and the key directors agreed to meet with some of the security analysts to explain a long-term policy that would result in short-term lower profits. One of the more affluent directors stated that he'd buy all the DCP stock that came on the market because he was convinced the company was really going places. He figured on making a killing in four years.

This case dramatizes how difficult it is to identify *all* the critical buyers. In most instances, Dennis Lahey reported that even seasoned salesmen missed the bankers as the true Feasibility Buyers. Even though they controlled only one function—finances—that function was a big one. It was up to them to decide whether it was financially feasible to convert production to robots. Their disapproval could easily have killed the sale. Ian and Tom Stuart had done a good deal of homework on the who, what, and how. But the who is always the pacer in formulating sales strategy. Without the correct identification of who the buyers are, the what and how are meaningless conjecture.

Another one of Dennis Lahey's cases focuses on the need to translate a dynamite sales strategy into a tactic that works. The case assumes that information is known about the who, what, and how of the buyers. An analytic comparison of differences and similarities has been done and a tactical approach for the presentation is being decided upon. As you read the case, make a few notes about how you would make that presentation. Be sure to assess the risks as well as the benefits of one particular tactical approach versus another. Then read Dennis Lahey's real-life narrative of what happened at the presentation.

Case 2: Deciding the Best Tactical Approach to Implement Sales Strategy

After the second day of the seminar on corporate planning, a group of attendees gathered in the hotel cocktail lounge. Most of them were chief executive officers of their companies. They reminisced on what they had heard that day and how it compared to their actual experiences.

Reilly Maxwell, president of ProsoTrol, reflected that although he was responsible for long-term plans for his company, others thought that short-term tactics might have a bigger impact. He told the story of how a salesman in one of the smaller branches turned in the biggest order ever received. In fact, it was the order that moved ProsoTrol from a fledgling company to a force to be reckoned with.

Chuck Kruger was a salesman for ProsoTrol, a brand-new manufacturer of electronic process control systems. The control system, PrTr 120, reflected state-of-the-art thinking. The company itself was less than two years old. Those two factors looked like they were going to cause Chuck a lot of problems in his upcoming sales presentation to Allegheny Paper Corporation.

Allegheny had been in the business of making industry-grade paper for 83 years. That grade was originally used for business forms and carbon copies. Now almost 80 percent of the output was used in the computer industry, fan-folded and pierced for computer printers. ProsoTrol had been invited to bid on the new process control system to be put on line 1 in the Bluefield Mill. The Big Three in the business were also invited. All companies were to submit a comprehensive written bid and make a two-hour presentation to the board of directors.

Chuck reflected upon the information he had about ProsoTrol and Allegheny as he planned out his sales tactics. ProsoTrol equipment was good. It was equal to or better than the competition. Price was also equal or better. The big drawback was lack of the big name and reputation that the other, more established competitors enjoyed.

Allegheny had been an established company for more than three-quarters of a century. Most of the members of the board of directors were descendants of the original owners. They had worked in the West Virginia mill for many years before being elected to the board. Their backgrounds and family ties were similar to those of the present labor force. Their education level was rather low. Few members of the board or the labor force had traveled much outside West Virginia.

The decision to go to an electronic process control system had not been an easy one. It was pushed primarily by Jack Morse, the plant manager, and S. W. (Swede) Olson, the company treasurer. Both were highly educated. Both had been brought in from the outside. Both were worried about the increase in production and reduced profits Allegheny was facing. Both believed that process control was the only way to ensure the long-term profits of the company.

Chuck tried to look at the situation from the point of view of the board members. They had to be worried about what could go wrong. They had been forced to make a decision they were not really happy with. They were concerned about turning over control of their paper making to fancy computers instead of their trusted professional paper makers. They were concerned about what the labor force would think, They were concerned about expanding the system to the five other lines if the experiment worked. Most of all, they had to be worried that the new system wouldn't work.

SOLUTION

From previous competitions Chuck was pretty sure how the other suppliers would gear their sales approach. They were used to dealing with very sophisticated buyers. They would pack their written bids with fancy colored pictures, statistics, and projected performance graphs. Their formal presentation would be multimedia, audiovisual. It would be beautiful, complex. It would be aimed at the technically sophisticated Feasibility Buyers, Jack Morse and Swede Olson.

Conversely, Chuck's approach was directed to the board of directors' fear of what could go wrong. Naturally, part of his written bid contained the basic facts and figures. But essentially it said that all of the bidders' products, including Chuck's, could get the job done for Allegheny if things were handled right.

The important part of Chuck's written presentation listed all the things that he thought could go wrong with any process control installation if it were not handled right. Then it specifically asked the board members to think of any other things that could go wrong and to list them. It offered no solutions but promised to discuss all the problems on the list during the formal verbal presentation. ProsoTrol was to be the last one to present.

This approach did a great thing for Chuck. It showed a realism that his competitors' anticipated optimism ignored. Chuck's credibility problem stemmed from the fact that his company was new and its technology was state of the art. This was compensated for somewhat by Chuck's belief that any of the competing systems would work if problems were correctly anticipated and their solutions planned for. Chuck's written proposal focused attention on problem errors and technology. Thus it set the stage for undercutting his competitors, who had been in business longer and so had a history of failures not yet shared by Chuck's fledgling firm. By focusing all his buyer's attention on the potential problems of a new system installation, Chuck was able to turn his company's use of state-of-the-art technology into an advantage. His company's new technology was designed to eliminate the problems that his competitors had experienced in past installations.

By asking the board to list all the pitfalls of the installation, Chuck's choice of tactic gave each member an arsenal of specific questions to ask the unsuspecting competitors during their formal presentations. It forced the board to put subconscious fears into a concrete written format that Chuck felt he could deal with because he was prepared. He knew the questions that were coming.

Chuck's final stroke of genius was his opening statement at the board presentation. He said, "Okay. We know we're going to have to put in process control to keep Allegheny current. We've got a list of all the things that could go wrong during the installation. I have worked out the ways to prevent many of them from occurring. I would like to use my two hours to discuss with you how to keep the rest from happening.

"You've worked in the mill. You know your people. You know the machinery on which we are going to install our control equipment. I would like to draw upon your experience to come up with a plan to prevent the problems we can and to deal with the ones we can't."

Within a short time the board was actively involved with

positive suggestions. The two-hour meeting finally broke up four hours later with an installation plan all but roughed out. The vague fears and concerns had been dealt with and put to rest. Somewhere in those four hours, although the subject was not brought up formally, it became understood that ProsoTrol was the system that would be installed.

Reilly Maxwell shared with his seminar group the follow-up to the story. The installation went well. ProsoTrol got the order for the other five lines without competition. The success story was written up in paper industry magazines and resulted in many more orders.

As this case study demonstrates, the choice of a sales tactic is just as important as the formulation of the sales strategy. Chuck was in a difficult position. His company was new and he was quite aware that his competitors would call attention to that by damning him with faint praise.

By virtue of the fact that he was talking to the board of directors, who were the Economic Buyers in this particular sale, rather than Jack Morse and Swede Olson, who were the Feasibility Buyers, Chuck was very aware that he would be unable to use his major weapon effectively—ProsoTrol's state-of-the-art technology. The details of the technology were beyond the understanding of his Economic Buyers. So Chuck chose a tactic that turned all those disadvantages into advantages. By correctly pointing out that any of the systems would achieve the results Jack Morse and Swede Olson needed, Chuck successfully focused the board's attention on what could go wrong. The major concern was which one of the systems would have the fewest problems.

Selling what can go wrong is a common variation of the negative sell. The Negative Tactic is designed to produce instant credibility, as we will see in the next chapter. Credibility is what Chuck needed because his company didn't have much. It hadn't been in business long enough. On the other hand, Chuck's company didn't have a history of problems. Furthermore, what could go wrong was really the area the board was concerned with. Board members know Murphy's Law well. What can go wrong will go wrong, and always at the worst possible time. Or as Chuck said, things will always be more screwed up than you think. The board liked that.

By admitting up front that things could go wrong, Chuck was instantly recognized as an honest man. And answering each board member's "what can go wrong" questions allowed Chuck to explain in detail the state-of-the-art technology that would have gone unheard or misunderstood had he presented it in lecture form. He found during his presentation that when he reached the technical limits of one board member, another would chime in and ask additional questions until finally the entire group understood exactly what Chuck's company did technologically that was different from what his competitors did. This would not have happened if the questions that Chuck was answering were rhetorical ones he invented himself, or if he had just stood there and lectured the board.

Chuck never said that his system was perfect. Had he done so, nobody would have believed him. But he counted on the fact that the board members had already been sold on the results of an electronic process control system, provided somebody could reassure them that the indirect and hidden costs of the change were not going to be monumental. So Chuck convinced them that ProsoTrol fit the bill. The lesson is that the best strategy still relies upon a good tactic to implement it, and without the correct choice of tactics a good strategy is worthless. However, only by formulating a sales strategy for Allegheny Paper was Chuck able to thoroughly analyze his strengths and weaknesses vis-à-vis his competitors in this particular selling situation. He was able to do this to a degree that he could choose the proper tactic to use rather than stand up in front of the group and make a blind canned presentation.

Advocate selling dictates skill in choosing the correct tactic as well as skill in developing a formidable sales strategy. The next chapter details six of the most successful sales tactics used by Advocate Salesmen. Certain tactics are better used in certain situations. If more than one tactic is applicable to a given situation, the Advocate Salesman may choose the one that best fits his personality. But he should be skillful in using all of them in order to be successful.

CONCEPT 14

Sales Tactics

One man's strategy is another man's tactic. As noted before, General Patton and Field Marshall Montgomery had a strategy for conquering North Africa. However, their strategy was subordinate to Eisenhower's strategy for invading Europe; therefore Montgomery and Patton's actions in North Africa became a tactical application of Eisenhower's overall strategy. Eisenhower's strategy for invading Europe was a tactical application of Roosevelt's and Churchill's global strategy to win the war in Europe and bring peace and freedom to all Western nations. Therefore, in practical application, the difference between a strategy and a tactic is the level of application and front-line risk. A tactic can fail and the strategy survive, but the reverse is almost an impossibility.

To put it on a simpler plane, if you are lost in the woods, you must first see the forest for the trees. Yes, even in that situation a strategy must be developed. If you simply pursue one tactic after another with no real system or design, you'll never get out alive.

Once a sales strategy has been designed, the best tactics become visible for the strategist to choose. Form follows function, and the function of strategy is to achieve a goal. The form tactics take is dictated by that goal. Only the tactics that can achieve the goal are worth considering once the strategy has been formulated. For example, if a salesman realizes that the difficulty he is going to have in a new territory is customer awareness of his company and the product he is selling, he must formulate a *strategy* to make customers aware of the benefits and features of his products, the success and credibility of his company, and of course his location, ability, and willingness to serve. The only *tactics* the salesman has available to fit his customer-awareness sales strategy are (1) direct mail and/or media advertising, (2) telecommunications, and (3) face-to-face personal calls.

From now on, the numbers dictate which tactics he should consider. In effect, the salesman will have to devise a tactical application of his time whereby he can (1) call directly upon the most potentially lucrative customers in his territory, (2) telephone potential customers he would like to see in person but does not have time for, and (3) write the rest a series of letters designed to make them aware that he, his company, and his products exist. The mix of these tactics is now entirely dependent upon the time and financial resources available to the salesman.

The message of this chapter is that tactics are dictated by strategy. Many salesmen become proficient in only one or two tactics and build their strategy around these limited abilities rather than focusing on the particular environment of the sale. Such salesmen are swordsmen rather than duelists. Swordsmen use swords very well. But should a swordsman anger somebody proficient with a bow and arrow or a pistol, he is in a great deal of trouble. Duelists recognize that in order to succeed they must be proficient in all weapons. Similarly, salesmen who call themselves advocate professionals must be proficient in all tactical applications of their trade. Otherwise they will succeed only in those situations where the elements of the sale *naturally* lend themselves to their specific tactical talents. The successful Advocate Salesman effectively reacts to the sales environment and adapts his style when the natural elements of the sale do not lend themselves to the tactics he prefers.

There are indeed situations when tactics have to be employed because there is no strategy. These are basically defensive and reactive tactics. During the Battle of the Bulge in World War II, the German attack decimated the Allied forces. The Allied generals were forced to react from a tactical standpoint because they had no strategic plans to combat an unexpected successful German offensive. The tactical decision to defend Bastogne to the death broke the back of the Germans' offensive because they had not planned to expend the resources necessary to dislodge the "battling bastards of Bastogne" from their do-or-die reactive tactical position. Of course, no general in his right mind would advocate reactive tactical decision making as an overall plan to achieve a strategic goal. Yet many salesmen employ this policy.

Salesmen have a product. They have a pitch. They have a brochure and a three-piece suit. They know the generic makeup of buyers who have purchased their services before. So they go to the Yellow Pages or their lead file and select a group of prospects who are in the same general business as their present customers, making careful note to get the address right. Then they stop by for a little chat. If they are lucky enough to see to the buyer, they don't ask questions of a strategic nature. They disengage their brain, open their mouth, and instruct their tongue to play back the canned sales pitch they have memorized with uncanny precision. This isn't selling, it's order taking—much like an Order Taker clerk handing a buyer a catalog then standing by as the buyer browses through the pages. The only difference is that the canned-pitch salesman is using his tongue instead of a catalog.

A canned pitch and catalog are primitive tactics to expose the customer to the benefits and features of your product. Choosing a successful strategy necessitates learning something about your customer, be it an organization or an individual, so that you can adopt a selling tactic that will convince your buyer. Let's look at a few tactics that skilled Advocate Salesmen use.

The Explorative Tactic

Every Advocate Salesman is faced with a chicken-and-egg situation when making cold calls. By definition a cold call is an information vacuum. But only by making the call can the salesman get any information. The Explorative Tactic enables a salesman to develop the information he needs when he has an opportunity to sell but no knowledge of his buyer.

The Explorative Tactic dictates that the salesman ask *specific* questions of his potential buyer. These questions are designed to separate the problems the buyer might have with the seller's product from the problems the customer needs to solve with this purchase. The salesman needs to know the results the customer is expecting to achieve. None of this information is particularly clear in the customer's mind when he is shopping. This is true whether the customer is a purchasing agent or a department store shopper.

The buyer's answers, voice inflection, body language, and

emphasis all give the salesman clues as to exactly what type of buyer he is. This provides information for answering the who, what, and how questions that are vital to developing a sales strategy.

Once these questions have been answered, a quick sales strategy should be formulated. There is no need to formalize a sales strategy on pages and pages of paper. Good salesmen recognize the answers to who, what, and how as soon as they hear them. When the buyer is an organization instead of an individual, it takes longer to get the answers to those questions and the information is more complex, but the process is the same.

In general, asking a buyer about a specific problem will generate answers that are rooted in (1) something that happened to the buyer in the past; (2) something the buyer is attempting to achieve in the present; or (3) a result that the buyer wants to achieve in the future.

This is invaluable data for the Advocate Salesman. He can separate these concerns and form a picture of the sales situation he is faced with. If a concern is related to the past, the buyer is probably looking for a solution that will either correct the cause of a problem or diminish the effects of the problem if the cause is uncorrectable. If the customer is concerned with achieving results in the present, he is really seeking to make things better than they now are for himself, his project, or his organization. A concern with the present gives the Advocate Salesman a very big clue that the buyer is a Doer—he wants to achieve results over and above those he has already achieved.

If a concern is related to the future, it's a sure bet that the buyer is seeking a product or service that will deal with a potential problem whose cause he's already anticipated and analyzed. Therefore he is looking either to prevent the problem from happening or to reduce its seriousness if the problem is inevitable. "Please send this contract by registered mail so the post office doesn't lose it, but make sure you send a xerox copy by regular mail in case they do," instructs the attorney. "I'd be lost without that copying machine," he adds. The copying machine justifies its cost again!

Bob Johnston was in advertising. He and his boss bumped into a new prospect over lunch at the club and were invited to join him. Dale Kline, Bob's boss, whispered that they had better just smile a lot. Neither of them knew enough about this buyer to risk saying anything decisive that could turn out to be witty, simple, and wrong. Bob agreed. So instead of answering the buyer's questions, Bob countered each one with a specific question designed to gather information. The buyer was not offended. Instead, he seemed to appreciate the fact that Bob and Dale were paying attention to detail. At the end of lunch, Bob and Dale compared their notes. Their buyer's three main concerns were (1) choosing the name of a new product for which he was directly responsible; (2) determining why sales of another product under his control had fallen off a full 5 percent during the last eight months; and (3) presenting a proposal to the board of directors to initiate major product modifications to meet present market needs as he perceived them.

The 5 percent fall-off of the old product was a *past*-related concern. It required either an analysis for cause or the generation of an alternative that would replace the business if the cause could not be found or eliminated. Choosing a new product name was a *present*-related concern. The name had to have internal appeal as well as appeal to the marketplace. If the product proved successful, Bob's buyer would greatly improve his professional standing and personal solvency. The buyer's concern over his presentation of major product modifications to the board of directors had *future* implications. The board meeting was two months away.

"I think we've got a good shot at this account," Bob said to Dale. "Simply stated, the man's problem is that (1) he has hold of an old product that isn't doing well, (2) he has at least one new product coming out which he hopes will offset the losses of the old product, and (3) he's thinking about correcting the entire situation by recommending radical product modifications to the board. All we have to do is formulate an advertising campaign that corrects his 5 percent decline in market share and we win. If you recall, Coors Beer came out with a punch-top can that just wasn't acceptable to the public. People cut their fingers. Coors could have changed the top, but then either Coors or its wholesalers would have been stuck with old inventory worth hundreds of thousands of dollars. So Coors simply bit the bullet on dealer/wholesaler relations and informed the public that the new snap-tops were now available, but if they bought one of the old-style cans they would be getting a collector's item. Coors's volume bounced back! Eventually so did that of the wholesalers! No one abandons a winner!

"In our case," Bob noted, "it will take further exploration

to decide on the best campaign to deal with the cause of the 5 percent decline. Our buyer's present need to choose a correct product name is probably tied to his past problem," Bob went on. "I would guess his new product must at least offset a profit loss that's gone 5 percent sideways. So if we handle his past concern properly, we can make him a real hero. And if we handle his present concern properly, he's a great big double hero. In other words, if we can recover the market loss on the old product and also create a winner with the new product, he's going to win the corporate Medal of Honor with two clusters.

"Nevertheless," Bob continued, "our major effort must focus on solving his future problem—his presentation to the board of directors. The board is the real buyer. The board is the heart of our 'who' and 'what.' If he doesn't get approval to modify the product line, there won't be a need for a new advertising campaign. The effort that we put in will be wasted if the board presentation fails.

"If you notice," Bob went on, "all his concerns seem interrelated. They involve past problems, present decisions, and future plans. But the only real common tie is product performance. Our buyer appears to be a Doer, but he doesn't know what he needs, so if we make a presentation to him that is directed toward solving his past problem with the old product, making his present new product a winner, and, most important, helping him successfully convince the board that he can gain the product market share it wants, we will get the business by default. He'll be so dependent on our alternatives that he wouldn't dare give the business to anybody else. If the board approves his plan, it is also approving us. We made the plan.

"Lunch is on you," Bob concluded. "Let's get to work."

At the next meeting with their buyer, Bob and Dale were well prepared. However, the who, what, and how of the board of directors was still relatively unknown. Therefore Bob and Dale could not formulate a sales strategy that would guarantee a close. They were in a minisale situation. Bob and Dale decided that their best next step was to sell the buyer on providing them with the information necessary to sell the board of directors. They concluded that the board probably knew as much or more about the company's product situation as their buyer. Therefore their major concern was credibility at the presentation. Bob and Dale needed to devise a strategy and choose a tactic that would make their credibility unquestionable. In-

stead of offering solutions, Bob and Dale again asked questions
at their next meeting with their buyer.

Reluctant at first, the buyer warmed to answering their
questions. He began to see the drift their line of inquiry was
taking. Bob summarized his and Dale's conclusions about the
buyer's three major concerns. Separating those concerns and
highlighting them was a revelation to the buyer. He hadn't
done that before. As a consequence, he provided immediate answers to Bob's second set of questions. These focused on the
buyer's past concern—the loss of old product market shares.
Ten minutes later Bob identified the cause as customer complaints about quality. Several phone calls and further analysis
revealed that production had purchased two additional pieces of
high-speed equipment. The company was experiencing problems with quality control. This coupled with a tight production
schedule due to high seasonal demand caused a relaxation in
quality control standards that would probably cost the vice president of manufacturing his job. However, it proved to Bob, Dale,
and their buyer that they could make a good case at the board
meeting for recovering the market loss of the old primary product. It certainly gave Bob and Dale a clear insight into the tack
their advertising campaign should take. They would need to
reassure consumers that all products were guaranteed and instruct them to immediately return defective products for new
ones at local service centers. They would stress ethics and credibility. After all, everybody knows that anyone can make a mistake. The mistakes that are not corrected cause loss of reputation.

Having assured themselves that they could correct the
cause of their buyer's past concern, Bob and Dale shifted the
discussion to their buyer's present concern—choosing the new
product name. They no longer had to focus on using the new
product to offset the market share loss of the older product.
They were convinced it would be able to hold its own again. So
instead of serving as a replacement product, the new product
could be looked upon as a vehicle to achieve its own market
share. Bob focused the discussion on what the new product was
designed to accomplish for its ultimate consumer. Thirty minutes later he and Dale looked at each other sharply. Their
buyer's product was going to be marketed throughout North
America.

"The name of your product," Bob cautioned his buyer,

"must reflect what the consumer might want it to do in all cultural and geographical areas of this continent. If that is an impossible task, then the name must be something abstract, noncommital, and nondescriptive. An old snake oil salesman I read about had the same problem three generations ago. So he called his product Alpha and sold it as far as he could travel in those days. When customers asked what *results* Alpha produced, he told them whatever they wanted to hear. He also charged whatever price the market would bear. He sold perceived value instead of real value. He made a fortune!"

Bob and Dale were gathering very pertinent information for their buyer's board presentation. He was impressed. As a consequence, there was no need for Bob and Dale to ask the buyer if they could accompany him to the board presentation. He thought of the idea himself. He requested that they back him up with facts, figures, and layouts. He asked them to discuss alternative product names and advertising thrusts that would consider the cultural and geographical market differences. In effect, he asked them to make the sale for him!

The Explorative Tactic put Bob and Dale in a position to have their buyer readily answer questions about the nature and personality of each member of the board of directors. They could now formulate the necessary sales strategy to make their buyer's presentation to the board a success. The buyer cooperated because he and Bob and Dale were no longer in an adversary situation. They were on the same team. He not only cooperated, he cooperated with enthusiasm.

Getting out concerns may appear awkward at first, but if you make those concerns your minisale, your buyer will politely cooperate even if he is not yet convinced that he has a real interest in what you are selling. Budget concerns, results concerns, and personal job-related concerns are all areas to approach. Sooner or later the buyer will begin to understand the thrust of your questions and will volunteer information if he sees something that can be of benefit to him. Your analytical approach to his problem will impress him so he will at least allow you to help organize the data he is dealing with.

Separate his data into concerns that deal with the past, the present, and the future. For concerns that deal with the past, you must seek a way to correct the *cause* or work for an adaptation that will negate or diminish the seriousness of the problem. For concerns that deal with the present, you must understand what results your customer *wants* to accomplish and those he *must* accomplish. Then ascertain the resources that he has to accomplish them with. For concerns that deal with the future, ascertain where the *pitfalls* and *critical areas* are located so that problems can be prevented or blunted.

The Exploratory Tactic is a two-edged sword. It can be used when there is a strategic need to gather additional information effectively. Or it can be used as a defensive tactic when there is an information void. The who, what, and how are all based on open-ended assumptions.

The Consultive Tactic

Every assumptive sales strategy is dangerous until its assumptions are tested. Here too the salesman is faced with a chicken-and-egg situation. How does he develop a sales strategy based on solid data unless he has a tactic to test his assumptions? Some tactics lend themselves better to testing assumption than others. The Consultive Tactic, like the Exploratory Tactic, is an excellent tool to test strategic sales assumptions. The Consultive Tactic also relies on motivating the buyer to answer specific questions. However, unlike the Exploratory Tactic, which deal with concerns, the Consultive Tactic is aimed directly at objectives that the customer is trying to accomplish with the purchase of a particular product or service. The level of detail is different. The approach is different. The questions are different. Good Advocate Salesmen are adept at using each tactic appropriately.

The Consultive Tactic is used to sell need. In setting objectives for your buyer, you are helping him build a set of specifications around your product. But you haven't yet mentioned your product. You've only talked about what your product accomplishes and what it costs. If he buys the objectives and the cost is within his resource boundaries, you've made a sale. Therefore the Consultive Tactic naturally follows the Exploratory Tactic. In both cases you are serving in an advisory capacity, even though the situation is really adversarial.

Most salesmen sell a product or concept that is related to the product's description. They pitch what the product will do without considering what the buyer may want to accomplish. It is a truism that if you involve the buyer in the decision-making process, he will begin to think that buying is his idea.

Some buyers pride themselves on never being sold anything. They *buy* what they need! There are people who suspect that these buyers are talking to some very competent Advocate Salesmen.

The Consultive Tactic isn't new but, like sex, every generation thinks it invented it. The Consultive Tactic allows you to crystallize in your buyer's mind what he is trying to accomplish *before* you present him with an alternative to accomplish it. Let's face it. If buyers are unsure about why they want something, they certainly can't be sure whether they want it. How better to gain their confidence, build credibility, and appeal to their self-interest than to help them crystallize their specific needs, wants, and goals?

The Consultive Tactic puts the salesman in the role of adviser. This is very difficult for some salesmen because they feel much more comfortable talking about a subject they know rather than entering into that murky world of what the customer thinks he wants.

Salesmen who memorize pitches won't touch the Consultive Tactic. They are horrified by the possibility of losing control. The tactic requires some of the same interpersonal skills that a good doctor or lawyer uses. The salesman must guide the discussion to areas of importance and *never lose control.*

Again, questions are the key to successful use of the Consultive Tactic. By asking questions, the salesman appears to be earnestly trying to familiarize himself with the buyer's problems. The buyer is appreciative and, because the salesman has asked a question, feels obligated to respond. Like a good psychiatrist, the salesman follows each question with one that delves deeper into the subject. Should the buyer go off on a tangent, another well-phrased question will put the discussion on a track that is ultimately going to meet the salesman's aims. If questions are kept relevant to areas which fit the product, the customer will eventually blurt out a product application that has the potential to produce benefits and results. Hurray! Results are the name of the game. The product is merely a means to achieve those results.

Consultive selling is the art of having the customer *tell you* how to best present your product. It offers the additional benefit of allowing you to play a nonthreatening and nonconfrontive role. The consultive approach is always appreciated by the customer. In the general discussion that ensues from your questions, your buyer will give you clear signals as to what his particular buying motivators are—need, greed, fear, self-approval, approval of others, and safety. He will also identify himself as a Doer, Waiter, or Watcher and as an Economic, Feasibility, or Implementive Buyer. He will confirm your qualifying assumptions about him and his company or cause you to reassess *before you have made your pitch!*

In walk-in businesses like residential real estate, it is virtually impossible to gather data on who, what, and how before the sale. Thus the salesman who ignores the Consultive Tactic is at the mercy of the buyer. He knows only what the buyer has deemed important enough to tell him. The smart Advocate Salesman will take a page out of Judy Ellis's book.

Judy Ellis is a top-drawer real estate salesperson—a real Doer piranha. She once told her people that in a typical real estate sale the customer talks and the salesman nods his head appreciatively. Meanwhile, his mind is racing through the listings he has. He loses control! If the salesman doesn't have control, he is reduced to the role of a multiple-listing catalog salesman and Order Taker.

Judy is expert at using the Consultive Tactic. She grasps control of the sale and the attention of the prospect—all with a big smile, of course. "A house is a house is a house," she says, "but do you want it for shelter? Speculation? A rental property?" This approach forces the prospect to ask himself, "Why am I here?" By handling this miniconfrontation smoothly and with good humor, Judy is able to immediately qualify her prospects. Lookie-loos disappear. Qualified prospects always give her an answer. Lookie-loos can't.

If the prospect's answer is shelter, she asks whether he has any particular needs. Children, for example? Pets? A desire for privacy? What type of lifestyle does the family enjoy? Near the beach? Outdoor living? Trees? A fireplace? A pool? As the answers come back, Judy and her prospect build a set of purchase specifications together. Each answer draws the prospect closer to Judy and closer to buying.

In one instance, a prospect indicated a desire to live close to the water. At that time Judy had no listing of homes on the water. She countered by asking the prospect and his wife if they had ever lived in the mountains. They had not. So Judy told them the story of another customer who had found comfort, serenity, and a feeling of closeness to nature and family when he bought a house that had an acre and a half of land and a yard full of shade trees. This story and all the images it conjured up instantly erased their stated desire to live by the water. It created instead a desire to live in the woods. The prospects never even realized Judy was selling. High praise for the Consultive Tactic.

To this day, Judy swears that the family bought 24 oak and maple trees that incidentally had a 4-bedroom colonial house located among them. More important, her buyers were *grateful* to Judy for suggesting a lifestyle that they hadn't considered before. Every other real estate salesperson had tried to sell them the beach house they originally thought they wanted! By using the Consultive Tactic, Judy was able to gently dissuade her prospects from a specification that she couldn't meet. She was an adviser, not a seller. That's how her customers perceive her and that's why they bought. Judy is a supreme Advocate Salesman.

Judy keeps various mental checklists to help her formulate questions about the results people want and the resources they have to achieve their goals. Her real estate checklist includes the amount of space or number of rooms her buyers seek, the flexibility of that space to meet the changing needs of the family, the location of the home, and the compatibility of their space requirements with their personal objectives. Personal objectives include the family's image of itself, its plans, and leisure interests like tennis and golf. The proximity of recreation facilities is always a good selling point.

Judy's financial resources checklist includes the amount of capital her buyers have, the costs and expenses their cash flow can bear, and whether they expect to achieve a return on investment from the house or simply live in it. In short, Judy's mental checklists of questions to ask her prospects enable her to accurately uncover objectives that the buyers have not been aware of themselves.

As we saw earlier, buyers react quickly when they are made aware of something they truly want. Automatic transmissions were once a thing of the future, dreamed about only by design engineers. Nobody else really thought much about them. People were too busy trying to learn how to work a clutch when they were stopped on a hill. The need for an automatic transmission was there. Detroit knew it. As soon as it was invented, car manufacturers sold it at a premium. As soon as it became standard, they brought back stick shifts and clutches. Then they sold those at a premium. The genius responsible for that could sell rodents rat poison (on a cash basis only).

Creating need is what selling is all about. The Consultive Tactic is a way to *find* need. It is a face-to-face tool to create your own market research. Pleasant, unobtrusive, yet penetrating questions will separate the customer's real objectives from his perceived objectives—what he really wants versus what he thinks he wants. This is the real service the consultive Advocate Salesman can perform for his buyer.

The Consultive Tactic folds neatly into the selling process Alan Jay Weiss outlined in the preceding chapter. In order to properly implement it, every salesman needs a mental checklist of categories broad enough to formulate additional questions. Once he tests his basic assumptions of why a customer is interested, he can develop an instant strategy and choose the correct tactic to make the sale.

Objective-Setting Checklist

People
   Motivation and attitudes
   Skills and abilities
   Performance and productivity
   Development and growth
   Health and safety
Ideas and Processes
   Security, propriety position
   Adaptability
Organization
   Relationships among units, functions, people
   Communications
   Responsibility and delegation
   Formal and informal organization
   Coordination
Output
   Quality
   Quantity
   Pace and timing

Material
   Sources and availability
   Quality
   Handling and storage
Money
   Capital or fixed
   Costs and expenses
   Return
External Influences
   Economic trends
   Competition
   Company image
   Legal and government
Facilities and Equipment
   Space
   Flexibility and adaptability
   Location
   Compatibility
Personal
   Goals and plans
   Family
   Strengths and weaknesses
   Interests

The questions asked by the salesman will enable buyers to determine whether they have thought through all the results they want to accomplish and the resources they have to accomplish it with, and to test themselves for hidden objectives. Each individual Advocate Salesman should devise his own specific checklist, but the one presented on the opposite page, which is from Kepner-Tregoe's *Results Planning Manual*, will provide a good start.

The Assumptive Tactic

The Assumptive Tactic is a departure from the advisory role. However, it does not place the salesman in an obvious adversary position, as does the Negative Tactic, which will be discussed shortly. The Assumptive Tactic is in between. It requires a well-thought-out sales strategy based upon thorough knowledge of the buyer—be it an organization, a group, or an individual. The beauty of this approach is that additional data may be gathered to strengthen or change the strategy *during* the sale. If your strategy proves invalid, then instantly evaluate whether the Assumptive Tactic is still the best arrow in your quiver. If not, switch tactics instantly to accommodate the new facts you have gathered and go on from there.

When you are trying to establish need for your product and trying to position it for high priority in order to close, your biggest problem is going to be indecision from your buyers. The way to have these maybes work for you rather than against you is to use an assumptive sale. If a buyer hasn't said no, assume a tacit yes and move on to the next step. As long as the buyer doesn't have to commit to spending money, he will probably allow you to proceed in order to resolve his own indecisiveness.

For example, if you are trying to sell need for a particular training program within an Economic Buyer's organization, you can begin to establish that need by showing him the productivity results from similar programs in other industries. You can also raise questions about the work attitudes of people within his organization. You should then state that you are going to—rather than ask if you may—see the vice president of manufacturing and arrange to talk to certain key supervisors within the manufacturing hierarchy in order to pull together an attitude survey. You will present him with the results at the end of the month. You should assume that he will not object, and *do not give him an opportunity to do so.*

Move right along and ask for the name of the person responsible for manufacturing. Then, thank your Economic Buyer for his time and march down to see the vice president of manufacturing. Naturally you will tell him that you just came from the CEO's office, where you discussed a results-oriented training program he is sure to be interested in. Of course, you assume he agrees with his boss and move right along to the important stuff. You need to meet several key supervisors who will provide the basis for your attitude survey. Look for motivational signs in the VP of manufacturing that might differ from those of the CEO.

Always maintain control of the sale. Don't ask the VP to set up the meeting with the key supervisors; just ask him to identify who they are. When he does, he'll be giving you the people whose word he takes. These are his Feasibility Buyers. They are also Implementive Buyers in their own right. At this point if you ask the VP of manufacturing to do any real work, like call a meeting, you're dead! You'll lose control. Don't even ask him where the supervisors are located—you may give him a chance to tell you to come back tomorrow. He's done enough for the day. Thank him very much for his time and ask someone else (the receptionist if you have to) where these people can be found now that you have their names.

You are now moving through the chain of beneficiaries rapidly and assumptively. When you finally talk to the supervisors, drop the names of the executives you've already talked to. They will assume that management is already in favor of your proposal. This will create a halo effect. (Everybody wants a halo. The way to heaven is to be a good boy and *obey* the commandments.) This, coupled with the need for approval of others and safety will almost guarantee your success. The supervisors want to be part of the team so they can have self-approval too.

Through your attitude survey you now have the marvelous opportunity to sell the benefits of your program. Pretty soon you will have the groundswell of a positive consensus flowing back to the CEO through both direct and indirect channels. He, of course, will assume (now you've got it) that everybody else in the chain took a critical and objective look at your proposal, just as he did. That assumption becomes reality, and your program is sold.

As this example demonstrates, successful sales strategy can be formulated by knowing the structure of an organization and the functions of the individuals within that organization even if the names of those individuals are unknown. Who, what, and how information can be gathered and incorporated into your strategy during normal sales conversations. This information will either strengthen your sales strategy or call immediate attention to its weakness. The chief executive officer in the previous situation is obviously the Economic Buyer. The vice president of manufacturing is the Feasibility Buyer. The key supervisors are the Implementive Buyers, and the attitude survey people are end users. The chain of beneficiaries is established.

If you have sold similar industries before, your sales strategy can be based on primarily assumptive information. But bear in mind that it is critical to test those assumptions. Be prepared to switch tactics instantly if any critical part of your sales strategy crumbles under an invalid assumption. To stay on the safe side, you should try to gather valid data *before* formulating your strategy. Do not fall into the trap of being so successful in formulating an assumptive strategy that you fail to make the effort to gather data. That's the lazy man's way to failure.

The Assumptive Tactic is a primary premise for direct-mail solicitations. Recipients are assumed to have an interest in the products offered. Assumptive selling is dangerous when no real who, what, and how knowledge is available. However, the Assumptive Tactic applied to direct-mail and subsequent face-to-face selling situations can be very effective if the proper sales strategy has been formulated previously.

Moe Crantz formed a highly technical data processing company that specialized in recovering overpaid Social Security taxes. Moe discovered that when the Social Security laws were written back in the 1930s, wages paid to employees who were absent due to illness were exempt from Social Security taxes. This exemption was designed to encourage companies to provide paid sick leave and other benefits for their employees. At the time, the portion of the employees' wages that was taxable for Social Security was almost minuscule. During the early years, employers ignored the situation. An employee would have to be on sick leave almost a full year before the exemption went into effect. As a consequence, in later years while employers centralized their payroll systems on high-speed computers located at company headquarters, they allowed the absentee records to remain in local facilities. After all, the resident manager is the best judge of whether an employee is abusing sick leave, and there was a tacit understanding that many local managers would permit sick time as a method of compensation when it was beyond their authority to increase wages.

Not surprisingly, the Social Security Trust Fund went bankrupt in the late 1970s. Congress enacted radical changes in the taxable base. It was finally increased to well over $30,000. No longer would an employee receive that "extra raise" in August or September when his Social Security withholding ceased because he had reached the limit of his taxable base.

Moe found another piece of information that was interesting. Labor laws in all states had long made it a *criminal* offense for an employer and its officers, directors, and agents to willfully overwithhold wages from an employee.

Moe knew that every corporation had a chief financial officer who was also a company watchdog. Not only did he keep his eye on corporate funds; he also scrutinized the legalities associated with the fiduciary responsibility of all officers and directors. So Moe formulated an assumptive strategy that chief financial officers, officers of the corporation, and directors were not aware that they were in criminal violation by willfully overwithholding their employees' wages. Moe drafted a letter addressed to this group in companies that employed 10,000 or more workers. Moe's letter called attention to the fact that (1) withholding Social Security taxes for wages paid on sick day was illegal and (2) now that the employer was formally notified of this error, if he continued the practice he could be held criminally responsible under the labor laws of both the state and federal government. The balance of his letter was devoted to explaining the services and benefits produced by his company, Payroll Recovery Systems, Ltd. Moe selected a rifle shot rather than a broad-based mailing on the assumption that major corporations would have the biggest problem consolidating field absentee records under one roof.

This assumption proved correct. The response was overwhelming, and Moe followed up each sale diligently. He also assumed the basic reason corporations were so interested was to recover the company's portion of the overpayment.

Moe called on International Can Corporation in St. Louis, confident that he was going to make an easy sale. He ran as-

sumptively down his list of why it behooved the corporation to effect a recovery for its employees and was amazed to find a stony silence at the end of his presentation. Moe had expected a quick close. International Can's chief financial officer was an accountant. He was receptive to adding any outside income to the balance sheet. It was pure profit. However, the personnel and labor relations people were hostile to Moe's proposal. Moe had missed some vital links in the chain of beneficiaries in his strategic assumptions.

Personnel and labor relations people never publicly admit their corporation has made a mistake. Like high priests of any religion, they refuse to acknowledge the deity can do wrong. Moe had a problem. He could no longer work on the assumption that every responsible executive in International Can wanted to do what was morally, ethically, and legally right.

Moe switched to an Exploratory Tactic and found that International Can had a past problem with its labor force. The labor people were afraid Moe's project would revive it. While he was mulling over this information, the chief financial officer hit Moe with another unexpected problem. The Tax Department, which was responsible for overwithholding sick pay in the first place, had a major concern about Moe's proposal. The company possessed massive holdings of raw forest land to provide pulp for its paper mills and cardboard for its packaging divisions. The company was carrying the value of that land on its tax books at the original purchase price of 30 years ago. The vice president of the department was certain a sick-pay recovery would goad government auditors to retaliate by assigning a present-day value to those forest lands. The tax result would have been catastrophic.

Moe was shocked. None of these executives was one bit concerned about the employees who had erroneously and illegally been deprived of their wages over the years. He was astounded, and he made the mistake of telling the executives so. Moe moralized with them. Moe lost the sale! Not being entirely stupid, Moe postponed his next three appointments. Then he sat down and rethought his strategic assumptions.

Moe's primary assumption was that all responsible executives would morally, ethically, and legally realize they had an obligation to their employees to recover any taxes that were overwithheld. That assumption was patently invalid. Moe had made the tragic mistake of not testing his assumptions. He had

forced himself into a situation where he could use only the Confrontation Close and that close had failed. He had not sold individual needs. He had not gone into the who or the what in any level of detail. Moe had blown it.

But Moe was not one to make the same mistake twice. His subsequent presentations were based on the strategic assumption that labor management was his enemy, personnel did not want to admit to an error, and tax management had something to hide. While this assumption did not always prove true, Moe found that it never hurt his sales presentation. It had been the converse that killed him. Moe correctly strategized that the chief financial officer would be the executive most interested in the services of Payroll Recovery Systems, Ltd. But he no longer assumed that any other executives within the company shared Moe's benevolence toward the overworked and underpaid workers whose wages were being illegally withheld. As a result, Moe's fees shot up to $5 million a year.

You would think that Moe would have learned all the dangers of using the Assumptive Tactic. He thought so too, but he hadn't. Even in the hands of experts, the tactic requires a sound sales strategy. After several profitable years and an unbroken string of successes, Moe was asked to discuss the services of his company with one of the nation's major defense contractors. Under the administration's austerity budget and attitude of peace at all costs, defense contractors were in serious need of operating capital. Moe's assumptive presentation went well, although he had taken his usual precaution of meeting with each key executive individually before pulling them together in a group. But the manager of payroll taxes, an Implementive Buyer at best, threw him a curve. He insisted that the Internal Revenue Service be allowed to audit Moe's figures. This was an unusual step because once Moe's work was certified by internal auditors, the corporation invariably took a credit against its future taxes. Thus it received its money instantly. Neither company employees nor Moe was to be paid until the IRS audit was complete.

Moe reflected for a second. One certainly valid assumption was that this company needed money right away. So Moe agreed to the contract provision. He wound up hating himself for almost two years. During the six months it took Moe's firm to do the field work, the nation elected a new President. His client successfully sought the government loan guarantees neces-

sary to keep it afloat and a viable producer of America's might. As a consequence, Moe's assumption was no longer valid.

No one in the company was now in a hurry to receive the millions of dollars in overpaid Social Security taxes. The government was providing the company with several billion dollars at little or no real interest. The money due from the Social Security refund was drawing 20 percent interest. So the payroll tax manager settled back and notified the IRS in a one-paragraph letter that the company had a claim of several million dollars in overpaid Social Security taxes. He requested an audit at the government's convenience.

Moe knew that the convenience of the Internal Revenue Service could be anywhere from six months to three years. Moe helped himself to a stiff Chivas Regal. He shifted gears. Moe chose the Consultive Tactic. He talked to labor and personnel people about the impact of delaying valid refund payments to their workers. Most had been laid off, and their unemployment benefits and union benefits had expired. Personnel's reply was after having laid off 65,000 people, how much more damage could be done? Union management was in bed with the company, and the union president had just been elected to the board of directors. A sweetheart contract was in the offing.

Moe was in trouble and he knew it. While his company was still financially solvent, he knew that his million-dollar fee was going to be delayed for an indeterminate period. Meanwhile he was going to pay interest on his out-of-pocket expenses.

To compound the matter, Moe's partner had proved inept at operational management. As a consequence, Moe had to cover those bases himself and correct the problems. Moe's company was extremely profitable but he was now in a cash bind, and the assumptions behind his strategy were the cause. The assumptions were wrong—not all of them, but some of them. The ones that were wrong were critical.

Management didn't care when the employees were paid. The union was necking with management, and the company no longer needed the money. Moe realized that the only guy on his side was the employee whose wages had been overwithheld, so Moe took a classic adversary stance with his buyer. He had his public relations firm release statements that his firm had recovered millions of dollars in overpaid Social Security taxes for the firm's workers and that the company had contractually agreed to pay those employees 30 days after the audit had been approved and the refund received. Much to his surprise, Moe found the name of his firm on the front pages of most business sections of the leading newspapers across the United States. He was an instant welcome guest on many of the talk shows he used to watch in the morning. The result was a foregone conclusion.

The corporate conscience was now awakened. A telephone call to an Internal Revenue Service regional director produced an instant audit. Within three months the company received its money, the employees received their money, and Moe received his fee. The crisis was over. But Moe was a salesman. He never forgot the lesson. The Assumptive Tactic is viable only if the assumptions and the sales strategy that the salesman has devised are *accurate*. Leave no stone unturned on the who, what, and how. Failing to motivate the manager of payroll taxes properly had almost cost Moe his company.

But there is a happy ending. Though Moe had made serious mistakes in his sales strategy, he was still one of the best assumptive salesmen around. He correctly assumed that the federal government would start to feel a drain from sick-pay recoveries on its already bankrupt Social Security fund and close the loophole. While such legislation was pending and when his profits were at their peak, Moe put his company on the block. He sold it to Pershing Industries, Inc., of New York City for several million dollars six months before legislation was introduced to eliminate the sick-pay exemption. "Caveat emptor," Moe replied, when his buyers threatened to sue. "I didn't know they were going to pass that legislation any more than I knew the stock I sold last month was going to go down. Let the buyer beware!" Moe Crantz was an Advocate Salesman. So were his buyers. They had simply made a wrong assumption in their decison to buy Moe's company.

The Negative Tactic

Most tactics are positive. Yet there is a time when the Negative Tactic has more impact and value to a sales strategy than a positive one. The power of negative selling is that no one expects it, particularly the buyer. Buyers expect to be sold. When a seller withdraws his proposal, in fact refuses to sell, the buyer is intimidated. Something is wrong with him! As long as you don't reject him completely, you can turn the tables and have the buyer sell *you.*

The Negative Tactic has a very wide range of applications. It can be made to relate to a personal level (the reluctant, but ultimately willing virgin) or a global level (self-serving platitudes denouncing war just prior to declaring it), and everything in between. Some types of products naturally lend themselves to the Negative Tactic.

Franchise salesmen are adept at using the Negative Tactic to reach the vanity of a buyer. They challenge his self-approval to the point that *he demands they sell him a franchise.*

Franchising developed when some people thought they had a hot idea for a product or a service but lacked the capital and commitment to risk everything on it themselves. Need or desire for self-improvement is assumed, so prospects are usually generated through enticing ads in the newspaper that imply high returns for the person buying their franchise and expertise. All that is needed is a little money!

From initial contact, the sale is negative. "Please send us a statement of your net worth, sir, and we will evaluate whether or not you are qualified as an investor in our franchise! Also you will find a section in the application for you to list your skills, training, and business experience. This too will help us decide." That sets the tone!

The buyer, at first affronted, now greedily realizes that he just might have hooked onto a real "winner!" He wants to be one of the first to get in on the ground floor of what's obviously going to be another McDonald's. From that point on his main concern, from reading the prospectus to selling meetings with the franchisors (yes, the buyer sells the meetings with the sellers), is to impress upon the sellers what a qualified candidate he is.

The franchisor, of course, allows himself to be convinced, little by little. Finally, the buyer makes the sale. He is allowed to spend his hard-earned money to take a risk that the franchisor himself wouldn't take. By golly, he *knew* he was qualified!

There is some justice in this world. The president of a prominent marketing group in Fort Lauderdale, Florida, tells the story about a customer who had franchised over 150 family restaurants. The franchisor's complaint was that the franchisees were making all that money—just as he told them they would—and he was making only a 10 percent override. The consultant laughed and remembered that he still had a tape recording of a meeting seven years ago in which the very same man was chortling because some damn fool from Idaho had just paid him a $50,000 franchise fee to open a restaurant. Now the place was doing over $1 million a year—just like he said it would! Not being a cruel man, the consultant did not play the tape or ask his client who drew up the contractual revenue-split arrangements in the first place.

Negative selling has its place in every sale. It can very easily be used as a step-up device. Retail salespeople who sell need will invariably tell a customer to whom they have just sold a new skirt that it won't look right without a matching blouse, shoes, and purse.

Productivity consultants use the negative sell to extend their time. One prominent consulting group averaged three months to complete a job. Their top salesman invariably sold six-month contracts. By accompanying him on a sales call and keeping his mouth shut, the president learned how he did it.

After wrapping up an $800-a-day per man, $80,000 three-month contract, the salesman launched into a discussion of "negative aspects of the sale." The president was horrified, but the buyers, who had just agreed to an $80,000 sale, were most interested. They encouraged the salesman to proceed. The salesman controlled the meeting.

On the blackboard the salesman listed areas of impact that were beyond the scope of his original proposal. In fact, he showed additional areas of benefit that could be derived by the company if it utilized the people *already on the job* to handle *additional* problems. The payout would be great, he demonstrated, and all that was needed was a little more time (at $800 per day per man, of course).

The management committee readily agreed and hardly realized that they were committing to an additional two and one-half months of consulting work. The president swallowed three Valiums and patted the salesman on the back. He had successfully used the Negative Tactic with a positive twist. The president had learned something valuable!

Moe Crantz, Advocate Salesman that he is, was as adept at using the Negative Tactic as he was using the Assumptive Tactic. When Moe knew that a customer was going to attempt to force a price discount, Moe would choose the Negative Tactic. Moe would first ignore price entirely and make sure that each one of his buyers was convinced that there was a need for a Social Security recovery in the first place. Moe would open his presentation with the comment, "I wish I could help you but. . . ." Then he would launch into the logistic problems associated with pulling all the records together into a central location and/or the expense of sending his people cross country to the various outposts where those records were located.

Moe knew full well that his buyers had been aware of the logistic problems when they considered doing the project internally. Moe was letting them know there was a possibility his people might not do the work either. They would then be faced with doing a job they had previously rejected as too disruptive and costly. Moe explained that his company had a backlog of business easier than theirs and deeply regretted having to turn their business down. However, just before his buyers could react, Moe would add, "Unless," letting the word hang while he paused, deep in thought. Ultimately someone would break his reverie. "Unless what, Mr. Crantz?"

At that point, Moe would launch into a set of complex terms and conditions that were just a tad less of a burden to his buyers than if they did the job themselves. Moe would finalize the sale with a Negotiated Close, giving and taking on whose company would be responsible for which tasks. Thus tasks became the issue instead of price.

The genius of Moe's Negative Tactic was that it never occurred to his buyers to contact Moe's competitors, because the logistic problems he raised were real. His buyers assumed that every one of Moe's competitors would have the same objections. This was not necessarily true. However, had Moe argued price with his buyers, they would indeed have immediately asked another firm for a bid. Anticipating that, Moe's choice of the Negative Tactic removed price as an issue and created more important concerns that demanded his buyer's attention. By getting Moe to reluctantly agree to perform costly tasks, the buyers felt they had already gotten as much flesh from Moe Crantz as they were going to. And without bothering to confer, they agreed not to raise the issue of price for fear of unraveling the sale they had made.

As we learned in the Hero Close, salesmen for Dan Moran's management development company were experts at the negative sell. Once need had been sold and the program accepted by management, Dan's salespeople shifted to a very adroit use of the Negative Tactic.

Training managers are invariably on a tight budget and do not have much clout within an organization. They don't like to concentrate all their money in one type of development program. That's no fun, even though it might be appropriate. Therefore a training manager would tell Dan's salesman that in the next fiscal year he had budgeted to train only 8 percent of the middle-management population within his organization. The salesman would immediately react in horror.

"Impossible," the salesman would say. "How can you expect to have behavioral change within your organization if you do not train enough people in our Zed III management process to effect peer reinforcement?"

If the training manager was green enough to not understand "peer reinforcement," the salesman would launch into a lofty explanation. The reason most people do not speak more than one language in the United States, he would lecture, is that they have no one with whom to practice their newly learned skills. Thus learning cannot be reinforced.

If that didn't work, the salesman would resort to an easel pad. He would diagram his client's organization horizontally by function, then vertically by reporting relationships in order to show communication intercepts, or points where various levels of management teams would interface regardless of function. Without the salesman's explanation the easel pad looked like a checkerboard. But the Negative Tactic is mesmerizing. The training manager had been told he was wrong. The checkerboard lines on the easel pad were telling him why. After a while he believed he was wrong, and he probably was.

Even though the salesman was pontificating, he did know that a certain percentage of people must use the same management process in order to instill it within an organization. He did not really know whether that magic figure was 8 percent or 40 percent. His company's goal was to sell as much management training material as possible at the highest price the market would bear. As a consequence, Dan's salesmen were told that 90 percent of the population was the only safe figure to sell against. No wonder salesmen like people.

After his discussion with the training manager, Dan's salesman would try to close on a larger population with the good old, never-fail Hero Close. But the best close sometimes fails. If the salesman discovered the training manager did indeed have budget restrictions, he would march up to a line manager Economic Buyer and restate his position. This end run wouldn't make the training manager a hero by any stretch of the imagination, but the salesman would be careful to blame the "budget system" rather than the man.

With the Economic Buyer, the salesman would use fear as a motivator because the buyer already had a substantial investment in achieving his own objectives through the training Dan's company offered. But the salesman was telling him he was about to lose the benefits of that investment because the implementation plan the training manager had devised was wrong! If the situation warranted, the salesman would risk the ultimate extension of the Negative Tactic and say, "In fact, Mr. Economic Buyer, if you really insist upon implementing the program this way, I suggest we put a hiatus on training for a full two years and then start over from scratch when your budget considerations are more elastic." In effect, he would withdraw the opportunity to buy.

If the buyer accepted, the salesman was in deep trouble. But normally this gambit merely opened the subject for discussion. A Negotiated Close of some figure between the 8 percent budgeted by the training manager and the 20 percent the salesman insisted on usually resulted. When you consider that materials were priced at $265 per participant, you can understand why Dan's mentor, the old chairman, could afford to hire only the most sophisticated Advocate Salesmen during the years he was trying to expand his business.

Martha Lewis used a variation of the Negative Tactic when she told the managing partner of that very prestigious consulting firm that she only wanted him to write an article. She was not trying to sell him. She did not add the word "now." He subsequently saw the value of advertising in Martha's publications from the response he received from the article he wrote—exactly what Martha had counted on. Martha had tried other tactics with this customer and they hadn't worked. Martha knew her buyer well. She had the who, what, and how down pat, and her choice of the Negative Tactic enabled her to succeed at last.

Don't ever be afraid to revise your tactic if it doesn't work. The only sin is reverting to a tactic that failed before. One of the best selling combinations is the Negative Tactic coupled with

Integrity Close Number One. But beware. The Negative Tactic demands great credibility on the part of the seller, his company, and his product. Who cares whether someone representing an unknown company selling a useless product is reluctant to let you buy unless you meet his terms and conditions?

The Parable Tactic

Advocate selling requires flexibility. Both hard-sell and soft-sell tactics need to be mastered for a true Advocate Salesman to represent himself as a professional. The Parable Tactic is sometimes called the Analogy Tactic.

The difference between parables and analogies is that parables conclude with a moral or obvious truth. Analogies simply end with a conclusion. Using the Parable Tactic, you can deal with a sticky situation by describing a similar situation that happened to somebody else. Therefore you are not directly confronting the buyer with a set of unpleasant facts related to him. You are merely telling him a story. Both parties can maintain an aura of sophistication and politeness if the salesman resists the temptation to moralize. There is no need to rub the buyer's nose in the point. If he's alive and conscious he'll get it. If the buyer proves to be thin-skinned, a good Advocate Salesman will back off and say, "Well of course I didn't mean you, Mr. Buyer. Wherever did you get that idea?"

Parables are vicarious learning experiences. From childhood we are conditioned to *expect* that a parable will depict the terrible consequences that will befall us if we do not behave. It is no small coincidence that the Bible is an almost continuous parable. Aesop's fables are parables. So are many children's stories. Invariably they portray the frustration, violence, and unhappiness that will befall us if we don't follow the self-evident truth at the end of the story.

The Parable Tactic is especially effective when there is a significant conflict between what the buyer wants and what the salesman thinks he should have. Safety and fear are great motivators around which to build the Parable Tactic. "Hobie" Harper was a top-of-the-line insurance salesman. Hobie used to say that you cannot tell your customer he is going to die. Everybody thinks dying is for the other guy. Hobie realized the only way to induce a man to buy more insurance was to ram his head through the family car windshield and let him watch the blood drip. Hobie would insist on making his presentation to both the wife and the husband. He would begin with the stated objective of merely wanting to consolidate the family's insurance in order to reduce premiums. Hobie's real objective was to sell as much insurance as Hobie thought the family needed.

After his buyers were warm, comfortable, and relaxed, Hobie would allow the husband to explain how he was already insurance poor. Hobie would nod and say, "I understand. Sometimes I think I have too much insurance myself." Then he would casually launch into a horror story. With the gentle aplomb of a mother telling "Hansel and Gretel," Hobie would describe the tragedy of Joe's terrible automobile accident. "Wasn't it a shame about his wife, Mary Ann?" His buyer's wife would invariably ask, "What about Mary Ann? Is she doing all right?"

Then old truthful Hobie would reluctantly paint a picture of a fallen lifestyle and deprivation. These tragedies occur all the time. There was no need to invent them. The files of his company were filled with heart-rending letters from widows and children pleading that their husbands or fathers surely had had no real intention of canceling the policy. When the prospect squirmed and his wife became uncomfortable, Hobie would throw out his hooker: the kids. The wife, regardless of reality, always felt she could fend for herself. Though she hadn't taught in the 15 years since she graduated, she never wavered in her belief that she could. Never mind that professional teachers with 20 years' service were being laid off. The kids were her Achilles' heel. So Hobie would tell another parable where the husband and wife were killed in a common disaster. The story would be along the lines of poor Cinderella who was forced to live with a wicked stepmother and stepsisters as a result of her parents' demise.

Only in Hobie's story, there was no Prince Charming to come to the rescue.

At the end of the evening, Hobie would talk about consolidating the family's insurance premiums. Inevitably, the husand or the wife would bring up areas of noncoverage they were both subconsciously aware of. They were frightened. Hobie bragged that he never sold anybody anything. He said, "All I had to do was choose my stories wisely and tell them properly. In the end my buyers were rooting through my briefcase to get brochures I couldn't find quickly enough." But you've got to know your buyers. Different people have different insecurities. Your parable must play on the particular insecurities of your buyer. Otherwise you are wasting your time."

Everybody likes a story. And there is some strange quirk in human nature that thrives on stories of disaster. So people will always listen. Only after a while does the listener conclude that the disaster described could befall him. Even then, if the salesman knows his business, the buyer rarely realizes that the salesman has chosen the story deliberately.

Parables are a wonderful way for the Advocate Salesman to appear subordinate to his buyer. As Hobie said, "If I stood up and lectured the husband and wife on their need to buy more insurance, they would throw me out of the house. Who needs a sanctimonious, self-righteous salesman telling them how to run their lives? But the parables allowed me to play the role of a storyteller.

Need Salesmen, Relationship Salesmen, and even Order Takers can effectively use the Parable Tactic. When Harold Bowe was selling franchises, he invariably instructed his salesmen that if a customer wavered they should tell a success story about a man who made a million dollars. "If the buyer brings up an objection," Harold would go on, "change the subject and then take out a picture and testimonial of a successful franchisee retired in Palm Springs and talk about his success story. That will get the conversation back on track very quickly." Parables are an effective way to bring back a customer who's off to a bad start.

The Parable Tactic is a credibility builder. Dan Moran used it well. Every salesman in the company knew the involved story of how the chairman and his partner had left General Research Ltd. They worked long days and hard nights in the basement of the chairman's modest bungalow developing the technology necessary to teach the management processes for which their company was now famous. It was a beautiful story of benevolent self-sacrifice for the benefit of mankind. What the salesman didn't know was that Dan Moran had made it up. Although alarmed when he first heard it, the chairman realized that refutation would probably cost more than it was worth, so when someone asked if the story was true, he would smile noncommittally and nod. Myth became fact. Every company salesman who retold the story to customers was convinced that the events really occurred.

The Predator Tactic

Soft and subtle tactics are probably the mainstay for most salesmen in the adversary business of buying and selling. However, as in war, tougher tactics are sometimes called for. Unlike war, these tactics must conform to the legal rules of the day. The Predator Tactic is what the name implies. It is a predatory attack on a buyer. Why should such a tactic even be discussed?

Business ethics, business moralities, and business practices rarely keep pace with each other. The robber barons of yesteryear who made this country great would find themselves in jail today for doing what they did. When asked whether his father had ever broken any laws, one of John D. Rockefeller's sons replied, "No, but many laws were enacted because of him."

When a salesman faces a situation involving murky ethics, he is forced to ask himself exactly what he intends to do. Smart Advocate Salesmen learn to use members of the legal profession to prevent trouble from happening rather than run to them with a hopeless case after it happens. There is need for the Predator Tactic. George Bordeaux found himself in just such a situation.

Remember George? Well, he received a significant promotion. He was named manager of national accounts for the Institutional Food Service Division of his company. This meant that George was now selling public hospitals, colleges, airports, and institutions instead of private plant and industry locations. George was quite pleased with himself.

In one of his first major sales, George learned the rules of predatory play the hard way. The King County, Tennessee, school district had routinely let its food service contract out for bid. George's office was duly notified. Like any good Advocate Salesman, George began to identify his buyers. He worked diligently, gathering and testing objectives with everybody remotely concerned with the quantity and quality of the school district's food service. George covered the chain of beneficiaries very well. He believed his bid had the best balance between quality and cost. Bids were required by law. As a precaution against losing on a technicality, George asked for and received permission from his company to hire a local attorney who made sure that his proprosal conformed to King County bidding rules and regulations. Andrew J. Brown, Esq., was present with George at the board meeting the day bids were opened. George was elated to learn that his bid was 3.1 percent lower than that of the closest competitor.

However, when the chairman of the school board finished opening the bids he took the unexpected step of tabling the motion to award the contract until it could be further reviewed by a select committee of board members.

"What does that mean?" George asked Andy Brown.

"I'm afraid that means you probably lost the bid, George," he replied.

"What do you mean lost the bid? I was a full 3 percentage points under," George protested vigorously.

"George," the attorney went on, "let me give you the facts of life. Bidding is just a ritual that school boards go through in this county. They award the contract to whom they want. The firm which presently has the contract hasn't lost a bid in nine years. When people like you underbid them, the school board examines the winning proposal with a fine-tooth comb. Invariably they reaward the contract to the current vendor on the basis of real quality versus perceived quality. Neither the public nor the press can argue with a decision to pay a little bit more so our children can have nutritional food. Motherhood, the American flag, and all that, you know."

George blew up. His lawyer ignored him and said, "George, why don't you just shut up and let me give you some advice? If you really want this contract I suggest that you see Reba Jane Welsh."

"Who is Reba Jane Welsh?" George retorted.

"Sit down, George," Andy Brown said, "and let me give you a bit of King County history. Your competitor has a very astute public relations policy. Cafeteria managers are instructed to solicit relationships with various teachers and administrators within the school district who hold real power. They are literally fired if they don't. The vendor will cater food for members of the board during their election campaigns at no cost to the candidate. In addition, sandwiches and hot meals can always be counted on to be delivered to people who have an official capacity with the school board at the same price a child pays for a meal in school. A child's meal is subsidized by the federal government. These 'favors' are subsidized by your competitor. But nobody can fault them. The practice is 'technically' impeccable and legal."

"How does Reba Jane Welsh fit into this?"

"All right, George, you're getting your first lesson in the ritual of doing business in this part of the country. Reba Jane Welsh and her sister Dinah are middle-class products of a past generation who surpassed their peers and achieved an education. Reba Jane and Dinah were going to make something of themselves. They were determined. There weren't many jobs open to women in King County and there were even fewer jobs open to minority women, but they made it. As teachers they were competent. But instead of sitting back and enjoying a success unrivaled by their peers, Reba Jane and Dinah chafed under the restrictions their gender, status, and job imposed on them.

"Like many women today, they suffered greatly at the hands of male peers. You can't blame them for wanting to even the score. The political environment of academia is judgmental, subjective, and intense. The man who said the reason campus politics are so vicious is because the stakes are so small knew what he was talking about."

"What does that have to do with our situation?" George asked, exasperated.

"Patience, my friend, I'm getting to that," Andy went on. "Enter Tom Welsh. Mr. Welsh was a minority politician when the time for a minority politician had come. On top of that, Tom Welsh was a shrewd minority politician. Tom was elected district leader of King County's powerful Liberal Party. He was both benevolent and tough, and his first wife was a very shrewd behind-the-scenes politician in her own right. With his initiative and her advice, Tom took complete control of the county organization three years later. For ten years they ruled together; then a disaster befell Tom Welsh. His wife literally ran off and left him and their 14-year-old daughter for a postman. Isabel Welsh, or Belle, as she was called, decided that she wanted happiness instead of power.

"Lonely and depressed, and used to the advice of a woman at home, Tom met and married Reba Jane. Tom solicited her advice, as he had Belle's. However, Reba and her sister were different from Tom's first wife. Where Belle Welsh fantasized on a statewide and national basis, Reba and her sister had a small-town focus. Belle was satisfied with reflected power. Reba and her sister wanted real power. So they gave Tom encouragement and support only when he turned his attention to running the affairs of King County. If he sought state or national office they were outwardly pleased but inwardly appalled, and they let him know it in subtle ways. Tom finally concentrated on the business of running the county."

"Okay, what's the point?" George said.

"In case you didn't know," the lawyer replied, "school boards are elected by the public. There is a primary slate presented by both parties in May of each year of a school board election. The survivors of the primary election face each other in the November general election. Since the Liberal Party dominates this county, whoever wins the party's nomination in the primary election is a shoe-in in November's general election. To continue this lesson in basic civics," Andy went on, "the political parties involved can throw an open primary, as the Conservative Party does in this county, whereby anybody who wants on the ballot can get on if he has the filing fees and petitions signed. Or they can follow Tom Welsh's Liberal Party rule of a closed primary whereby the only candidates for the school board on the ballot are those endorsed by the county committee."

"Now I see it," George exclaimed. "All the Liberty Party school board members at the meeting tonight—and that's most of them—were personally picked by Tom Welsh."

"You got it," his attorney replied. "And it took you only a little longer than I thought it would."

"Okay, exactly what does Reba Jane Welsh have to do with all this? You know my company. I can't pay bribes or make contributions to political organizations. We're a national company and work to maintain our integrity. I know that regional outfits and some privately owned local companies will cut all sorts of deals in this business, but I don't want to. I can't and won't do business that way."

"Now you're ready for the second part of the story, George. We've established Reba Jane Welsh's background. We've established that the politics in academic circles is vicious. And we've established that your competitor has maintained a very intense public relations campaign to include powerful people in King County. Your competitor has ties to Tom Welsh. However, Reba Jane and her sister Dinah have suffered traumatically under the bigotry of those who control the civil service bureaucracy of the King County school district.

"From the superintendent on down, all the principals of the King County school district are white Anglo-Saxon Protestants.

Don't make a judgment, George. Just accept it as a fact. Some assistant principals are black and some are Irish or Italian Catholic. But the real power of the school district bureaucracy rests with the King County WASPs. Your competitor had an interesting problem to deal with. If he showed any real favoritism toward Reba Jane and her sister, he would have alienated the bureaucracy. On the other hand if he ignored them he would suffer at the hands of Tom Welsh. So he made certain never to offend Reba Jane and Dinah and took care of old Tom every time his organization threw a bash to raise funds or present a candidate.

"Allow me to introduce you to Reba Jane Welsh and present your case as it really occurred. If you explain you are trying to offer a major improvement in food quality at a reduced cost but are being denied your just and earned right because of favoritism, you will provide her with a defendable altruistic reason for donning her armor, mounting her horse, and charging out to slay the people who shunned and demeaned her in the past.

"She won't ask for money, but I suggest that you make sure that Tom's little shindigs are well catered if you want to keep the contract longer than two years. And if I were you I'd show Reba Jane and Dinah a little bit more attention than they've received in the past, but that's all. No bribes, nothing outside the scope of what's normal and legal according to the canons of King County, the State of Tennessee, and the government of the United States of America.

"By the way, if you're successful, as I'm sure you will be, my bill will be triple what we anticipated. You'll be paying for what I know, not for how long it took me to explain it to you."

George's company got the job.

George and his attorney did not do anything unethical or illegal. Influence is a way of life. Old-boy networks are housed in brownstone buildings in every major city of the world. Country clubs, alumni groups, business associations, and fraternal orders are all nests of the quid-pro-quo way of doing business. The fact that Reba Jane Welsh wanted to show her peers that she had power was not George's problem. It was Reba Jane's. A long time ago George had decided to let people live their own lives and not be critical of a lifestyle different from his.

Political influence is but one type of problem an Advocate Salesman may run into in the area. Different alliances are made for different reasons. Clearly a salesman must know what he is up against before he can deal with it. A good sales strategy will usually uncover the elements he must deal with if the assumptions are tested. In George Bordeaux's case it never occurred to him to make an assumption that the school district contract might be influenced by old-boy ties. Therefore it certainly wouldn't have occurred to George to use the Predator Tactic of political influence to counter the old-boy influence with which he was faced. Never having made the assumption, George could not have tested it. Therein lies the fallacy of all strategies, management or sales.

Most Advocate Salesmen start their own business. Their independent nature draws them into the ranks of manufacturer's reps and distributors who buy and sell on a local, regional, or national basis. Being small businessmen, they do not have the resources the big boys have to deal effectively with predatory buyers or other carnivores in the arena, so they have to resort to being clever.

There is an old saying in the high-back-chair haunts of the world's shakers and movers: "If you owe a bank less than a million dollars you have a creditor. If you owe it more than a million dollars you have a partner." Lockheed's and Chrysler Corporation's problems demonstrated that fact in this decade. But such is not the case with the independent salesman/businessman.

Jack Cabot and Carl Henderson had been friends for years. Both had successful manufacturer's rep businesses that offered noncompeting lines. They stayed in touch, shared customer information, and exchanged recommendations. It was a cozy relationship. But the overall expansion of their businesses caused them a mutual cash flow drain.

Jack and Carl met to discuss their common problem. Jack was a bit of a gambler. He had speculated freely and successfully in apartment houses. Carl was conservative. He kept most of his assets liquid or safe in Treasury bills. But both Jack and Carl were faced with the prospect of having to finance their expansion or be content with what they had.

Jack had a bank lined up that would talk to both of them. Carl was reluctant. Finally he agreed to meet with the bankers. To make a long story short, Jack easily was granted a loan of three-quarters of a million dollars secured by the apartment houses he owned. Carl, on the other hand, refused to pledge anything other than the assets of his company. Both firms had a healthy balance sheet but no inventory. However, the bankers were reluctant to loan Carl money on that basis. Finally they compromised. They loaned Carl $250,000 at an interest rate one point greater than that for the $750,000 loan to Jack.

Jack thought Carl was crazy. He told him so. For some time their relationship was strained. During his expansion, Jack took on a line that competed directly with Carl's. His rationale was that Carl would not be able to expand his business into the same areas in which Jack was now operating. Therefore it was not a breach of the friendship they had enjoyed for years.

Carl felt differently, but kept it to himself. He knew he didn't have the operating capital to compete with Jack. Then came the recession. Profits plummeted. Cash flow went negative, and it took Jack twice as long to dismantle his expanded operation. Both Jack and Carl went to the bank to renegotiate. The bank refused and threatened to sue. Neither Jack nor Carl could meet the terms the bank demanded. They walked away, waiting for the lawsuit that was sure to come.

Both were served within two weeks and the battle was on. Carl's attorney sat down with the bank's attorneys and showed them the note. The loan was unsecured. Carl's company was a corporation with an active board of directors and several shareholders in addition to himself. Carl had taken the precaution years ago of putting his land, house, and other tangible assets of his estate into a trust owned by his wife and children. Carl's personal assets couldn't begin to pay off the debt, so the bankers reluctantly agreed to restructure Carl's debt the way they did Chrysler's. In five years Carl paid off the loan. His credit is still Triple A.

On the other hand, Jack didn't fare very well. The bank sued, and when Jack's lawyer asked the bankers to play fair, the result was attachment proceedings on Jack's property. Before the attachment hearing, Jack attempted to transfer all his assets into his wife's name by way of a postnuptial agreement backdated five years. The lawyer who did that for him, even though Jack was the one who thought of it, knew it wouldn't work but charged him $1,000 anyway. The end result? Not only did Jack lose his properties; he had to pay $25,000 in penalties and face a very irate judge unimpressed with Jack's short-term maneuvers.

To make matters worse, instead of going bankrupt as he should, Jack used what cash he had left to maintain the few assets that remained, including his house. Carl tried to help, but Jack was beyond help. Their friendship disintegrated. When Jack's money finally ran out, his house went into foreclosure and Jack into bankruptcy.

The moral of the Jack and Carl story is simple. No matter how good a salesman you are, there are practical elements you must deal with just to stay alive in the business arena. Let's face it, if you're not in the arena you're not going to sell. If you can't sell, you can't make any money.

Jack's lawyer had advised him not to secure the loan with his house and tangible property. Jack didn't take the advice. Carl's lawyer had advised him not to secure the loan with his house or tangible property. Carl did take the advice. Carl won. Jack lost. The banks were negotiating the conditions of each loan. Carl negotiated less money but he also took less risk. Jack allowed the banks to tie up his assets. Carl did not. When it came time for repayment Carl was in a position to bargain and Jack was not. The sad part about Jack's situation was that the tangible net worth of the assets that the bank attached was far greater than the $750,000 loan that Jack owed it. But banks are not in the real estate business. They sold off his apartments at auction. This meant that tangible assets of $1,400,000 in a good market were sold at auction for $750,000 to satisfy the bank's immediate demand. The banks had won, and were not the least bit concerned about being fair to Jack. All they wanted was their money. No wonder salesmen like people.

Other buyers are equally dangerous. As Carl grew older, he decided that he wanted to retire and sell his business. With no inventory, Carl's major assets were his customer relationships, backlog, and excellent goodwill. Carl found a large firm that was willing to pay $2.2 million for his company, or three times his annual profits. He was surprised. The contracts were written and the buyers were anxious to close. Carl was patting himself on the back for doing such a good selling job. The $2.2 million was a nice price.

But in retrospect Carl didn't remember doing much selling at all. The buyers were interested from the beginning. Now they were pushing for a fast close. Traditionally conservative, Carl begged time before putting his name to the documents. He looked up his old friend, Dean Erickson, an astute litigator specializing in contracts. Dean went over Carl's agreement point by point. His conclusion was ominous.

"This is a dangerous contract," he told Carl. "They have you warranting that your business is going to be at least as profitable in the next three years as it has been in the last three."

"Nothing wrong with that," Carl replied. "In fact I expect there's going to be an increase."

"Only if they manage your company as well as you did, Carl. Don't forget that."

"What are you saying?" Carl retorted.

"Quite simply, Carl," Dean said. "If you sell them the business and they muck it up, under the terms of this contract they can refuse payment even if the fault is theirs. This is particularly true in the service business. There are some real predatory buyers out there," Dean went on. "It's not unusual for a big outfit to buy a perfectly healthy small company like yours and then find some reason, usually a warranty or a representation, to claim fraud or misrepresentation."

"I'd sue them," Carl shot back.

"Certainly you would, and you'd burn up all your assets fighting a court case that's going to last at least three years. Meantime, your enemies are allocating one-sixth of one percent of company revenues, including yours, toward paying legal fees. If they lose, all they are going to wind up paying is probably what they agreed to in the first place. If you hit them with legal fees and other damages, they'll simply appeal and keep the case in court for the next ten years. Meanwhile, the out-of-pocket expenses will bankrupt you."

"What should I do?" Carl shouted back

"Fairly simple," Dean said, "I'll insert a clause that clearly states they are buying an 'as is' business. They are aware of this, and thereby waive their right to rescind the contract under state or federal law. This clause won't stop them from taking you to court but it will sure make it easy for you to win. If they ever file against you, let me know and I'll have a demurrer in the hands of a judge in 30 days."

Carl returned to his buyers and showed them the changes he made to the contract. For the first time he hit solid resistance. It centered on the specific clause Dean had insisted on. Two weeks later Carl and Dean had lunch.

"You were right," Carl said. "Those guys would have had me in court three months after I sold the business. I was only going to get $350,000 up front. The rest of the payments were on the come. I would have had to live on the $350,000 plus pay my legal fees—I would have been broke in six months."

"I gather you told them you weren't going to sell," Dean said.

"I told them to go to hell," Carl said.

Six months later Carl read about a lawsuit that had been filed by his ex-buyers against one of his competitors for breach of contract, misrepresentation, fraud, and rescission of a sales contract. The case dragged on for four years.

Several years later, when Carl and Dean Erickson were sitting around a pool in Miami, they reflected upon that particular situation. Dean volunteered, "You know, Carl, in this life I've learned a few important things. I've learned that people who sell integrity usually need to. And I've learned never to count my money while I'm still in the game. But most of all I've learned to know when to fight and when to quit, when to walk and when to run."

Wouldn't it be wonderful if we could somehow inculcate that wisdom into our children's heads so they wouldn't have to learn it themselves?

Epilogue

Why be a salesman if you're not going to advocate your company's position, your product, and yourself—in that order?

The customer's needs and objectives fall into a separate subordinate category. Your buyer can live without you and will not suffer any pain by cutting your feet off at the ankles. However, a salesman can also live without a particular buyer. There are thousands of buyers in the world and thousands of products, all looking for good salesmen.

Harsh as that philosophy may sound, if everybody understands it and does business that way, which in fact people do, then it merely establishes the groundrules of the arena.

In order to be a good Advocate Salesman and do justice to your company, your product, and yourself, you need to first understand yourself and what kind of salesman you are. Then you need to understand the buyer and what kind of person he is or what kind of people and philosophy make up the organization you are trying to sell. Third, you need to understand the selling environment or, more precisely, the arena you are in. Just as a visiting football team needs to know the nuances of the stadium in which it is about to play, so salesmen need to know the expected rituals and tacit buyer/seller understandings that exist in the customer's environment. *The salesman is always on the buyer's home ground.*

Good Advocate Salesmen know how to formulate sales strategy and have developed the skills necessary to devise a tactic that will work on the particular buyer in his particular arena. A master archer who cannot also use a sword will never survive a battle fought in a driving rain. Advocate Salesmen have mastered all the selling tools.

Most important, remember that the only way to be absolutely certain you haven't been rejected is to close the sale and make sure it sticks.

Good selling!

Index